EVALUATION PRACTICE
Thinking and Action Principles
for Social Work Practice

ELIZABETH DEPOY
University of Maine

STEPHEN FRENCH GILSON
University of Maine

THOMSON
─────★───── ™
BROOKS/COLE

Australia • Canada • Mexico • Singapore • Spain • United Kingdom • United States

THOMSON

BROOKS/COLE

Executive Editor: *Lisa Gebo*
Assistant Editor: *Alma Dea Michelena*
Editorial Assistant: *Sheila Walsh*
Marketing Manager: *Caroline Concilla*
Marketing Assistant: *Mary Ho*
Advertising Project Manager: *Tami Strang*
Signing Representative: *Linda Larrabee*
Project Managers, Editorial Production:
  Stephanie Zunich and Kelsey McGee
Print Buyer: *Vena Dyer*

Permissions Editor: *Connie Dowcett*
Production Service: *Kaila Wyllys,*
  G & S Typesetters, Inc.
Text Designer: *Jeanne Calabrese*
Copy Editor: *Cynthia Lindlof*
Illustrator: *Hoby Van Hoose*
Cover Designer: *Roger Knox*
Cover Image: *Hoby Van Hoose*
Compositor: *G & S Typesetters, Inc.*
Printer: *Transcontinental Printing*

COPYRIGHT © 2003 Brooks/Cole, a division of Thomson Learning, Inc. Thomson Learning™ is a trademark used herein under license.

ALL RIGHTS RESERVED. No part of this work covered by the copyright hereon may be reproduced or used in any form or by any mean—graphic, electronic, or mechanical, including but not limited to photocopying, recording, taping, Web distribution, information networks, or information storage and retrieval systems—without the written permission of the publisher.

Printed in Canada
1 2 3 4 5 6 7 06 05 04 03 02

For more information about our products, contact us at:
Thomson Learning Academic Resource Center
1-800-423-0563

For permission to use material from this text, contact us by: **Phone:** 1-800-730-2214
Fax: 1-800-730-2215
Web: http://www.thomsonrights.com

Library of Congress Control Number: 2002101769

ISBN 0-534-54391-X

Brooks/Cole–Thomson Learning
511 Forest Lodge Road
Pacific Grove, CA 93950
USA

Asia
Thomson Learning
5 Shenton Way #01-01
UIC Building
Singapore 068808

Australia
Nelson Thomson Learning
102 Dodds Street
South Melbourne, Victoria 3205
Australia

Canada
Nelson Thomson Learning
1120 Birchmount Road
Toronto, Ontario M1K 5G4
Canada

Europe/Middle East/Africa
Thomson Learning
High Holborn House
50/51 Bedford Row
London WC1R 4LR
United Kingdom

Latin America
Thomson Learning
Seneca, 53
Colonia Polanco
11560 Mexico D.F.
Mexico

Spain
Paraninfo Thomson Learning
Calle/Magallanes, 25
28015 Madrid, Spain

CONTENTS

PART I | **BEGINNINGS** 1

CHAPTER 1
Introduction to Evaluation Practice 3

Definition and Scope 4
History 6
Political Context of Evaluation 13
Theoretical and Value-Based Foundation
  of Evaluation Practice 14
Main Points 15
Exercises 16

CHAPTER 2
The Conceptual Framework of Evaluation Practice 17

Overview of the Model 18
Principles and Assumptions 19
Deductive Reasoning 25
Inductive Reasoning 26
Main Points 30
Exercises 30

CHAPTER 3
Roles and Responsibilities of Social Workers in Evaluation Practice   31

Managing People   32
Analytic Axes   32
Evaluation Practice Ethics   40
Main Points   41
Exercises   42

PART 2 | THINKING PROCESSES OF EVALUATION PRACTICE   43

CHAPTER 4
Identifying Social Work Problems and Issues   45

Definitions   46
Thinking Processes in Articulating Social Problems   48
Problem Mapping and Force Field Analysis   49
Main Points   57
Exercises   57

CHAPTER 5
Obtaining and Organizing Information   58

Diverse Purposes of Information in Evaluation Practice   59
When to Review Information in Evaluation   61
Mechanics of Information Review   63
Main Points   72
Exercises   73

CHAPTER 6
Ascertaining Need   74

Distinction Between Problem and Need   75
Choosing Needs Assessment Action Strategies   78
Main Points   83
Exercises   84

CHAPTER 7
Examining Need with Previously Supported Approaches: Designing Experimental-Type Inquiry 85

Using Experimental-Type Design in Needs Assessment 86
True Experimental Design 87
Nonexperimental Designs 91
Thinking Process of Experimental-Type Design Selection in Needs Assessment 93
Main Points 96
Exercises 96

CHAPTER 8
Obtaining Information in Experimental-Type Needs Assessment 97

Introduction to Measurement 98
Instrumentation Structures That Are Useful in Experimental-Type Needs Assessment 101
Main Points 110
Exercises 110

CHAPTER 9
Ascertaining Need in Unexamined Contexts: Designing Qualitative Inquiry 112

Underlying Tenets of Naturalistic Inquiry 113
Selecting a Design in Naturalistic Needs Assessment 123
Mixed-Method Designs 124
Main Points 125
Exercises 126

CHAPTER 10
Setting Goals and Objectives 127

Introduction and Definitions 128
Objectives 129

Deriving Goals from Need Statements   134
Action Process of Writing Process Objectives   135
Action Process of Writing Outcome Objectives   136
Main Points   137
Exercises   138

PART 3 | REFLEXIVE INTERVENTION   139

CHAPTER 11
Intervention Selection and Reflexive Intervention   141

Translating Goals and Objectives into Interventions   142
Selection of an Intervention Approach   143
Reflexive Intervention   147
Main Points   148
Exercises   149

CHAPTER 12
Thinking Processes of Reflexive Intervention   150

Elements of Reflexive Intervention   151
Main Points   160
Exercises   161

CHAPTER 13
Action Processes of Reflexive Intervention   162

Introduction to Design Selection in Reflexive Intervention   163
Experimental-Type Process Assessment Designs   163
Naturalistic Inquiry   167
Mixed-Method Design   172
Process Assessment Questions Posed by Diverse Groups   172
Selecting a Method—Guiding Questions   173
Main Points   175
Exercises   175

PART 4 | ASSESSING OUTCOMES 177

CHAPTER 14
Thinking Processes in Outcome Assessment 179

Introduction: Outcome Assessment as One Step
  in Evaluation Practice 180
Definitions 180
Essential Elements of Outcome Assessment 181
Main Points 184
Exercises 186

CHAPTER 15
Action Processes of Outcome Research: Looking at Group Outcome 187

Four Steps of Outcome Assessment 188
True Experimental Design in Outcome Assessment 188
Using Nonexperimental to Quasi-Experimental Approaches
  in Outcome Assessment 189
Alternative Strategies to Attribute Outcome to Intervention 194
Main Points 196
Exercises 196

CHAPTER 16
Outcome Assessment Using Idiographic Designs 198

Definition of Idiographic Designs 199
Three Idiographic Design Types 199
Main Points 207
Exercises 207

PART 5 | CONCLUSION 209

CHAPTER 17
Sharing Evaluation Practice Knowledge 211

Reporting and Using Knowledge 212
Evidence 212

Questions to Guide the Selection of a Reporting Format
and Strategy   214
Structures   216
Use of Evaluation Practice Knowledge   220
Main Points   221
Exercises   221

CHAPTER 18
Conclusions   222

Continuous Process of Evaluation Practice   223
Joshua   223
Individual Problem   224
Systemic Problem Identified by Joshua   226
Jennifer   227
Systemic Problem   228
Evaluation Practice: Upholding the Social
Work Commitment   231
Go For It!   232

APPENDIX   233

Data Analysis   233
Level 1: Descriptive Statistics   234
Level 2: Drawing Inferences   237
Level 3: Associations and Relationships   239
Naturalistic Data Analysis   239

GLOSSARY   241

BIBLIOGRAPHY   247

INDEX   251

PREFACE

Two major intellectual and practice trends created the impetus for this book. The first is the increasing call for systematic inquiry in social work practice. Since the 1970s, when the term *empirical practice* was first coined, the field of social work has joined other professions in asserting the importance of an evidence-based approach to practice (Thyer, 2001). It is curious to note, however, that despite this recognition, there remains a separation between systematic inquiry and practice in our educational preparation as well as in the field.

A serious consequence of this separation has been the mistrust and maligning of each camp by the other. Practitioners suggest that they do not need empirical evidence to support the value of practice; researchers and evaluators question the claims made without the support of empirical evidence of the value of practice (Berlin & Marsh, 1993).

The second important trend is the change in the meaning of *empirical* and its impact on the nature of professional knowledge. Traditionally, the term has been reserved to describe the knowledge generated by experimental approaches to research. However, with the increasing use and respect for interpretive approaches to inquiry, knowledge generated through these diverse methods has joined the ranks of empiricism. Experimentation and replicability, while still respected, are outdated as the sole criteria for empirical knowledge. We use the term empirical in its most contemporary sense to mean the logical and systematic acquisition and use of evidence to support knowledge claims. The resultant impact of this expansive approach has been an acceptance of multiple ways of knowing beyond top-down methods of research. We believe that this democratic and contemporary view of empirical knowledge has the capacity to garner support from practitioners who have not found strict adherence to quantitative methods relevant to their practices.

Capitalizing on these two trends, we have written this text to meet the challenges from social work educators, practitioners, and scholars (Roche, ed., 1999) to examine and revise current boundaries in social work curricula and practice. Our aim is to provide a framework for the integration of systematic inquiry with practice that can be used by all social workers.

Unlike previous usages of the term *evaluation practice* and others, including *evaluation, evaluation of practice,* and *program evaluation,* the model of evaluation practice that we have developed and advance in this text provides the evidence-based structure within which diverse social work theories and skills can be organized, examined, and verified.

Unlike traditional notions of evaluation, which focus primarily on practice assessment, our model comprises three elements: (a) clarification of the problem, need, and intervention goals and objectives; (b) examination of the process through reflexive intervention; and (c) examination of the outcome. The important roles of context, values, and purpose in evaluation practice provide the conceptual backdrop for each of these elements.

The text is organized into five sections. Section 1 introduces the model of evaluation practice and the diverse roles that social workers play within the model framework. Section 2 provides a discussion and illustration of the first element of the model. We define *social problem* and distinguish it from need and then proceed to discuss how current knowledge shapes the rationale for and approach to intervention. The chapter on establishment of intervention goals and objectives completes this section.

Section 3 details the second element in evaluation practice. We have created the term *reflexive intervention* to describe our vision of thoughtful and rigorous practice in which social workers apply systematic inquiry to scrutinize how they practice.

Section 4 discusses diverse approaches to assessing the outcome of practice. Section 5 concludes with two chapters, one on sharing evaluation practice knowledge and a final chapter that walks the reader through the full sequence of evaluation practice.

HOW TO USE THIS BOOK

We have organized the book to be used in multiple ways. Instructors, practitioners, and students can use all or part of the text to elucidate the application of systematic inquiry to each phase of social work practice. At the beginning of each chapter, the element of the model that we are addressing is highlighted in the model graphic. Each chapter contains a conceptual rationale and set of guidelines, details on how to conduct evaluation practice, and two types of examples for illustration. Along with examples from actual evaluation practice, we follow two fictitious characters, *Joshua Williams* and *Jennifer Savoy*, throughout the text to provide illustrations of evaluation practice in action.

We italicize new terms and boldface terms found in the glossary to help you identify which parts of the text are most useful for you to read or reread. *Joshua* and *Jennifer* appear throughout the text and are identified in an alternate font. As you will come to see, our discussion of evaluation practice is not prescriptive or mechanical. Rather, we pose a series of thinking and action processes through which social workers make and enact decisions about how to conduct, report, and put evaluation practice to use.

At the end of each chapter, we summarize the main points and suggest exercises to help you experience and become proficient in the thinking and action processes of evaluation practice. In addition, we have included a glossary, an extensive bibliography, and an appendix on data analysis for further information.

We believe that evaluation practice not only advances the integration of practice and inquiry, but provides a creative framework through which practice wisdom and learning can be incorporated into the knowledge base of our profession. Through application of this model to all domains of practice, we can articulate the process, outcome, and value of social work intervention to practitioners within our own profession as well as to a full range of colleagues, peers, and consumers.

ACKNOWLEDGMENTS

We thank those whose ideas have contributed to our work: our students, teachers, and colleagues at the University of Maine, Virginia Commonwealth University and throughout the United States, our families, and especially Lynn, who has a unique approach to defining problems. We are also grateful for the helpful comments of the following reviewers: Frank Baskind, Virginia Commonwealth University; John Gandy, University of South Carolina; Wallace J. Gingerich, Case Western Reserve University; Steve Marson, University of North Carolina—Pembroke; Paul R. Raffoul, University of Houston; Ronald Reinig, Edinboro University of Pennsylvania; and Michael J. Smith, Hunter College.

BEGINNINGS

PART I

INTRODUCTION TO EVALUATION PRACTICE

CHAPTER I

Definition and Scope

History

Political Context of Evaluation

Theoretical and Value-Based Foundation of Evaluation Practice

Main Points

Exercises

DEFINITION AND SCOPE
What Is Evaluation Practice?

In this text, we discuss and illustrate an innovative and comprehensive model that we have named *evaluation practice*. Unlike traditional approaches to evaluation, the evaluation practice model is designed to integrate evaluation thinking and action with social work practice. Evaluation practice is a comprehensive means for social workers to examine and respond to social problems and issues and to describe, examine, and assess the efficacy of content and skill-specific practice.

Both historically and currently, evaluation has been taught and treated as separate and distinct from social work practice (Unrau, Gabor, & Grinnell, 2001). Some evaluators (Grinnell, 1999; Yates, 1996) suggest that evaluation is an end process to examine the extent to which a desired outcome has been achieved. Others (Patton, 1993; Rossi, Freeman, & Lipsey, 1999) describe evaluation as ongoing for the purpose of using feedback to improve practices. Many evaluation scholars and texts combine both outcome and process evaluation (Rossi et al., 1999). And finally, as the field of evaluation grows and diversifies, many evaluators have developed methods to examine parts of practice as they differentially relate to and influence intermediate and final outcome.

All these models are presumed to exist apart from and provide the empirical systematic structure to "look in" on practice (Berlin & Marsh, 1993). Current thinking and scholarship, however, call for the integration of systematic inquiry and scrutiny with practice (Hess & Mullen, 1997; Kirst-Ashman & Hull, 1999). Consistent with this challenge, we formally name our approach evaluation practice and define it as the *purposive* application of evidence-based thinking and action processes to the definition and clarification of social problems, and to the identification of what is needed to resolve them and of the way in which and extent to which problems have been resolved.

Does this definition remind you of any field? Consider "thinking and action processes," "systematic," "logic," and "evidence." These are the foundations of both research and practice thinking (DePoy & Gitlin, 1998; Roche et al., 1999). Building on the work of DePoy and Gitlin, thinking and action processes are the two essential elements in systematic inquiry. Thinking processes are the systematic logic strategies that are used to clarify concepts, organize and apply knowledge to the development of research queries, and plan approaches to obtain and use evidence. Action processes enact the plans that result from thinking processes.

There is significant debate in the field of evaluation regarding the distinction between evaluation and research (Alkin, 1990; Thyer, 2001). On the one hand, some suggest that despite its empirical and systematic activity, evaluation is not research because it focuses on the assessment of value rather than on the production of knowledge (Sadish, Cook, & Levitan, 1991). On the other hand, scholars such as Weiss (as cited in Alkin, 1990) claim that evaluation and

> **BOX 1.1** | **EXAMPLE — PURPOSE IN EVALUATION PRACTICE**
>
> You are a substance-abuse rehabilitation social worker in a section of your agency that is specifically set up to assess and intervene with professionals (physicians, attorneys, social workers, and such) who have set up their own appointments or have been referred by employers or licensing boards. You have been given the task of determining the extent to which the program met the goals of promoting sobriety for clients. How do you design such an evaluation? You know that your program is based on the theoretical framework of social learning theory, in which group discussion and therapy are used to promote behavioral changes toward sobriety and in which vicarious learning occurs to further support sober behavior. However, you also know that even though you can observe behavior in therapy and see changes in that environment, you have no way to ascertain sobriety once clients leave the treatment center. You develop a set of procedures to measure sobriety at six months following the completion of your program and find that 20% of your clients maintain sobriety. Your program is defunded, and you are no longer able to work with the population of professionals. Had you realized that the purpose of the evaluation was to determine continuation of funding, you might have selected other evaluation measures, such as learning and desire to be sober, because these two indicators are highly associated with sobriety, even if sobriety is not likely to occur until several iterations of treatment.

research are not distinct fields. She draws our attention to the role of evaluation in systematically examining practice as a basis for developing practice knowledge.

We transcend the debates by asserting that evaluation practice serves both research and practice and bridges the gap between the two. Evaluation practice is grounded in logic and the systematic thinking that undergirds all evidence-based thinking processes. However, unlike other forms of inquiry, the purpose in evaluation practice is explicit and is a major determinant of the scope and approach chosen by the inquirer (Rossi et al., 1999; Unrau et al., 2001). The centrality of political purpose is the element that we suggest sets evaluation as a distinct subset of research. Also, the thinking and action processes of evaluation process provide a reasoned, evidenced-based structure for practice thinking. Consider the example in Box 1.1.

Can you see how important purpose is in evaluation and how you might design the evaluation to meet the practice, administrative, and funding purposes? Both approaches to evaluation suggested in Box 1.1 would give you valuable information, one looking at long-term outcomes and the other, at intermediate outcomes. The choice to examine intermediate outcomes (those that lead to but are not final desired outcomes) may have resulted in continued funding so that your program would be available for readmission of those individuals who needed continued intervention. However, the evaluation of intermediate outcome would not have given information about the overall sobriety rate derived from each full session of intervention.

This example illuminates the importance of systematic, comprehensive approaches to practice that can aid the social worker in identifying what information is needed, not only for direct service but for indirect areas such as policy and funding. Knowledge of indirect practice issues will enhance the likelihood that the social worker can attend to purpose as a critical influence on the evaluation practice method selected. Keep this important example in mind as evaluation practice thinking and action processes are introduced.

Reasoning in Evaluation Practice

Inductive and deductive reasoning form the basis for evaluation practice thinking processes. Moreover, the two major research design traditions, naturalistic and experimental-type inquiry, are based on these logic structures (DePoy & Gitlin, 1998), and thus they are used to guide thinking and action and to support claims regarding the processes and outcomes of intervention. The logic structures in evaluation practice are defined not only by the questions to be answered but by the political context, nature of the practice to be evaluated, purpose, and intended use of the knowledge generated by evaluation (Chronbach, 1982; House & Howe, 1999; Rossi et al., 1999).

HISTORY

A brief history of evaluation will help in understanding its development and current context in social work practice. According to Sadish et al. (1991), evaluation is an inherent human trait. Humans in daily living automatically assess what they think, do, observe, and experience. Even more expansive is the role of evaluation in evolutionary psychology, in which mutations are evaluated for their capacity to produce desired change by determining the degree to which these changes resulted in enhanced survival (Buss, 1998). Although evaluation has been characterized as an inherent biological activity, we look toward the field of evaluation scholarship to inform current evaluation practice.

According to Rossi et al. (1999), systematic program evaluation was first addressed in the field of public health and education. Between World War I and World War II, evaluation slowly expanded; and researchers such as Lewin, Lippitt, and White became well known for their work in the application of scientific method to determine the outcome of practice efforts in several fields, including public health and psychology.

The scholarly field of evaluation became well known and extensively practiced in the late 1950s and early 1960s, when evaluation theories were developed to guide practice. Due to the extensive amount of money spent on social programs by the federal government, the value of these expenditures in achieving desired outcomes was subjected to scientific scrutiny.

Three major phenomena were responsible for the current field of evaluation research: the need for accountability as social programs grew in scope and number, the increase in the sophistication of research and statistical methods, and the explosion of computer technology (Alkin, 1990). With these three factors operating, methods texts, journals, academic programs, and the professional field of evaluation have taken hold and are now commonplace in practice, education, and scholarship in social sciences and social work practice. Current evaluation is based on skepticism, the need for accountability, fiscal conservatism, and a history of ineffectual social programs (Gambrill, 2001).

Most approaches to evaluation in the current social service context do not merely examine desired outcomes and processes by which these outcomes were achieved, but expand to many other arenas. Included in these are cost-effectiveness and containment, differential comparisons of approaches to defining and resolving social problems, and examination of the influences of contextual and change factors on program process and outcome (Royce & Thyer, 1996; Thyer, 2001).

We build on past efforts, such as evidence-based practice and empirical practice (Thyer, 2001), by proposing evaluation as the implementation of three major thinking and action process areas: *problem and need clarification, reflexive intervention,* and *outcome assessment.*

Problem and Need Clarification

Because of the complexity of defining and understanding social problems, methods to alleviate and/or address them are often unclear. As we so frequently see in social services, intervention initiators frequently do not specify a social problem but jump directly to an intervention that they believe is needed. Why that approach to intervention is needed and to what social problem it responds are unfortunately omitted from the thinking and action processes of many social service efforts. Without clear understanding of what problem is being addressed and without evidence supporting the means needed to address it, we cannot demonstrate the value of our practice. We can look at Fisher's (1973) classic work that questioned the efficacy of casework. Without a clear articulation of the problems that casework intervention is addressing, how can intervention effectiveness even be discussed?

The clarification of the problem is critical to any service effort because how a problem is conceptualized, who owns it, who is affected by it, and what needs to be done about it are all questions based in political-purposive and ideological arenas. Thus the problem forms the basis on which all subsequent evaluative activity takes place and provides the ultimate foundation for the implementation and continuation of interventions.

Such questions must be posed and answered by professionals in social work and human services if the efficacy of practice is to be assessed and demonstrated. In the case of clinical practice, if mental illness, conceptualized as a chemical imbalance, were the problem and a cure for mental illness were determined as a need, it would seem futile for clinical social work to be the selected intervention. If, however, isolation leading to emotional pain was the problem, the need for clinical social work as an intervention becomes viable, and the outcome of intervention is both "doable" and reasonable to expect.

At multiple system levels, we assert that a clear and well-supported understanding of problem and need is essential to social work practice. Without problem and need clarification, interest groups may define problems differently and thus expect different outcomes from the same intervention. To illustrate, meet *Joshua Williams*, one of the two individuals whose life and work will serve as examples to illustrate concepts and principles throughout the text. Consider the scenario from our first case history.

At 35 years old, Joshua Williams was finally feeling some sense of accomplishment in his life. It had not always been this way. As the first of two children born to Mary and David, much of Joshua's childhood was spent feeling disconnected from his peers and his family, except for his younger sister, Magdalene. Despite their having died at different ages and from different causes, both his parents were active alcoholics. Much of Joshua's childhood remains either forgotten or quite vague.

What Joshua does remember is that during the later part of his primary school years and then throughout his middle school years, he was engaged in what he terms "minor acts" of juvenile delinquency. These acts included shoplifting, drinking alcohol, breaking and entering, suspension from school, malicious mischief, vandalism, destruction of property, fighting with classmates, and school truancy. He speaks of these activities with remorse, knowing full well that his actions have influenced who he is today. Also noteworthy was Joshua's poor performance in school, an important determinant of his future professional direction.

Joshua's use of alcohol increased significantly during high school with regular-to-daily use/abuse, including periods of increased tolerance, blackouts, driving while drunk (although he was never arrested for such use), increased numbers of hangovers, public intoxication, and general perception by others that he was an active alcohol abuser. His use of alcohol interfered with his participation in and successful completion of high school, although when he was 17 years old, graduating from high school was not a priority for him—alcohol use was. Despite erratic attendance, poor assignment-completion rates, a general attitude of indifference, and periodic assignment to a counseling group by the school social worker, Joshua did graduate, but with poor grades and noncompetitive test scores on college entrance examinations.

The summer following his graduation from high school marked Joshua's first serious attempt at sobriety. Joshua signed himself into an inpatient detoxification unit, only to leave against medical advice a few days later. The next four years of his life were marked by several periods of voluntary inpatient and outpatient treatment, along with attendance at several meetings of Alcoholics Anonymous (AA). On his 22nd birthday, Joshua again signed himself into an inpatient county-based alcohol treatment unit. This event marked his first sustained period of abstinence from substance use and his continued participation in AA; and this period of recovery is ongoing today. At the same time, he also attempted to secure vocational rehabilitation services so that he could enroll in and complete his college education. His assigned vocational rehabilitation counselor was very reluctant to support Joshua in seeking an academic degree, documenting in his notes that Joshua was "alcoholic, unreliable, and unprepared due to poor performance in school and on college entrance examinations." Only after insisting that the full treatment team meet, including his social worker, was Joshua able to obtain funding for his plan of recovery and sustained and substantive employment. Over the course of his efforts at recovery, his work to pursue the goals he wanted, and his undergraduate course work, Joshua developed an interest in political science and public policy, leading him to major in political science and minor in public policy. During his senior year, reflecting back on the critical role that grades and tests had had on his life, Joshua decided to pursue a joint degree in social work and law with a practice focus on public policy, and with particular attention to public education law and policy.

How would you define the problem for which Joshua sought help? Some, such as the vocational counselor, might see it as alcoholism. Others might view the problem as behavioral, emerging from a family system in which Joshua learned substance use. Even others may see Joshua's problem as unemployment and lack of skills. Joshua, even with the recognition that his alcohol abuse was problematic, clearly saw a more critical part of the problem as the influence of childhood school performance on adulthood options. Each view would beget a different set of goals and interventions to resolve the stated problem. We will revisit Joshua throughout the text to illustrate evaluation practice at multiple system levels.

In evaluation practice, a clear understanding of need must be based on credible evidence. Although we may make claims on what type of intervention is needed to resolve problems, accountability in making informed professional decisions is dependent on the presence and organization of empirical evidence of need. Without such evidence, the basis for provider, policy, payer, and administrative decisions cannot be ascertained.

Consider Joshua again. His first period of sustained recovery occurred when he was 22 years old. At the same time he decided to engage actively in changing his life on several other levels, including his economic level. Key to this economic change was his attendance and graduation from a college or university. Although Joshua was clear on what his "problem" was and what he needed to do to resolve that problem, the vocational rehabilitation counselor had made a different assessment. For the counselor the empirical evidence of need was Joshua's history of substance abuse and his past attempts at recovery. The crux of the dilemma for the counselor, or perhaps the social worker, was determination of what constitutes credible evidence of need. Clearly, Joshua's prior history of abuse and relapse could not be ignored when administrative decisions were made regarding the allocation of resources to fulfill a need. But what role should the direct empirical evidence as provided by the individual, group, or community take? If the empirical presentation of need is defined solely in terms of day-to-day sobriety, the initial decision not to provide resource support for an individual's education might have been warranted. However, once that presentation of need was expanded to include multiple and complex understandings of problem and need, many directions emerged for the establishment of goals and objectives to guide an intervention and define expected outcomes.

Setting goals and objectives for intervention derives directly from need. In Chapter 5, we explore goals and objectives in detail and look at the manner in which each need statement gave rise to different opinions about what goals and objectives were to be achieved in Joshua's recovery.

We now move to the second element in the evaluation practice model. We have named this step reflexive intervention.

Reflexive Intervention

In research texts, particularly those that present naturalistic methods, reflexivity is an important construct. Typically, **reflexivity** is defined as self-examination for the purpose of ascertaining how one's perspective influences the interpretation of data (Denzin & Lincoln, 2000; DePoy & Gitlin, 1998). Here we expand the term to denote the set of thinking and action processes that we believe should take place throughout interventions. By using the name reflexive intervention, we make explicit the intervention action processes, resources, and influences that are part of evaluation practice. Thus, the objective of reflexive thinking processes in our model is not limited to an individual but is applied to the sum total of the intervention and scope of influences on the process and outcome of intervention.

Reflexive intervention involves three important foci: monitoring process, resource analysis, and consideration of indirect influences on the intervention.

Monitoring Process or Process Assessment Monitoring process or process assessment is the element of evaluation that examines if and how the intervention is proceeding. Unlike Scriven (1991), who views monitoring as a process whereby an individual or group oversees the expenditure of resources in relation to actions performed, we agree with Rossi et al. (1999) regarding the expansiveness and importance of this part of the evaluation practice process. We see monitoring as an essential evaluation practice action in which the actual implementation of an intervention is systematically studied and characterized. Monitoring process not only examines the scope of the intervention, but scrutinizes the intervention processes to determine who they affect, to assess the degree to which goals and objectives are efficaciously reflected in the intervention, and to provide feedback for revision based on empirical evidence. The primary purpose of monitoring process is to ascertain if an intervention was delivered as planned so that attribution of outcome can be positioned properly.

We will use the example in Box 1.2 to illustrate the link between monitoring and outcome assessment.

> **BOX 1.2**
>
> ### EXAMPLE — TEACHING WORK SKILLS TO YOUNG CRIMINAL OFFENDERS: LINK BETWEEN MONITORING AND ASSESSMENT
>
> Suppose we find at the end of a behavioral intervention to teach work skills to youth who perpetrated criminal offenses that they did not learn the necessary skills. An automatic response would suggest that the program failed and should be revised or discontinued. However, sound monitoring might lead to other conclusions. Suppose we learn in the monitoring action process that the teaching staff worked with youth on attitudinal changes rather than on specific work skills. Although the intervention may not have been implemented as specified, monitoring revealed that the staff, in their assessment of the youth, realized that attitude change was a necessary prerequisite to skill acquisition and modified the intervention and time line to address this very important element of work ethic. Do we conclude that our program failed, or has the monitoring illuminated a necessary revision?
>
> Can you see how monitoring enhances knowledge of what happened and why or why not the goals and objectives were achieved?

> **BOX 1.3**
>
> ### EXAMPLE — TEACHING WORK SKILLS TO YOUNG CRIMINAL OFFENDERS: DETERMINING COST
>
> We might look merely at the financial cost of salaries and day-to-day operations of the intervention and draw conclusions about the amount of dollars spent on each client to effect attitude change without having achieved the end goal of youth employment. This focus might lead us to believe that the intervention is too costly to continue, as the goal of employment is not attained. What if we expand our resource analysis to the cost of unemployment for these clients over a lifetime, something that may occur without the prerequisite step of attitude examination and change? The cost of not continuing the intervention in this scenario might greatly outweigh the cost of funding a modified and possibly longer intervention.

Resource Analysis Similar to monitoring, resource analysis occurs throughout the intervention and requires reflection. When we think of resource analysis, cost in dollars for services rendered is the most commonly examined resource. In our model, we expand reflexive intervention beyond cost factors to include the full host of human and nonhuman resources that are used to conduct an intervention and that are related to its need and outcome. In Box 1.3, we continue with the example from Box 1.2.

> **BOX 1.4**
>
> **EXAMPLE—TEACHING WORK SKILLS TO YOUNG CRIMINAL OFFENDERS: EXAMINING INDIRECT INFLUENCES**
>
> What if the youth in our program discussed in Boxes 1.2 and 1.3 lived in a remote rural area in which they were uncertain of job opportunities. You have noted that they lack enthusiasm about skill acquisition. A reasonable explanation for this lack of enthusiasm could be their awareness of the limited potential for obtaining a job in the area, regardless of their skills. This factor is an example of an external influence that needs to be considered in intervention process and outcome.

Consideration of Indirect Influences on the Intervention Part of the process of reflexive intervention must be a consideration of factors external to the intervention that affect both process and outcome. Without widening the scope of examination, it is difficult to determine why or why not change is occurring in the desired direction. The example continues in Box 1.4.

Many evaluation texts and scholars refer to what we are calling reflexive intervention as process or formative evaluation. These functions are included in our conceptualization as we will discuss in detail later in the text. However, we selected the term reflexive intervention to denote what we consider to be the ultimate purpose of formative assessment and an essential obligation of every social worker; that is, the generation and/or use of systematically derived evidence to scrutinize and revise interventions. The term *reflexivity* is both descriptive and comprehensive, and thus we have chosen it to denote a process of "looking inward" while simultaneously acknowledging and addressing the influence of contextual factors on intervention processes.

Outcome Assessment

Outcome assessment is the action process of evaluation practice that is most familiar. It answers the question "To what extent did the desired outcomes occur?" In addition, it examines the parts of an intervention and its context that related to outcome, as well as differential outcome resulting from influences such as the intervention processes themselves, the target populations, the complexity of outcome expectations, and so forth. Although the aim of outcome assessment seems obvious, to judge the value of an intervention in its achievement of goals and objectives, outcome assessment serves many other important purposes. Outcome assessment provides empirical information on which to make programmatic, policy, and resource decisions that influence and shape social and human services at multiple levels (Unrau et al., 2001).

POLITICAL CONTEXT OF EVALUATION

We wish to emphasize the importance of the political nature of evaluation. In our experience, evaluation practice is the *politicalization* of research thinking and action processes within social work practice at multiple system levels; that is, the field of evaluation practice uses inquiry as political and purposive. But what do we mean by this statement? Evaluation practice provides the empirical "power" to guide and/or justify decisions about social programs and interventions. The decision to devote resources to a particular area of social concern is always a matter of power in decision making and action, given the scarcity of dollars allocated to social programs (Alkin, 1990).

We now introduce the case history of Jennifer Savoy, whose experience also serves as an example throughout the text. As a result of complications from polio, Jennifer's primary education was divided between classes at the hospital and homeschooling with her father and mother acting as her teachers, using textbooks provided by the local public school district. When not in the hospital, Jennifer was often confined to her home because of either the immobility created by her various leg and body casts or the lack of accessibility to classes at her elementary school. At the elementary school, the fourth-, fifth-, and sixth-grade classes were held on the second floor of a building that did not have an elevator. Fortunately for Jennifer, her middle school was on only one level, with just a few steps up to the front entrance. The back of the building, however, was ramped to allow workers, delivery people, and cafeteria staff to bring equipment, supplies, and foodstuff into the building. Although the building housing Jennifer's high school had two stories, she could select classes that were held in classrooms on the first floor.

One of the big problems for Jennifer during high school was trying to convince school administrators, her teachers, the guidance counselor, and the school social worker that she wanted to attend college and therefore would need college prep courses. Unfortunately, many of these classes were offered only in classrooms on the second floor. Jennifer's mother and father had been very active in the parent-teacher association. Because of the level of their activity, Jennifer's parents had learned how to "work" with school officials, including the school board, to push the school district to meet Jennifer's educational needs.

Much of her public school education took place prior to the formulation of regulations in 1978 resulting from the Rehabilitation Act of 1973, and her bachelor's and master's degrees were awarded prior to the enactment of the Americans with Disabilities Act of 1990 (ADA); therefore, Jennifer's educational experiences have included little in the way of accommodation to her disability, despite her significant mobility impairments. Following receipt of her doctoral degree in 1995, she secured a position as a teacher in a public high school in her community. At age 44, Jennifer has begun to experience a variety of new musculoskeletal symptoms.

As you can see from reading this scenario, the allocation of dollars to render the school building accessible may not have been valued, and thus, students who were unable to navigate architectural barriers such as stairs were essentially denied a full and equal education. The decision to restrict Jennifer from classes was not based on her disability, but rather on a larger political question of resource allocation. As we proceed through this text, we urge you to pay close attention to the significant role of political power and resource allocation in all elements of the evaluation practice process, from problem definition to use of reflexive intervention and outcome assessment findings to improve future intervention. All evaluation practice is value based, as are interventions and all levels of social work intervention. Let us consider this point in more detail now. As we look at values, consider our two individuals, *Joshua* and *Jennifer*. As we will see later in the text, *Joshua's early experience created a clear political agenda for him in the area of standardized testing inequities exhibited by the students in his state. Similarly, Jennifer's personal experience as a mobility-impaired student influenced her commitment to universal access to education.*

THEORETICAL AND VALUE-BASED FOUNDATION OF EVALUATION PRACTICE

As we will see in the chapter on problem clarification, all social problems are statements of value. What is a problem to some is not a problem to others, or how the same problem is conceptualized may differ among groups and individuals. The application of a theoretical lens through which to view and explain a problem complicates problem definition even further (Sadish et al., 1991). Thus, the need to clarify the approach to a problem and the value base of the problem is critical in the evaluation practice process and comprises the first major thinking process of our evaluation model.

This need to clarify one's approach is evident in both *Joshua's* and *Jennifer's* stories.

For Joshua, if the social worker were to take a narrow definition of the problem and a narrow view of intervention, it would be possible to limit the problem identification to the need for permanent sobriety. This approach, with the primary value on individual sobriety, would not address the economic or career issues that are associated with substance abuse nor would such an approach be expanded to look at cause of substance use in this population. The decision to intervene to render sobriety an individual responsibility may then not attain the goal of permanent sobriety, if rigid value restrictions on expanding the scope of intervention to career development and other areas of social worth are maintained.

For Jennifer, by limiting the problem identification to recognition of her work barriers, with the response being the elimination of those barriers specific to her, the larger issues of overall lack of access and barriers would not be addressed. Although Jennifer might be better able to perform some of the tasks associated with her job, the larger issue of community access to schools would go unaddressed.

What do we mean by value base? A value is what we believe to be desirable and/or important. A value base is a composite of individual, group, social, and cultural beliefs about what is just, correct, and desirable (Rokeach, 1973). You can now begin to see why the clarification of value is so important in evaluation practice. Clearly, what one individual or group values, another might not. One group may believe, for example, that youth who perpetrate crimes are "bad kids" and thus would advocate for the need for punitive intervention and outcome. Another group might see these youth as victims of unjust social systems and thus would value rehabilitation and large-systems change as concurrent interventions. Each addresses the same problem, youth crime, but conceptualizes the problem and need differently as a function of value difference.

In Joshua's example, the social worker might view the problem of substance abuse as an individual failing, while others may look at the phenomenon as a cause of stress associated with family and social worth.

We can now begin to understand theoretical lenses as critical factors in the thinking processes of evaluation practice. If we see youth crime through a behavioral theoretical lens, then our need would suggest behavioral intervention as the intervention of choice with individual behavior change as the desired outcome. If we apply a social justice theory to the problem of youth crime, however, the need for large-scale social intervention, such as affirmative action, might be indicated, with equal opportunity as the desired outcome.

If we look at access barriers, as in the case of Jennifer, as individual barriers, then we would approach the problem through accommodations designed to meet the needs of individuals. However, if we looked at access barriers as a social issue, we more likely would use social theories to suggest universal design for public buildings.

MAIN POINTS

1. Evaluation practice is a comprehensive framework that integrates evaluation thinking and action within social work practice.
2. Evaluation practice is a means to examine and respond to social problems and issues, within which content, skill-specific theories, and skills can be organized, examined, and verified.
3. Evaluation practice is designed to bridge the gap between research and practice.
4. A formal definition of evaluation practice is the purposive application of evidence-based thinking to the definition and clarification of social problems, and to the identification of what is needed to resolve them and of the way in which and extent to which problems have been resolved.
5. Evaluation is based in inductive and deductive logic structures.

6. Evaluation practice has emerged from a rich history of the intersection of inquiry with economic and accountability concerns.
7. The three elements of evaluation practice are problem and need clarification, reflexive intervention, and outcome assessment.
8. All evaluation practice is value based and purposive.

EXERCISES

1. Consider *Joshua* and *Jennifer*. What do you believe the problems are in each case?
2. What values are implicit in your problem statements?
3. What do you think would be the most desirable outcomes for the problems that you stated for each?
4. What values are implicit in your selection of outcomes?
5. Compare your responses to those of another reader who has responded differently than you have. Compare and contrast the values that each of you holds and how these values have guided your thinking processes about evaluation practice problems and desired outcomes.

THE CONCEPTUAL FRAMEWORK OF EVALUATION PRACTICE

CHAPTER 2

Overview of the Model
Principles and Assumptions
Deductive Reasoning
Inductive Reasoning
Main Points
Exercises

FIGURE 2.1 | MODEL OF EVALUATION PRACTICE

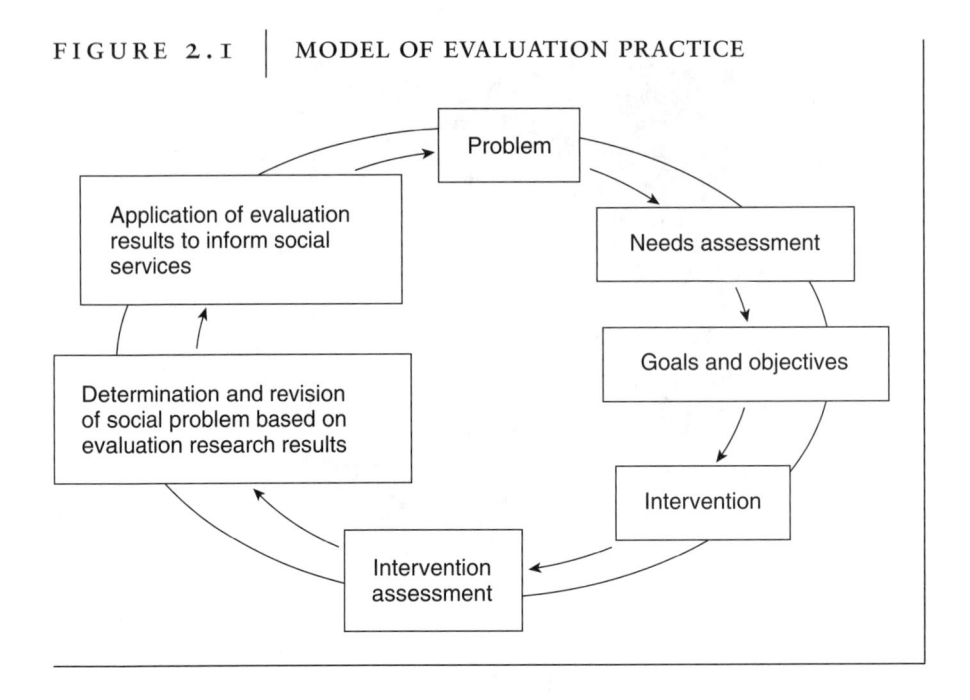

```
                          Problem
                             │
  Application of evaluation  │
  results to inform social   ▼
  services              Needs assessment
        ▲                    │
        │                    ▼
  Determination and revision  Goals and objectives
  of social problem based on       │
  evaluation research results      ▼
        ▲                      Intervention
        │                          │
        │                          ▼
              Intervention assessment
```

OVERVIEW OF THE MODEL

In this chapter, we examine the evaluation practice model and its elements in detail. Figure 2.1 depicts our view of evaluation practice as multidimensional. The graphic illustrates the model as a sequential, nonlinear set of thinking and action processes. We have used a continuous shape to depict the larger purpose of evaluation practice in social work as knowledge building. Engaging in evaluation practice is an ongoing process of generating and applying systematically generated knowledge to the identification and resolution of social problems.

In Figure 2.1, the three areas of evaluation discussed in Chapter 1—problem and need clarification, reflexive intervention, and outcome assessment— are further broken down into steps, which are sequential and ongoing.

In the clarification stage, we specify a social problem or problems to which our professional activity is directed. We then look at what is needed to resolve the problem, in part or in total, and establish goals and objectives that will guide the intervention to fulfill the need. As we implement intervention, we engage in reflexive intervention, in which practice, resources, and influences are elaborated and monitored. This step helps us to clearly understand what we are doing, using, and being influenced by and how we are proceeding to meet our goals and objectives.

As we move to outcome assessment, we base our success criteria on how well the goals and objectives were met. Our final step begins the process again, in which we use findings to guide and inform future practice.

We now clarify the assumptions upon which this model is based. Knowing these principles will help you understand evaluation practice not only as a sequence of steps, but as an essential practice action embedded within an ethical, value-based context.

PRINCIPLES AND ASSUMPTIONS

Evaluation practice is grounded on the following principles:

1. All evaluation is value based.
2. Evaluation practice is political.
3. Evaluation practice may have multiple and competing audiences.
4. Evaluation practice may have multiple and competing purposes.
5. Evaluation practice should be the purposive application of rigorous inquiry-based thinking and action to examination of practice need, process, and outcome.
6. Evaluation thinking and actions should provide a meta-framework for systematic practice thinking and actions.

We now explore each of these critical principles.

All Evaluation Is Value Based

We briefly introduced the principle of value-based evaluation practice in Chapter 1 and will now examine it in greater depth. What are values, and what do we mean by value based? **Values** are defined as beliefs and opinions about what is desirable or undesirable, important or unimportant, and correct or incorrect. There is significant debate in the literature on how and the degree to which values influence behavior. By our definition of evaluation practice advanced in Chapter 1, however, all evaluation activity is value based, and thus the role of values in evaluation practice must be recognized as primary to the planning, execution, and use of evaluation knowledge. But what roles do values play in evaluation design and conduct?

Evaluation practice is value based because its primary purpose is to examine how and the extent to which an intervention resolves a social problem. As we will examine in depth later in this chapter, social problems themselves are statements of value. What is desirable, and what requires change? You might note that the word *value* is the root of the term *evaluation* and thus serves to remind us of the essential role that values and ethics play in social work evaluation.

The recognition that diverse groups have differing and sometimes competing values and thus define problems in diverse ways suggests the complexity of evaluation practice thinking and action. What problem(s) an intervention is designed to address, how the intervention is designed to address the problem, and who and what are being evaluated for what audience(s) and purpose(s) can be both confusing and complex to decipher. Sound evaluation practice takes these factors into account to assure the appropriate and purposive use of the new knowledge resulting from evaluation practice process and findings (House & Howe, 1999). Rossi et al. (1999) remind us that social problems change over time as well. Consider *Jennifer*.

Currently, Jennifer is employed as an English teacher in one of the high schools in her community. When she was 40 years old, she began using a wheelchair. Today her needs for accommodations and workplace adaptations are supported by the employment provisions of the Americans with Disabilities Act of 1990 (ADA). When she was a child, getting into and out of the building and classroom were viewed as "her problems"; limited access issues in current legislative rhetoric locate the problem of environmental access barriers within the social, cultural, and institutional environments. Physical and environmental barriers are viewed as being socially constructed and therefore need to be removed and/or supplanted with other means of reasonable access. The responsibility for access therefore falls to the employer, community, and social institutions. The determination of how to accomplish equal access falls to the employer and not to Jennifer. These changes in the definition of a problem and in strategies for intervention are significant, as the locus of responsibility has shifted away from an individual to the community. These changes do not mean the barriers that Jennifer faced in public school will disappear. Many of the problems for Jennifer will remain the same, but the response has changed through the passage of legislation. What was once considered a private issue has become a public problem.

Evaluation Practice Is Political

As discussed previously, evaluation practice deals in large part with the distribution of resources. Those resources can be human, programmatic, financial, intellectual, and so on. Regardless of the type of resource, when resource distribution in the form of intervention and desired change enters into a process, stakeholders emerge, sometimes with competing perspectives (Chelimsky & Sadish, 1997). Of particular importance to the evaluation practice process is how power and position control resources and come to define the target for change, how change should occur, and how it should be recognized.

Because we define evaluation practice as the politicalization of inquiry, some might err in thinking that rigor is not as important as it is in research conducted for the purpose of knowledge and theory generation and testing. Quite to the contrary, it is imperative that evaluation practice be ethically conducted and methodologically sound. In evaluation practice, political purpose informs rather than obfuscates the use of the findings. Political power, dissonance among groups, and stakeholding, whether explicit or implied, play essential roles in the conceptualization, conduct, and use of evaluation findings (House & Howe, 1999). Political considerations, along with other ethical and methodological factors, influence each thinking and action step in the evaluation process.

The passage of the ADA in 1990 highlighted significant changes in political power. This legislation brought disabled individuals such as Jennifer into the mainstream by asserting the protection of their civil rights. In Jennifer's case, the right to access is both conceptually different from historical treatment of mobility-impaired individuals and fiscally demanding in that compliance with the law requires the expenditure of resources.

Evaluation Practice May Have Multiple and Competing Audiences

Because of the value-based and political nature of evaluation practice, audiences may be multiple. But what do we mean by audiences? **Audience** is an individual or group of individuals that has a role in some or all thinking and action processes of an evaluation, including the initiation, receipt, and use of findings. Beginning with problem identification and proceeding through all steps to the use of findings, diverse groups from which multiple perspectives emerge may be involved. These audiences can change throughout a single evaluation practice process or remain stable. The social worker(s) may constitute one of the audiences as well. The following example shows how the concept of audience plays out in evaluation practice.

Earlier we met Joshua. Among the many roles that he occupies in his life is that of state legislator. He was elected to the legislature when he was 28 years old. Because this is a "part-time" legislature, he also holds a position in a public nonprofit agency dedicated to poverty law work. As a legislator, his primary interests involve employment, health, and education. One of the responsibilities of publicly elected officials is to help resolve social problems, often through the enactment or the repeal of legislation. Perhaps nowhere else in evaluation work is the political nature of the process as clearly apparent as in the area of legislative activity. From the beginning process of problem identification through devising alternative solutions, it is likely that many actors will have distinctively different problem definitions, suggestions of alternatives for problem resolution, and determinations of the impact and consequences of the variety of possible courses of action.

For Joshua, this "conflict" became readily apparent in response to what was presented to him as the public school students' "low scores" on standardized academic achievement tests. Public school students in several neighboring states were also tested using some of the same instruments, so it was possible to directly compare the test results of students in his state, and within various counties in his state, to the test results of students in other states. It was argued by some that these results demonstrated not only the "poor performance" of students but the failure of students to learn needed material.

Because, as we noted above, one of Joshua's areas of interest was education, this issue was brought to his attention. What makes this seemingly straightforward problem emerge as one with multiple and often competing audiences? For Joshua, the road to seeking a solution involves meeting with multiple audiences with multiple definitions of the problem and perhaps multiple alternatives or solutions. One audience may argue that the performance on standardized achievement tests does not reflect the "true" measure of one's capabilities, but reflects only what has been predefined by an elite few as important to learning and therefore does not test what has been learned or identify what and how youth need to learn. Another audience might agree that the test scores are substandard but that the causes for students not performing well include large class sizes, poorly maintained classrooms and buildings, and lack of equipment or outdated equipment such as computers and science laboratories. Another audience might argue that the teachers are not prepared and that without competition between schools for student attendance, schools do not have an incentive to have their students achieve better. Solutions in this case might be raising the standards for hiring teachers, instituting a system of merit pay for teacher and student performance, and supporting competition among schools through the creation of charter schools and tax-support incentives for private schools. Of course, there are many more possible explanations for the performance of students on standardized tests, as well as for the identification of solutions to the problem. For Joshua, both the identification of the problem and the selection of solutions will involve a politicized evaluation process that will have multiple audiences competing for his attention and support.

Evaluation Practice May Have Multiple and Competing Purposes

This principle, although seemingly contrary to traditional understandings of systematic inquiry as bias free, is critical to the planning and conduct of evaluation practice and central to our definition of evaluation practice. By definition, evaluation practice is purposive because of its aim to empirically examine intervention value and integrity, and/or to inform intervention change. However, let us consider this principle in more detail. Even though all evaluation has the same basic purpose of empirical scrutiny of intervention process and/or outcome, each study is initiated for particular purposes within the context of practice assessment and conducted and used for those purposes. Factors such as the problem that the intervention addresses; the identified targets of intervention, audiences and stakeholders; and the political issues associated with service delivery all impact the manner in which the basic purposes are actualized. For example, evaluating program integrity for some may mean elaborating best practices with clear evidence, while for others it may mean determining the degree to which an intervention achieved a success criterion as a basis for program revision or elimination. Both are purposively designed to examine intervention integrity, but each has a potentially different outcome for the practitioner, client, funder, and so forth.

Returning to the issue faced by Joshua and the poor performance on standardized achievement tests provides us with a very good example of this principle. If we think about Joshua as a practitioner, then we might also consider him to have multiple clients. Clearly, part of the client system would be the students who are now attending, and those who will in the future attend, public schools in his state. As a legislator responsible for maintaining an educational environment that best equips students for their futures, Joshua has an educa-

tional quality oversight responsibility. As a legislator responsible for assuring funding of public education as well as other public concerns, including some health services, roadways, recreation areas, and state safety and protection, he must assure that sufficient fiscal resources are available for a wide variety of services. As such, Joshua has a fiscal oversight responsibility. It is clear that the history of education is replete with examples of change and adaptation. Joshua also has the responsibility to attend to program evaluation findings that may suggest the need for significant change in the delivery of public education. The ability to be innovative can be an important quality for a legislator. Following any one or all of his public responsibilities may lead Joshua to support a variety of conclusions and outcomes, each having a basis of being "right" within its own framework and according to its own criteria of achievement.

Evaluation Practice Should Be the Purposive Application of Rigorous Inquiry-Based Thinking and Action to Examination of Practice Need, Process, and Outcome

This principle is not new but is the synthesis of the previous assumptions and the ethical foundation of evaluation practice as we see it. As previously mentioned, evaluation practice is conducted for explicit and implicit purposes. Evaluation practice has a primary impact on service users, program developers, policymakers, and practitioners but also broadly informs practice knowledge through incrementally adding empirical knowledge to health and human service practice (Alkin, 1990; Thyer, 2001). Not in spite of, but in our opinion, because of the complex context of evaluation practice, such as stakeholding, resource distribution, political purpose, and competing values, rigor must be upheld in all thinking and action processes of evaluation practice. Rigor means that regardless of evaluation design, practice must be carefully and soundly planned and executed with all thinking and action processes being clearly articulated, conforming to high standards of inquiry, and being well justified so that the audience understands the knowledge generated and the context and process through which knowledge was derived. This principle becomes even more important when evaluation is not welcomed by practitioners or others who are wary of the intended use of empirical knowledge derived from it.

Jennifer now has work accommodation and access needs that have presented themselves since she started to use her wheelchair on a regular basis. It is somewhat common for some employees with disabilities to have accommodation and access needs evaluated by someone other than themselves. Additionally, following the enactment of the ADA, a set of building adaptation and modification codes and guidelines was developed. To respond to Jennifer's needs, the "evaluator" will have at a minimum two audiences, Jennifer and the administrator of the public school, who is responsible for approving and overseeing suggested changes. Jennifer will be in the position of presenting her needs, as she sees and understands them, to the evaluator, who will then interpret them and make recommendations to the school administrator.

In this process, the extent to which the evaluator views Jennifer's accommodation and access needs in the same light as she does may be open to question. Jennifer may hope that there is at least an equal match, if not even new insights and suggestions, but may not see the evaluator as an ally because of her past experience with similar situations, in which solutions to her access needs were scaled down due to cost factors. For the school administrator, any suggestions or recommendations that the evaluator may make—equipment purchase, environmental modification, schedule changes, and so forth—in great likelihood will have a fiscal impact and possible staffing impact. Although the school administrator may feel a responsibility to respond to Jennifer's needs, having to draw upon a limited budget and needing to rearrange work responsibilities and schedules may pose significant conflicts. Given these constraints, the evaluator's assertion of needed changes may be seen by the administrator as costly and coercive. As such, the evaluator may enter the process under a cloud of mistrust and exit with one or both parties unsatisfied.

Evaluation Thinking and Actions Should Provide a Meta-Framework for Systematic Practice Thinking and Actions

Although inquiry and practice are conceptualized as separate curriculum areas, the logical thinking and action processes that are used in evaluation practice are similar to the processes we use in all domains of social work practice (Berlin & Marsh, 1993; Gambrill, 1999). The separation of these curriculum areas seems to arise from the way in which inquiry and practice have been perceived as different by educators and practitioners. One difference lies in the perception of evaluation as outside and in judgment of intervention process and outcome. Another difference is based on the systematic nature of evaluation practice through which each logical step is scrutinized for its knowledge foundation, process, and outcome.

Unlike the current treatment of inquiry as distinct from practice, our contention is that regardless of the domain of practice, social workers need to use inquiry-based thinking and action to be aware of why, how, and what should emerge from what they are doing. Thus, while evaluation practice at its basic level is based on and perceived as closest to principles of logical inquiry, we suggest that it should inform social work practice in multiple ways. First, the model of evaluation practice builds on previous practice approaches such as empirical practice and evidence-based practice (Thyer, 2001). Our approach places the responsibility for scrutiny and excellence on the social worker. Second, evaluation thinking and action processes contribute to social work knowledge through incrementally adding empirically derived information to health and human service practice. Box 2.1 illustrates these points.

We now come to a discussion of thinking and action. As discussed earlier, while complicated by its context, all evaluation practice is based on two distinct forms of human reasoning: deduction and induction.

> **BOX 2.1** | **MISTAKEN IDENTITY OF THE PROBLEM**
>
> Suppose you are a clinical social worker and a new client walks into your office with the request for help. The client appears to be tired, sad, and shaky. Based on your observations, you begin by asking the client to set goals for counseling. If you take this route and omit systematic thinking and action processes, not only might you miss important data on which to make professional decisions but you may do harm. The client lets you know that he wants to feel better, happier, and more energetic. If you begin to explore depression as the problem that "needs" to be remedied, without systematically examining what is needed to resolve the client's problem of sadness, lethargy, and tremor, you missed important information, such as the client's medical condition of diabetes.
>
> Using principles of evaluation practice, you would systematically examine alternative explanations for the client's presenting problems. Once you had a solid understanding of the nature of the client's problem, you would then proceed to what is needed to resolve all or part of the problem. Each step would be based on a sound, logical thinking process. But where do values fit into problem definition? First, your choice of counseling is a value, in that you believe that counseling is "good." Second, you attribute the need for professional help to the client. Thus, you are agreeing that the client's problem as presented is an undesirable condition. If the client came to you with the problem of hating his neighbors because they do not go to his church, you might or might not accept that he has what you agree is a problem.
>
> Now that you agree that the client has a problem, using evaluation practice you would collect data on need, select a point of intervention, identify goals and objectives based on your knowledge and theory preference, implement reflexive intervention, and examine outcome to ascertain the extent to which the client "feels better." The actual approach that you take within the meta-framework of evaluation practice will depend on the substantive theoretical and domain-specific knowledge and experience that you hold and value.

DEDUCTIVE REASONING

Deductive reasoning begins with the acceptance of a general principle or belief and then proceeds to apply that principle to explain a specific case or phenomenon. For example, if you believe in behavioral theory, it is likely that you will reward your children for what they do well. This approach in evaluation practice involves "drawing out" or verifying what already is accepted as credible and correct. Deductive approaches to thinking lead the social worker to examine outcome with preexisting views of success. Evaluators typically use quantitative, experimental-type designs to conduct deductive inquiries (DePoy & Gitlin, 1998).

Consider Joshua again. For Joshua, deductive reasoning related to a programming decision regarding the delivery of quality educational services for children would take the form of establishing theoretically based and well-accepted outcomes, in this case perhaps performance on standardized achievement tests, and comparing the results among groups of students who have been exposed to different settings. It would be possible to compare the results for students in "nonchanged" settings to those of students whose settings had been enhanced by new equipment and building refurbishment, students who were taught by teachers whose salaries were tied to merit pay, or students who were in private school settings. This evaluation would provide four groups of students from which performance scores could be compared. This approach would require that decisions be made regarding the length of time between initiation of the changes and analysis of test results. Admittedly, an evaluation involving multiple years might not be satisfactory if any sense of urgency is given to the problem. Should time be considered a critical factor, it would be possible to identify students currently being educated in distinctly different settings, such as financially well supported schools, poorly funded schools that lack equipment and well-maintained buildings, and private and charter schools.

With the first approach, Joshua and the other evaluators would have more control over the "experimental" variables than in the second situation; however, the outcome measures accepted as credible or correct might remain the same. Both scenarios are based on the theoretical notion that knowledge is monistic and can be acquired by students and that students will illustrate their mastery of the knowledge on a test. The difference factors, such as the settings and teacher incentives, based on previous knowledge, have been identified prior to the evaluation implementation as well.

INDUCTIVE REASONING

Inductive reasoning is a type of cognitive activity that involves a process in which general rules evolve or develop from individual cases or observations of phenomena. The social worker, proceeding inductively, seeks to reveal or uncover a truth based on aggregation and analysis of the multiple perceptions of informed sources of knowledge. This approach assumes to a greater or lesser degree that the social worker does not know the "truth" but seeks it from credible involved sources, such as practitioners, literature, and clients. Intervention success criteria, sound intervention processes, and methods of intervention assessment then would be developed based on aggregated and inductively derived principles.

Based on inductive thinking, the social worker would not use testing as in the example above, but would observe each setting to see what factors emerge both to define learning and to differentiate the settings from one another. To summarize, in a deductive approach, the theory is established and the method for testing its application and efficacy is set prior to the inquiry. In an inductive approach, there are no previously established expectations that can be tested. Thus, observation is intended to reveal information that can be examined for emergent knowledge and principles.

How Thinking Processes Guide Evaluation Action Processes

Although both types of reasoning are used in any evaluation project, the overall process can be characterized as following the structure of one or the other type of reasoning. Each type of reasoning may result in different action strategies to derive evaluation knowledge.

Working deductively, the social worker assumes a truth before engaging in the evaluation practice process and applies that truth to the thinking and action processes. Evaluation practice based on deductive thinking would utilize experimental-type action strategies such as standardized testing and statistical analysis in needs assessment and process and outcome investigation. Problem statements would be drawn from preexisting theory and experience characterized in the practice and scholarly literature.

As discussed in our example of the use of deductive reasoning in developing an evaluation of student performance on standardized achievement tests, an initial problem statement would involve the establishment of a relationship between student performance on standardized achievement tests and admission to college and/or successful job performance. The link here would be between current achievements and defined measures of future success. In this situation, Joshua might turn to educational and career literature either to support or refute this connection. If there were little or no support in the literature for this link, then conducting this deductive evaluation might not be considered, and another course of action supported in conceptual and/or empirical literature might be followed. In either situation, without some support from preexisting literature and practice, the expense associated with the deductive evaluation considered here would not be warranted.

In an evaluation effort proceeding inductively, the intervention and desired processes and outcomes emerge from what is learned from those who will be receiving service. Action strategies might consist of open-ended interview, observation, and other forms of investigative actions that are characteristic of naturalistic, qualitative traditions. Interventions might be developed as a consequence of new insights and thus might include a broader array of services based on the emergent problem statements, needs, and issues identified by those who are considered to be knowledgeable.

An inductive reasoning approach in evaluation practice is used to reveal rules and processes (Patton, 1997), whereas deductive reasoning is used to test or predict the application of theory, processes, and rules to specific areas of concern. Both approaches can be used to describe, explain, and predict phenomena. Table 2.1 summarizes the major characteristics of each type of reasoning. As you can see by examining Table 2.1, induction and deduction, while not opposite, take alternative approaches not only to thinking and action, but also to the view and related credibility of knowledge derived from each approach. We suggest that both deductive and inductive thinking and related action are viable and credible approaches to evaluation practice and that they can be integrated as well, given the contextual factors of purpose, audience, and politics.

28 BEGINNINGS

TABLE 2.1 | CHARACTERISTICS OF INDUCTIVE AND DEDUCTIVE THINKING

Inductive	Deductive
No a priori acceptance of truth	A priori acceptance of truth
Alternative conclusions drawn from data	One set of conclusions accepted as true
Theory development	Theory testing
Examines relationships among unrelated pieces of data	Tests relationships among discrete phenomena
Development of concepts based on repetition of patterns	Testing of concepts based on application to discrete phenomena
Holistic perspective	Atomistic perspective
Multiple realities	Single, separate reality

Next, we illustrate how deductive and inductive thinking underpin thinking in all domains of practice. As we continue to explore induction and deduction, think again about evaluation practice as an organizing meta-approach to social work practice.

Applying Evaluation Practice Thinking and Actions Across Social Work Practice Domains

If you carefully examine the knowledge that you use to make practice decisions, you will see that the same thinking and action steps that we suggest in our evaluation practice model characterize direct practice reasoning and activity. Look at Table 2.2 for more detail.

As an example, *Jennifer* comes to you for clinical social work intervention. Look at how you might use evaluation practice as an organizing approach to intervention.

Jennifer was first married at the age of 40. Before she was married and because of the changes in her physical strength and capabilities, she called your office to set up an appointment. Most of your practice work had involved adults in their 30s, 40s, and 50s and their changing life circumstances. You have a particular interest in working with women and had sought out additional education and training as better preparation for your work. You had not worked with a woman with a disability, however, and little from your early training seemed to prepare you for your work with Jennifer. As a result of your initial interview, you consult the literature and find that Jennifer, like many women with disabilities, had not had many long-term romantic and sexual relationships. She

TABLE 2.2 | SOCIAL WORK REASONING AND EVALUATION PRACTICE

Reasoning in All Domains of Practice	Evaluation Practice
Presenting issue to be addressed by social work	Literature support and values clarification to identify and obtain a comprehensive understanding of social problem
Obtain information about the client/client group	Empirical needs assessment
Based on information, what approaches/skills do I use to intervene? What needs to be done?	Specification of goals and objectives, with process and outcome assessment indicators based on empirically supported needs statement
What about the intervention should be changed so that the best result is achieved?	Reflexive intervention
Was the intervention successful in achieving its desired outcomes?	Outcome/summative evaluation

was approaching 40 and had hoped to have a child by now. You found out in your interview that, as was also noted in some of the literature about women with physical disabilities, Jennifer had been actively discouraged by several health professionals from becoming pregnant and carrying out a vaginal birth.

The literature also introduced you to a relatively recently acknowledged post-poliomyelitis (post-polio) syndrome. Symptoms such as muscle fatigue and bouts of depression were common for many people who developed post-polio syndrome. As Jennifer's mobility needs began to change, from full-time use of forearm crutches to regular, though not full-time, use of a manual wheelchair, her experiences with the outside world began to change. As she approached her marriage, fears of sexual intimacy and general physical and emotional concerns were weighing heavily on her mind.

In your attempt to clarify the problem that will guide your clinical work with Jennifer, you discover that what may seem to be a private, individual problem with intimacy is also very much a public problem. The individual issue associated with Jennifer's relative "newness" to and fear of a romantic and sexual relationship is a common, socially constructed, and culturally promoted sexuality role of women with disabilities. Thus, Jennifer's failure to conceive a child during her 20s or early 30s, as for many women with, or without, disabilities, not only is a problem for her but is a large social problem, which places Jennifer in a public category for which health professionals have very limited practice knowledge.

Should you work with Jennifer in counseling to explore intimacy issues from a psychodynamic perspective as you have done with many other clients? As you proceed, you realize that this new area of work for you poses challenges to deductive strategies. How will you approach and examine the effectiveness of your work in accomplishing stated intervention goals? Will your work be short-term, ongoing, or episodic? What will the desired outcome(s) be, and how will you and Jennifer know that the intervention was "successful"? Will your work with Jennifer, and the necessary learning on your part, lead to future work on your part with other adults with disabilities? How will you help other social workers learn from your work with Jennifer? Inductive approaches to inquiry are indicated in a situation such as the one you face with Jennifer. As you can see, the application of inductive logic and systematic thinking from our evaluation practice model parallels your clinical reasoning approaches. The evaluation practice meta-framework makes explicit the thinking and action processes throughout your work with Jennifer and with the expanded social problem that contact with Jennifer reveals.

MAIN POINTS

1. The evaluation practice model comprises a set of thinking and action processes embedded within a purposive, political context.
2. Evaluation practice is based on a set of assumptions and principles.
3. Evaluation practice comprises three distinct but integrated thinking and action phases:
   a. problem and need clarification
   b. reflexive intervention
   c. outcome assessment
4. Each element of evaluation practice is founded in logical thinking and action processes, with systematically derived and organized evidence supporting each of these temporally sequenced processes.

EXERCISES

1. Think of an example of how you use deductive reasoning in your daily life.
2. Think of an example of how you use inductive reasoning in your daily life.
3. Compare and contrast each example for context, processes, and outcomes, and your comfort with each.
4. Describe a practice activity, and examine how it could be translated into an evaluation practice process.
5. Look at a mission statement of a service agency and extract the values implicit in it.

… CHAPTER 3

ROLES AND RESPONSIBILITIES OF SOCIAL WORKERS IN EVALUATION PRACTICE

Managing People

Analytic Axes

Evaluation Practice Ethics

Main Points

Exercises

MANAGING PEOPLE

In this chapter, we look at the diversity of roles and responsibilities that social workers and other practitioners have within evaluation practice. As you might expect, the context of evaluation practice, its purpose, and resources all factor into the equation of who conducts evaluation and how social workers interact with others who are involved in each step in evaluation practice. Defining roles and responsibilities reminds us that evaluation is a human process, and consideration of the values, interests, and perspective of each person involved is critical. As reiterated throughout the text, although practitioners, researchers, and evaluators often assert that they are being objective, we suggest that any human process cannot be free of preference or bias. That is not to say that evaluation practice is not rigorous. Rather, inherent in our model, bias and political stakeholding are important elements to be recognized and addressed.

One of the least understood elements of evaluation in general is the importance of the evaluator's skill in managing people. Theory and practice of group process, which are basic to all social work education, are therefore skills that social workers possess and apply to managing the human dynamics of evaluation practice thinking and action at multiple levels. Consider the example in Box 3.1.

ANALYTIC AXES

The example in Box 3.1 provides us with insights about the complexity of evaluation practice faced by a social worker. The roles and purposes of the evaluation not only influence the questions asked and methods chosen to answer them, but highlight the importance of clarifying the social worker's role, as well as the roles and preferences of diverse stakeholders. All of these challenges require significant skill in social and group process. Three analytic axes provide the decision structures through which a social worker can examine, clarify, and select the appropriate role(s) to take in the evaluation practice process:

Insider—Outsider

Scientist—Practitioner

Formative—Summative

Of course, the axes are not mutually exclusive, but each one does provide guidance in a focused area regarding answers to who, what, how, where, and why of evaluation. Thinking of where you fall on each axis provides definition of your roles and responsibilities in evaluation practice.

Insider—Outsider

This axis identifies where the evaluator is located in the thinking and action processes of evaluation practice from problem definition to final **summative assessment**. The insider typically occupies an integral role in the delivery of inter-

> **BOX 3.1**
>
> ### EXAMPLE — SERVING FAMILIES OF INDIVIDUALS WITH POST-TRAUMATIC STRESS DISORDER: MANAGING PEOPLE
>
> You are a social worker in a mental health agency. Lately you have noticed that family members of individuals being treated for post-traumatic stress disorder (PTSD) have been calling and requesting services for themselves. The agency is willing to address the needs of family members but does not necessarily know what help these family members are seeking. In this case, you accept the lead role in the thinking and action processes of problem identification and needs assessment. First, you find that the literature is very limited in describing the problems that family members may encounter in living with an individual with PTSD. At this point, you can proceed in many directions. Do you take the lead role in needs assessment? Do you work with an advisory group of providers and family members themselves? Do you provide the structure for needs assessment? Do you ask others to participate in developing and conducting the inquiry? Time, need for and/or desire to collaborate, agency structure and mission, resources to conduct needs assessment, and your skills in the thinking and action process, including managing the human element, may be important considerations in what role you take and what responsibilities you accept.
>
> Suppose you have already ascertained that support groups are needed to provide an outlet in which family members can share experiences and strategies for living with an individual with PTSD. The agency is willing to fund a short-term pilot program to be evaluated for its long-term continuation. Now what is your role in the process? If you are an insider who is committed to offering support groups, should you set the goals and objectives? Doing so might be perceived as self-serving. If you do not participate in specifying goals and objectives, it might be possible for others to disagree with you on the intended outcomes and set objectives that may not be attainable through support group interventions.
>
> Finally, what about intervention assessment? Who does it? You? An outsider? What about a team of evaluators? What perspectives and biases are operating, and how do you recognize and manage them to assure quality of service to a group in need? As you can see in this example, roles and responsibilities need to be clarified.

vention being evaluated, while the outsider is external and not involved in the intervention at all. On the insider extreme, the evaluator may occupy the role of director of a program or service being evaluated, or of primary social worker working with an individual client. The outsider may be a consultant hired by a funder or by the agency providing the intervention, or may be a government-appointed person or group to assure the adherence of interventions and providers to externally developed standards. Between the two ends of the continuum are an infinite number of positions that the social worker can occupy. The further from the extremes, the more complex the task of evaluation practice becomes. In Box 3.2, we revisit the previous example.

With the current trend for social, health, and human services to demonstrate efficient and effective use of resources, it is not unusual for evaluators to

> **BOX 3.2** | **EXAMPLE—SERVING FAMILIES OF INDIVIDUALS WITH POST-TRAUMATIC STRESS DISORDER: INSIDER—OUTSIDER**
>
> As an insider in the planning, development, and implementation of support groups for family members of individuals with PTSD, you are most interested in the process of connection and understanding of family members so that they would be able to provide support for individuals being treated for PTSD. Evaluation practice would therefore examine how family intervention was perceived by participants and if the group intervention resulted in ongoing support for families. However, on the outsider end of the continuum, the funder is more interested in how many family members utilized the service and the degree to which the intervention was cost-efficient in preventing future stress-related problems in family members. The social worker who is located at neither extreme of the insider-outsider continuum would have to address both perspectives, as well as others expressed by diverse stakeholder groups.

be outsiders selected by funders and policymakers to impose external summative standards of program success (Cherin & Meezan, 1998, p. 1). Although there is a belief in the objectivity of top-down external approaches, the criteria selected by outsiders are often not relevant success indicators to those who are insiders in the delivery of interventions; thus, underutilization of evaluation data to improve intervention process and outcome is a frequent phenomenon (Cherin & Meezan, p. 1). Moreover, as indicated in Chapter 1, the word *evaluation* contains "value" within it, challenging the assertion of evaluation as objective under any circumstances. In an ideal situation, we would agree with Cherin and Meezan, who suggest that the key to evaluations that meet the needs of multiple stakeholders on the full spectrum from outsider to insider is the conceptualization and implementation of evaluations as a learning collaboration among all stakeholders. However, the ideal is often not the practice. We turn now to a more detailed critical examination of how the location of the evaluator influences the thinking and action processes.

The agency-based evaluator, while cost-efficient, begins the evaluation firmly within the potential for a conflict of interest. As a primary stakeholder, an employee of the agency delivering an intervention may face an explicit, implicit, or unconscious obligation to provide an evaluation that is positive and possesses only a contained critique of the agency or organization. We are not suggesting that the evaluator is unethical. Rather, the inside evaluator has an interest, along with the agency administration and employees, to use empirical information to solicit resources in order to carry out the agency's mission. Tension between assuring the survival of an intervention and conducting rigorous inquiry is therefore not uncommon.

Another area of potential conflict for the inside evaluator involves the obligation to follow the direction and expectation of the supervisor while seeking to maintain sensitivity to the perspective and needs of the direct-service staff. A major part of the job of the administrator is fiscal management. It is therefore not unusual for direct-service staff to have competing agendas among themselves and between service and administration. Thus, the challenge for the insider evaluator may be to reconcile conflicting agendas, including his or her own competing alliance as a peer, employee, supervisee, and judge of all levels of service.

The outside evaluator is less likely to experience some of the competing demands that have just been identified. First, because the outsider will be contracted by a specific stakeholder group, which may be anyone of the several that we have identified, the primary relationship responsibility will be between the contracting stakeholder group and the consultant. However, outside evaluation is often met with mistrust from insiders, who perceive potential threat from the evaluator. Limited cooperation in an evaluation procedure limits not only the knowledge derived, but the use of the knowledge to improve intervention. Cherin and Meezan (1998) have found that outsiders who simulate an insider perspective by regularly engaging in communication with the evaluation participants have higher rates of impact on organizations than those who maintain distance. Collaboration with key decision makers and agency personnel is therefore a critical role and responsibility of the outside evaluator as a means to promote the best utilization of evaluation findings. According to Cherin and Meezan, "sensitivity to and the understanding of the political and social contexts of the organization by the evaluator in conducting the evaluation also has a significant impact on utilization and the acceptance of the evaluation process and evaluation findings" (p. 8).

Between the two extremes of the continuum are numerous and infinite positions. For example, an agency employee may be hired exclusively for the purpose of evaluation. Thus, while an insider to the agency, the individual is an outsider to direct-service staff. Evaluation may be conducted by a team of insiders and outsiders, bringing both the limitations and strengths of each position to bear on the thinking and action processes of the evaluation. Within this paradigm, the move toward participatory evaluation (in which multiple stakeholders, including service recipients, participate) has expanded the evaluator role beyond assessor to collaborator and group member (Patton, 1987). You can now see why knowledge and skill in group process is essential in evaluation.

Scientist—Practitioner

This continuum addresses not only the primary functions of one's job, but the underlying philosophical framework through which the social worker approaches his or her professional responsibilities. Before beginning our discussion of this continuum, we need to acknowledge the heavily debated and changing understandings of **science**. From our perspective, science is not limited to a logico-deductive method of investigation. On a broader spectrum, we suggest that science is a philosophical, theoretical, and epistemological lens through which one systematically examines phenomena, collects evidence, and uses evidence to develop, support, or refute a knowledge claim. We do not suggest a particular methodology through which scientists work, and thus are not eliminating any rigorous methods of inquiry from the domain of science. Rather, we distinguish the scientist from other roles by the focus of the scientist on the development of knowledge through systematic investigation (Schon in Chelimski & Sadish, 1997). The social work practitioner, at the other extreme end of the continuum, focuses his or her professional activity on the enactment of specialized skills and actions to resolve social problems, but does not see his or her role as knowledge generation. It is our contention that all social workers, regardless of their identification as scientists or practitioners, should be using evaluation practice as a meta-framework in which all practice activity takes place. If systematic thinking and action processes were explicitly used in social work practice, the distinction and tension between scientist and practitioner would be diminished. As such, all social workers, regardless of their practice focus and domain, would see themselves as contributing to the knowledge base of social work. However, we realize that our ideal is not the case, and we therefore proceed with the discussion of the scientist-practitioner continuum as we currently view it in practice, with the vision that this continuum will be moot in future social work practice.

As you can see, the distinction between practitioner and scientist is not a clear one, even in today's practice climate. Some argue that the mere practice of social work in and of itself creates new knowledge. We do not disagree, but suggest that practitioners do not see themselves as concerned as researchers with elaborating practice wisdom, testing it, expanding it to theory, and/or creating a foundation of knowledge that explains and advances practice. Similarly, scientists do not view themselves as focused on the actual delivery of services and interventions based on theory and knowledge.

The position of the social work evaluator along the scientist-practitioner continuum is therefore based in how one perceives his or her primary professional purposes and functions, how one thinks about professional activity, and how one allocates time to specific activities. The individual whose primary professional tasks are collecting and analyzing data, recording results and conclusions, and disseminating the knowledge derived therefrom in scholarly and professional environments is most likely to identify as a scientist. The individual who works primarily with client groups to achieve a practical solution to social problems would tip the scale on the practitioner end.

How the evaluator is viewed by others and by himself or herself on this continuum is important to how the evaluation will be conducted and used. The scientist provides evidence that is sought and well respected as "true," while the practitioner is characterized by his or her primary involvement in the delivery of interventions. The scientist is frequently seen as an outsider, removed from practice, objective, and systematic. The practitioner, on the other hand, is immersed in practice and is often perceived as an action-oriented insider rather than as a systematic evaluator. In the past two decades, however, there has been a call for social work to integrate systematic inquiry and practice. A recent text edited by Hess and Mullen (1997) advances models of researcher-practitioner partnerships, some of which suggest that the social worker must be both. Similarly, the terms *empirical practice* and *evidence-based practice* have been used to indicate the link between research and practice and to suggest that the practitioner is or should be following scientific logic in making practice decisions (Thyer, 2001). Moreover, the last two Council on Social Work Education Curriculum Policy Statements have mandated that social workers at both the graduate and undergraduate levels be educated in systematic evaluation of practice, thereby reducing the gap between inquiry and practice.

Although our ideal social work role would eliminate the scientist-practitioner continuum, social workers often engage explicitly in either practice or inquiry. As suggested by Hess and Mullen (1997), demands for accountability and examination of outcome can be best met by a partnership between scientist and practitioner. We concur for the short run and add the caveat that additional stakeholders, including the recipients of social services, be involved throughout in the thinking and action processes of evaluation practice. As indicated earlier in this chapter, collaboration increases the likelihood that the evaluation conduct and findings will be welcomed and used to improve intervention process and outcome, which is illustrated in Box 3.3.

Closely related to the scientist-practitioner and insider-outsider continua is the formative-summative axis. We now turn to a discussion of this important element of evaluation

Formative—Summative

As discussed previously, the field of evaluation historically has been divided according to two purposes: use of data about intervention input, conduct, and output to inform intervention improvement (formative); and use of intervention data to determine overall intervention worth and future status (summative). As indicated by Chen (1992), formative or process evaluation focuses on program implementation. We have included formative evaluation, also called monitoring, within reflexive implementation as described in Chapters 1 and 2 and elaborated in Part 3. Summative or outcome evaluations, on the other hand, determine whether "a program's goals are being achieved" (Chen, 1992, p. 11).

As indicated in Chapter 1, evaluation has expanded both conceptually and methodologically beyond this axis. Not only has evaluation been expanded to the entirety of conceptualizing and resolving social problems, but the methods used to examine problem resolution and how it occurs have diversified (Grinnell, 2001; Patton, 1987). Nevertheless, evaluation is still generally considered by most as meeting the purposes of intervention improvement and/or assessment of success (Tripodi, 2000). Even though our text is devoted to an expansive model of evaluation practice, we do acknowledge the roots and current major action processes of evaluation as formative and summative assessment. We therefore posit this axis as an important consideration in the thinking and action processes of evaluation practice, because how evaluation is conceptualized, conducted, and disseminated is significantly influenced by its perception as formative or summative.

BOX 3.3 | **EXAMPLE — SERVING FAMILIES OF INDIVIDUALS WITH POST-TRAUMATIC STRESS DISORDER: COLLABORATION IN EVALUATION PRACTICE**

Suppose that the social worker who initiates support group interventions for family members of individuals diagnosed with PTSD is not involved in setting or examining success criteria. The outsider scientist who conducts the evaluation tends to base success criteria on theory and research literature. In the absence of literature on family intervention related to PTSD, the evaluator selects support group outcome criteria that have been demonstrated in analogous populations. In our illustration, the scientist makes the decision to test family members for their levels of stress and their knowledge of PTSD. The evaluator selects standardized measures of stress and creates a knowledge assessment to be administered before participation and at three-month intervals. However, the practitioner knows that the family members who join the pilot support group have extensive knowledge about PTSD and may not have experienced reduction in stress during or following their participation in the group. The specific goal set by the support group members and the practitioner is the development of a network of relationships among families who can serve as informal and long-term supports in the community. Clearly, the scientist and the practitioner are not in agreement regarding the purpose and desired outcome of the support group. Even if the practitioner's goal is met, success will not be accomplished according to the investigation criteria proposed by the scientist. However, the scientist is baffled by the practitioner's stated goal for the group because there is no evidence to support the selected goal. The disparity between the evaluation and practical success criteria may be detrimental to the focus of the scientist as well as that of the practitioner, and in the scuffle, the client group becomes invisible. Collaboration between scientist and practitioner, or our ideal of the social worker as scientist-practitioner using evaluation practice as a meta-framework for all social work action processes, would provide a structure in which practical and empirically supported criteria for desired outcome could be examined and synthesized as the basis for expected outcomes.

Suppose that the social worker, the agency administrator, and a family member of an individual with PTSD form an evaluation team in which the problem is collectively identified; and multiple groups are represented in the statement of what is needed to address the issues faced by family members of individuals with PTSD, from the perspective of family members, professionals, and those concerned with fiscal efficiency. Goals and objectives can therefore reflect the desired outcomes and would include multiple approaches to assessment of process, outcome, and cost. This scenario would combine the advantages of the specialized knowledge of the evaluator-scientist with the knowledge and experience of the practitioner and client system.

Let's revisit Joshua to illustrate. If the problem to be resolved in Joshua's youth was identified solely as alcoholism by his social worker or vocational counselor, any intervention that did not produce permanent sobriety would fail. Numerous needs could be revealed to resolve the problem, such as removing Joshua from alcohol, or removing alcohol from Joshua's environments. Both of these needs could be met by permanently restricting Joshua to environments in which alcohol was not available or by eliminating alcohol from all environments such as in the days of prohibition in the United States. If formatively evaluated, the implementation of each strategy could be asserted and then examined for its efficacy. Of course, these measures are not within the domain of social work and are extreme examples of how problems that are identified by outsiders can be formatively characterized and summatively evaluated as successful or not successful regardless of the fairness or appropriateness of the intervention.

Let us look at one of many possible examples of sound assessment on the formative-summative axis. If the problem to be resolved were defined as substance abuse caused by feelings of worthlessness, the needs would be to promote a sense of worth and thereby reduce and ultimately eliminate substance use. Formative evaluation would examine the extent to which intervention goals and actions were being enacted and moving in the direction of the summative criteria of worth and sobriety. In this scenario, there are intermediate goals and objectives to be assessed and a feedback loop established from formative data to determine how each intervention process is producing a desired summative outcome. If sobriety were not immediate and permanent, formative data would be used to inform intervention change and to examine intermediate changes that would lead to the ultimate summative goal of sobriety and self-worth.

A synthesis of these three axes demonstrates the complexity of the roles and responsibilities of the social work evaluator, some of which are chosen and some of which are imposed. Clearly, these axes are interwoven and in no way mutually exclusive. For example, summative, outsider, scientist evaluation is what we typically think of when we hear that we are being evaluated. These three elements are combined in school evaluations where "objective" tests are used to measure what we learn and to form the basis of our school performance record. It is therefore not surprising that external summative evaluation is often intimidating and resisted. If we successfully meet the desired outcome criterion of learning class material but do not test well, we have failed.

However, let us consider how these three extremes could be useful to those being evaluated. Suppose an outside evaluator came into a class in which you were a student, to ascertain the extent to which students were learning algebra. The ultimate success criterion would be mastery of algebraic concepts. It might be possible for students to define how they wish to demonstrate this mastery, and thus the measurement of an externally imposed summative criterion could be tailored individually. Think of classes that you have attended in which you can choose how to demonstrate your mastery. If you test well, you might select that medium; if not, perhaps you would select a portfolio, oral presentation, or some other medium. Sound summative evaluation would capture the attainment of the goal through careful consideration of assessment method.

We have stated that the combination of formative and summative strategies is what we consider the ideal in evaluation practice. Knowing that an outcome occurred (summative) may not illuminate why it occurred. Only formative scrutiny can provide information on the degree to which an intervention and/or its parts produced the summative success criterion. Because problems, needs, goals and objectives, and interventions are complex, it behooves the social work evaluator to look at variability and diversity in the intervention processes. Consider your algebra class again. What if only some students mastered algebra? Without formative evaluation, how would you know what aspects of the class, students, or other influences may have contributed to a continuum of success? The link between formative and summative assessment is therefore one that we feel is critical if an evaluation is to yield findings that can be used to improve both interventions and outcomes.

Throughout our discussion of the multiple roles and responsibilities of the social work evaluator, it is apparent that evaluation thinking and action processes are fraught with ethical crossroads and dilemmas. We now shift our attention to ethical challenges and responsibilities of social work evaluators.

EVALUATION PRACTICE ETHICS

We begin our discussion with an illustrative scenario in Box 3.4.

Both the political nature of evaluation practice and the competing interest groups render evaluation practice processes complex and challenged by ethical dilemmas. For the social work evaluation practitioner, the framework and guidelines of the National Association of Social Work (NASW) Code of Ethics (2002) provide the ethical structure underpinning all social work professional activity. However, these guidelines are not readily clear and require careful consideration in ethical decision making. The NASW Code of Ethics, value of service, and its associated ethical principles posit that the primary goal of social work is to help people in need and to address social problems. On first blush, it would therefore seem that the agency would address the needs of the girls as well as the prevention of homelessness. However, what if the girls are not perceived as making decisions in their own best interests? What if their needs are clearly evident but in conflict with the funder's mission, values, and beliefs for the program?

The NASW Code of Ethics values integrity, with the associated ethical principle that social workers are to behave in a trustworthy manner. On each of the three axes and in all roles and responsibilities that we discussed earlier, NASW mandates that we must act honestly and responsibly in our relations with our agencies and organizations. By extension, for the agency-based evaluator a primary stakeholder may be justly considered to be the agency or organization. What decisions should be made and why? Should client-centered evaluation practice take precedence over other approaches? Sometimes, however, without the support from and evidence to show the value of an intervention to funders, policymakers, and administrators, client service may not be an option. Thus, the ethical codes of our profession direct us away from a prescriptive approach to decision making toward a consideration of the purpose of social work in promoting social justice and equal opportunity. Ethical decisions must be made on these bases. Moreover, in our opinion, the basis for resolving ethical dilemmas should be clearly explicated by the social work evaluator so that the value base

> **BOX 3.4 | EXAMPLE—ETHICAL DILEMMAS IN AN ADOLESCENT SHELTER**
>
> Jane is a social worker who is employed in a shelter for adolescent runaway girls. Her primary job is providing counseling to the girls in which she helps them make decisions about their futures. Jane, who has just accepted the position of evaluator, has been asked to conduct both summative assessment of resident high school graduation rates and reflexive implementation of the educational support program at the shelter. Because the shelter receives funding from the state, the state effort to achieve 100% high school graduation for all youth is a major aim of the shelter program.
>
> From her work with the girls, Jane knows that the educational support staff member, John, is not liked by the residents, and the girls are therefore reluctant to attend educational sessions that will help them pass their academic subjects. Jane also knows that John is strict but fair in his work with the girls; because he is serious in his work, he is perceived as a stern parent. As you can see, there are many ethical dilemmas in this case. First, how does Jane measure graduation when the likelihood is that these students will take longer to graduate than typical high school students and will follow an educational path different from that of typical students? What if the rate of graduation on time is poor among the residents, but the long-term graduation rate is 100%? Second, knowing that residents may not be tracked more than a few years after leaving the residence, how should graduation rate be reported, and how will it affect program funding? Third, how will Jane address educational support in process assessment, knowing that the girls do not like a competent social worker who is committed to his job? In the larger evaluative picture, what if the girls have goals in the program that they perceive to be more important than immediate high school graduation, such as locating a job so they can live independently and safely away from abusive families? How does Jane reconcile the conflict between the summative success criteria of the girls and those of the funder? There are many ethical challenges in this scenario, even beyond those that we identified. We have no answers to these ethical dilemmas other than to note that they exist and social workers must be aware of them and of the framework in which ethical decisions will be made.

of the evaluation thinking and action processes is clear and provides a contextual understanding for the evaluation knowledge that is generated and used.

MAIN POINTS

1. Evaluation practice is a process of human communication, and interpersonal skills and group process are therefore essential evaluation practice skills.
2. Three axes both define and are defined by evaluator responsibilities, values, and approaches: insider—outsider, scientist—practitioner, and formative—summative.
3. A synthesis of the three axes and their intersection is part and parcel of all evaluation practice thinking and action.

4. Two frameworks for ethical decision making are the NASW Code of Ethics and the responsibility of social workers to clearly define the value criteria on which they approach and consider ethical dilemmas.

EXERCISES

1. Select an article from a social work journal that describes an evaluation effort in social work. Identify the evaluator's role in each of the three continua presented in this chapter, and discuss your rationale for positioning the social worker.
2. Discuss how evaluation of process and outcome occurs in your agency or school, and examine the ethical dilemmas that are present in evaluation practice.

THINKING PROCESSES OF EVALUATION PRACTICE

PART 2

IDENTIFYING SOCIAL WORK PROBLEMS AND ISSUES

CHAPTER 4

Definitions

Thinking Processes in Articulating Social Problems

Problem Mapping and Force Field Analysis

Main Points

Exercises

DEFINITIONS

In this chapter, we examine the nature of social problems and illustrate specific techniques that can be used to identify and clarify problem statements. The problem statement forms the foundation for all thinking and action processes in intervention and assessment of intervention efficacy. Therefore, careful and systematic formulation of the problem statement is critical in evaluation practice. Further, unlike many texts that do not differentiate problem and need, we see these two processes as separate and distinct in nature. A **problem** is a conceptual-value assertion of what is undesirable, and a **need statement** is a systematically supported template of actions that are necessary to resolve all or part of the problem as it is stated.

Consider, for example, the following problem statement: "Substance abuse interferes with one's ability to function in employment." In this statement, what is undesirable? Substance abuse certainly is, as are limitations in employment. Conversely, by stating what is undesirable, a problem statement directly or indirectly indicates what is valued as desirable. Let us reword our previous problem statement to illustrate: "Substance abuse is a serious problem because it creates barriers in getting to work on time and doing one's job correctly." As you can see by this statement, what is desirable is the elimination of substance abuse as well as punctuality and "correct" work output.

Although we often consider problems to exist as entities outside ourselves, problems are contextually embedded in personal and cultural values. Thus, a problem statement is a social construction emerging from the values and interests of those who are naming the problem. As suggested by Rossi and Freeman (1999), a problem becomes "social" only when it attracts political attention and is positioned within the public arena of resource allocation.

In the case of Jennifer Savoy, one of the major issues for her involves physical and environmental access related to her use of a wheelchair. When she was a child, issues of access to buildings, including classrooms, were seen as her responsibility or problem. The problem statement would have been "Jennifer is unable to access public buildings." Can you see that this problem statement is located individually, so the logical solution to it would lie with Jennifer changing her behavior in some way?

A current statement of Jennifer's problem, however, might look very different given the significant political and value changes that have taken place over the past 20 years. The problem statement now changes: "The physical and environmental inaccessibility interferes with or blocks participation in community activities (that is, work, education, community living, securing healthcare services, and so forth) for people, like Jennifer, with physical disabilities." Although this scenario is the same as the one above, note that in the second definition, Jennifer's disability is not the locus of the "problem," and thus the solution is not her responsibility. Such a problem statement would suggest an environmental, public resolution to limited access.

Let us consider another example.

We have already met Joshua Williams. During high school and the four years following graduation, he was an active drinker, a situation that led to many complications for him, including employment difficulties. Following inpatient and outpatient treatment attempts, Joshua began a period of sustained recovery. He identified a key feature for his continuing recovery as enrollment in and completion of a college degree. His vocational rehabilitation counselor was very reluctant to support this plan, viewing Joshua as unreliable. Depending on whether you are the vocational rehabilitation counselor or Joshua, the problem statement would be quite different. For the counselor, the problem statement might be "Joshua has a significant history of alcohol abuse." In this problem statement, because of his history and the (implied) likelihood of subsequent use and abuse, the state's Department of Vocational Rehabilitation Services (DVRS) would be hesitant to resolve his problem by providing him with the financial and other service supports required to attend and complete the requirements for a college degree. They might be more likely to support community-based programs designed to monitor sobriety.

Joshua, however, has identified one problem as his own limited education constraining him from making changes in his life. He might also identify his substance abuse as a problem. For Joshua, those issues emerge from the primary problem of his limited education and boredom. The logical solution to Joshua's problem, as he defines it, is enrollment and success in higher education. You see here that different interpretations of problems can raise serious conflicts.

Thus, a well-developed problem statement in which values are clarified is essential if social workers are to examine their domain of practice and target intervention to social issues at all system levels. Also, without a problem statement, the foundation for ascertaining need is absent.

Ideally, social services are designed to resolve a social problem by addressing all or part of what is needed to remediate the problem in a valued direction. However, with the action orientation that is so characteristic of social workers, we typically move to interventions that we believe "work" but do not clarify the problem we are addressing. What do we mean by what "works"? While we are well-meaning in our efforts to quickly remediate social problems and diminish suffering, the omission of the thinking steps of problem clarification leaves us open to error and criticism. It is not unusual for social workers, when they are asked to be accountable, to be vague about the problem they are addressing or to avoid showing evidence beyond their own opinions to support the problem description, need, or desired outcomes (LaViolette, 2000).

In her study, LaViolette conducted interviews with clinical social workers. She asked them to describe the social problems/issues/concerns that they address in their practices and to identify how they know that their interventions are effective in producing desired outcomes. More than 80% had no formal mechanism to discern intervention success, and over 90% could not clearly articulate even one social problem/issue/concern for which their practice was initiated.

Similarly, in his seminal article in 1973, Fischer questioned the outcome of casework. Had social workers been clear about problem statements and desired outcomes, Fischer would not have been able to substantiate his claim asserting the failure of social work. We now turn to social problems and examine the thinking processes in depth.

THINKING PROCESSES IN ARTICULATING SOCIAL PROBLEMS

Although it may seem simple to specify a problem, problem clarification is an intricate task that requires careful and succinct thinking processes. Let us examine some of the common mistakes made in problem statements.

First, consider vague problem specification.

Here we can reconsider the problem specification as identified above by Joshua and his vocational counselor. Treatment, continued sobriety, degree and nature of DVRS support, enrolling in and attending college, and future sustained and substantive employment are all included in Joshua's problem. Thinking about just any one of these issues, we can get a sense of how complex Joshua's problem is. Consider the problem statement advanced by the vocational counselor: "Joshua abuses alcohol." Such a vague problem statement leads us nowhere. What would be needed to resolve this problem? The problem statement as it stands gives us no guidance or direction. As social workers, many of us are involved in providing treatment for substance abuse. For Joshua, what sort of intervention might there be, given the vagueness of the problem statement? Would our intervention include individual counseling, group counseling, cognitive, and behavior-based interventions, unannounced urine screens, deterrent medications, or other pharmacological cotherapies? Would residential treatment be appropriate? Without analyzing the problem and looking at its complexity, we would be guessing at how to proceed.

Another common mistake related to vague problem definition is failure to state the scope and complexity of a problem.

For Joshua's problem, if we had only delimited the problem with Joshua's desire to go to school as one method to attain and maintain sobriety, we would have been moving in the right direction. We could then look at the complex issues of substance abuse in light of facilitating Joshua's successful performance in school. In this instance, the following might be a sound problem statement: "Joshua abuses alcohol as a method to mediate depression and boredom."

In Jennifer's vignette, we focused principally on her career. Because we often think of high school teaching as classroom based, it is easy to limit a problem statement and thus overlook the wide variety of obstacles that Jennifer may face in carrying out her professional responsibilities. Even though her school may be accessible and her classroom modified to her height, range of motion, space requirements, ease of mobility, and so on, major access barriers often exist outside the classroom. Omitting these environments from the problem state-

ment can render useless any problem resolutions that may be moving in the right direction.

For example, suppose part of Jennifer's job involves taking her high school classes on field trips to museums, community lectures, and other activities. If the scope of access is delimited to the school building, Jennifer's capacity to use community resources for teaching may be impossible due to inaccessible transportation and community sites.

Stating a problem in terms of a preferred solution is another error that frequently occurs. Let us look at an example.

Consider Jennifer again. Suppose the problem statement were similar to this: "Jennifer lacks access to public transportation necessary to do her job successfully." This statement implies that the only solution to prevent job failure is to have access to public transportation. Can you see how the single solution is implied within the problem statement itself? How might we state the same issue so that multiple and feasible alternatives could be posed as resolutions? We could state that transportation barriers pose obstacles for Jennifer in carrying out her job. It may seem that we are mincing words here, but look at how a shift in the problem statement away from a preferred solution expands alternatives. For example, alternative transportation could be arranged for Jennifer while her students still access the community by public transportation; or her job could be modified to accommodate her limitations. Perhaps she might use virtual environments for her students to access community resources. Perhaps policy change to assure transportation access would be a long-term resolution as Jennifer finds methods to expose her students to community resources.

To avoid being limited by an incorrectly stated problem, thinking strategies to conceptualize and clarify the complexity of problems from multiple value perspectives are needed.

Here we propose a two-step method we have found very useful not only to expand the thinking process about a problem but to identify values and forge a direction for subsequent thinking and action processes in evaluation practice.

PROBLEM MAPPING AND FORCE FIELD ANALYSIS

Problem Mapping

The sequence that we present consists of two thinking processes: problem mapping followed by force field analysis. **Problem mapping** is a thinking process through which problems, no matter how they are initially conceptualized, can be expanded and grounded in value, literature, and evidence. Problem mapping is a superb tool to assist the social worker and user of a service to identify the context in which an intervention takes place, specify what part of the problem can be addressed, and illuminate what is needed to do so.

Problem mapping is a method in which one expands a problem statement beyond its initial conceptualization by asking two questions repeatedly: "What caused the problem, and what are the consequences of the problem?"

Let's work with this problem statement: *"Transportation barriers pose obstacles for Jennifer in carrying out her job."*

To conduct problem mapping, we first conceptualize a problem as a river. The initial problem statement that we just made is analogous to stepping into the river and picking up one rock. As we look upstream, we look at cause; as we map downstream, we look at consequence. Using our example, let's look upstream at two causes: *Jennifer's job does not consider mobility limitations; and public transportation is not designed for universal use. Let's continue to map upstream. The causes of this lack of consideration for mobility limitations might be that able-bodied administrators are unaware of how mobility limitations affect individuals in their ability to access community resources. Suppose we continue this line of thinking and look at what may have caused the lack of awareness. Although there may be many causes, for the sake of illustration, let's suggest that negative attitudes toward disability limit public education about disability. Looking upstream once more, we see that cultural values are responsible for negative attitudes toward disability.*

If we map upstream with our second cause statement, we would ask why public transportation is not designed for universal access. We might say that one reason is lack of awareness, which leads us to the same part of the map that we just constructed; or we might say that it is too costly to expand transportation to everyone. We would then realize that attitudes and values about disability would be responsible for the reluctance to spend resources on transportation access.

Now let's look downstream at consequences. One consequence could be that Jennifer cannot do her job. Another might be that Jennifer's student education is curtailed. What happens if Jennifer cannot do her job? The consequence is that Jennifer becomes unemployed, leading to the need for more tax dollars to provide public support for her and thus leaving less expendable money for those who work and have to pay higher taxes. What happens if student education is curtailed? We might see students ill-prepared for adulthood and work, leading to such problems as inefficiency, once again costing the individual.

Figure 4.1 illustrates the full problem map that we have just created. Each box above the initial problem is a broad answer category to what caused the problem. Once we identify first-tier causes of the problem we ask the question "What caused the cause of the problem" and so on until we reach cultural and/or social value statements. Below the initial problem statement, we repeatedly ask the question "What is the consequence?" As with the upstream map, we repeat this question about the consequences of consequences and so forth until we reach the impact of the problem on individuals. The problem map therefore expands the problem statement from cultural-social causes to personal impact and values and gives us many different places in which to intervene, as well as topical areas for further inquiry and specification.

As you can see, there are many causes and consequences for which social work will not resolve the problem in Figure 4.1. For example, we cannot reallocate money for universal access in public transportation. There are, however,

FIGURE 4.1 | PROBLEM MAP—JENNIFER

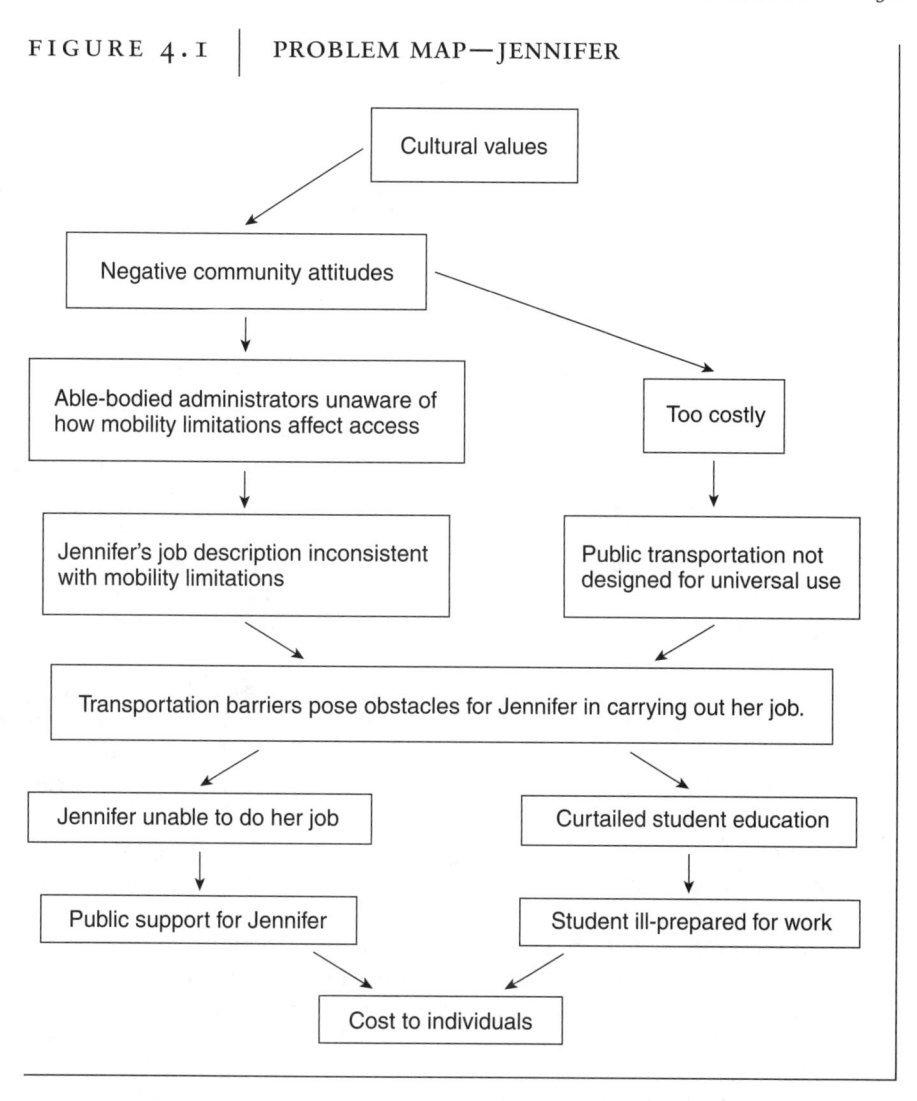

```
                          ┌──────────────────┐
                          │ Cultural values  │
                          └──────────────────┘
                                 ╱
                                ↙
              ┌──────────────────────────────┐
              │ Negative community attitudes │──────────────┐
              └──────────────────────────────┘              │
                        ↓                                   ↓
    ┌──────────────────────────────────┐          ┌──────────────┐
    │ Able-bodied administrators       │          │  Too costly  │
    │ unaware of how mobility          │          └──────────────┘
    │ limitations affect access        │                  ↓
    └──────────────────────────────────┘          ┌──────────────────────────┐
                  ↓                               │ Public transportation    │
    ┌──────────────────────────────────┐          │ not designed for         │
    │ Jennifer's job description       │          │ universal use            │
    │ inconsistent with mobility       │          └──────────────────────────┘
    │ limitations                      │                  ↙
    └──────────────────────────────────┘
                      ↘                        ↙
        ┌────────────────────────────────────────────────────────────┐
        │ Transportation barriers pose obstacles for Jennifer in     │
        │ carrying out her job.                                      │
        └────────────────────────────────────────────────────────────┘
                  ↙                                        ↘
    ┌────────────────────────────┐              ┌────────────────────────────┐
    │ Jennifer unable to do      │              │ Curtailed student          │
    │ her job                    │              │ education                  │
    └────────────────────────────┘              └────────────────────────────┘
                  ↓                                          ↓
    ┌────────────────────────────┐              ┌────────────────────────────┐
    │ Public support for         │              │ Student ill-prepared for   │
    │ Jennifer                   │              │ work                       │
    └────────────────────────────┘              └────────────────────────────┘
                      ↘                        ↙
                       ┌──────────────────────────┐
                       │   Cost to individuals    │
                       └──────────────────────────┘
```

numerous points of intervention in the arenas of both cause and consequence in the problem map. We could intervene at the macrolevel by creating community education programs about disability as a method to positively influence attitudes and policy. The disability rights movement has successfully accomplished this aim, resulting in the ultimate passage of the Americans with Disabilities Act in 1990 (Charlton, 1998). At the microlevel, we could work with Jennifer to find alternative ways and resources to accomplish her job in light of inaccessible public transportation. Each of these points needs further exploration and elucidation from credible sources, such as scholarly literature and research. We address the action strategies of literature review and support in Chapter 5.

Once the scope of the problem and the point of action are identified in the problem map, a force field analysis can be conducted.

Force Field Analysis

A historical overview will help us understand the context in which force field analysis was developed. *Force field analysis* is a planning tool that was developed by Lewin (1951) in the 1940s. This planning approach was based on "holistic psychology," which suggests that a network of factors affects an individual's decision-making process (Hustedde & Score, 1995, p. 5). Lewin (1951) was interested in the contribution to the analysis of phenomena and their subsequent actions of factors such as government, the kind of work an individual did, family members, and an individual's personal ambitions.

Lewin demonstrated force field analysis techniques by using elaborate diagrams of "life space" or "psychological space" pertaining to and affecting individuals (Hustedde & Score, 1995, p. 5). These diagrams appeared as a series of directional vectors depicting the nature and strength of the influence of relevant factors on the object of change. Lewin (1951) viewed group use of information and influences to set and attain goals as a systematic, collaborative thinking process.

There are several models of force field analysis in the social science literature that tend to share common elements (Brager & Holloway, 1992; Cohen, 1994; De Panfilis, 1996). The first commonality is the use of force field analysis for problem identification, analysis, and goal setting. A second common element is the thinking process of applying a relevant body of information to the identification of restraining and driving forces that impact goal attainment for resolving problems. Third, all models share the step of identifying which forces can be targeted for action. Thus, at its basic level, force field analysis includes a clear definition and dissection of a problem, specification of goals for resolving all or part of the problem, and a systematic identification of resources to achieve the goals that are targeted for intervention (Bens, 1994).

The scholarly literature on the use of force field analysis as a planning tool in organizational change reveals variations of Lewin's original model (Brager & Holloway, 1992; De Panfilis, 1996). In general, force field analysis provides a diagrammatic picture of all influences that maintain and/or impact a situation at a given moment. Through force field analysis processes, assessment and organizational change can be systematically planned if the following three areas are addressed: (a) a multilevel analysis of an issue, (b) inclusion of diverse types of information from numerous variables to examine the influences that affect a situation, and (c) an analysis of the factors that serve to affect the stability and change in a situation (Brager & Holloway, 1992). If these three elements are addressed, force field analysis can be used to examine the probability of reaching issue-specific goals that have been agreed upon through a structured group process of critical, collaborative thinking.

Given the history and use of force field analysis, we have found it very useful in further clarifying and honing the scope of the problem to which social work intervention is directed. Force field analysis is also an excellent tool in identifying primary and secondary targets of change, resources that can enhance problem resolution, impediments to be avoided or eliminated, and stakeholders who affect or will be affected by a social work action.

Where does one begin? Review the problem map in Figure 4.1. A specific element of the expanded problem was selected as the primary entrance into the overall problem. We now use that statement as the foundation of our force field analysis by translating it into an active statement: Disability awareness is limited.

Once the statement is active, it functions as a center point of analysis to identify what contributes to maintaining the problem, what factors could make it worse, and what factors could remediate the problem in part or in total. Although force field analysis can be done by a single individual, it is usually conducted as a "group think" activity (Brager & Holloway, 1992).

Following the clarification of the problem, participants in the analysis identify the driving (positive) and restraining (negative) forces that would affect movement toward the desired goal related to alleviating part or all of the problem. The forces can be grounded in evidence provided to the participants in the force field analysis process or can be brainstormed.

There are many forces that can be identified, but for illustrative purposes, we will work with just a few. The following are three driving forces that could be identified from literature and practice wisdom:

1. current civil rights legislation
2. public figures with disabilities, such as Christopher Reeve
3. the aging of the population

Three restraining forces might include the following:

1. devaluing of disabled individuals
2. fear of disablement
3. minimal exposure to productive disabled individuals in the community

Once these forces have been identified, each one is then rank-ordered to represent its perceived importance in maintaining the status quo or eliciting social change (Brager & Holloway, 1992). Directional problem articulation can then be targeted to a complex understanding of the problem in terms of its restraining and driving forces. Moreover, those factors that cannot be changed by the planning group can be identified and discarded as targets for action.

Looking at need and intervention planning based on the driving and restraining forces identified in the two lists, rank order and analysis of each would reveal that all are important and can be used and/or addressed by social work. Therefore, a social worker might collaborate with a disability group to develop a community education program about disability. The educational program would highlight the driving forces (civil rights legislation, public figures with disabilities, aging of the population) to raise disability awareness, thereby decreasing the restraining forces.

A two-phase approach to problem identification using mapping and force field analysis is depicted in Box 4.1. See also Figure 4.2, which follows.

> **BOX 4.1** | **TWO-PHASE FORCE FIELD ANALYSIS**
>
> **Phase 1: Preparation**
> Problem statement is clarified through constructing a problem map and identifying the arena for intervention.
>
> **Phase 2: Conducting the Analysis**
> Participants identify the magnitude of the problem and place it within a grid illustrating the severity of the problem.
>
> Based on literature, practice wisdom or other relevant information, participants identify and visually depict driving and restraining forces.
>
> Each force is rank-ordered as a target for intervention from most important to those that will not be addressed at all.

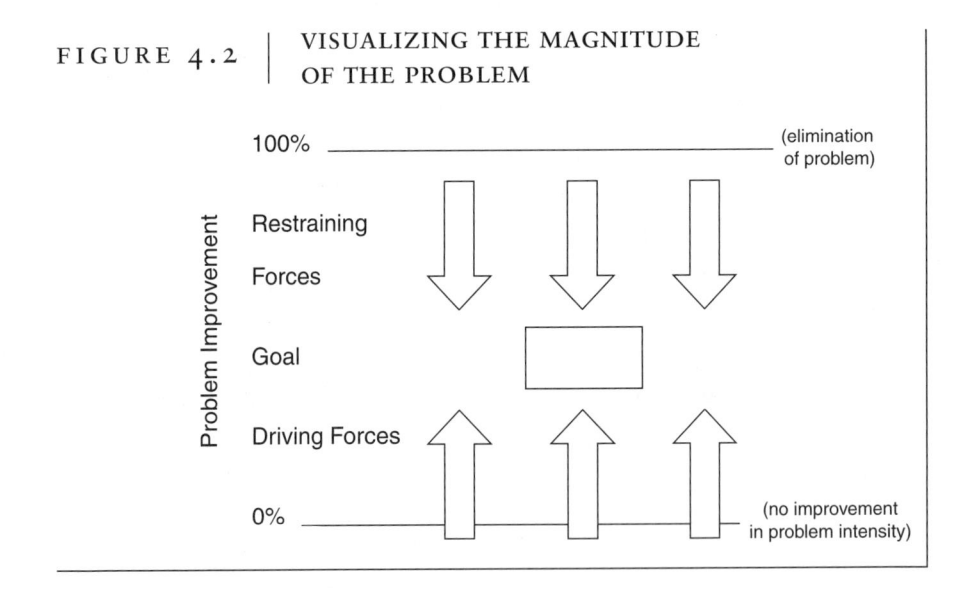

FIGURE 4.2 | **VISUALIZING THE MAGNITUDE OF THE PROBLEM**

Let us look now at Joshua to fully illustrate the two-phase model. We begin with the problem statement: *"Joshua abuses alcohol as a method to mediate depression and boredom."* Figure 4.3 shows our problem map.

In this problem map, there are many points of intervention for the social worker. For illustration, we choose two points that are within the domain of the social worker's agency: Joshua's immobilization and limited community resources. However, there are parts of the map that are not the domain of social work intervention, such as community burden.

IDENTIFYING SOCIAL WORK PROBLEMS AND ISSUES

FIGURE 4.3 | PROBLEM MAP—JOSHUA

```
┌─────────────────────────────┐      ┌──────────────────────────────────┐
│ Drinking is socially valued.│      │ There are no community resources.│
└──────────────┬──────────────┘      └─────────────────┬────────────────┘
               ↓                                        ↓
┌─────────────────────────────────┐   ┌──────────────────────────────┐
│ He has a family history of      │   │ His friends also use alcohol.│
│ alcoholism.                     │   │                              │
└─────────────────────────────────┘   └──────────────────────────────┘
                        ↘           ↙
               ┌──────────────────────────────────────┐
               │ Joshua abuses alcohol as a method to │
               │ mediate depression and boredom.      │
               └──────────────────────────────────────┘
                        ↙           ↘
┌─────────────────────────────────┐   ┌──────────────────────────────┐
│ Intoxication limits productivity.│   │ Alcohol increases depression.│
└──────────────┬──────────────────┘   └─────────────┬────────────────┘
               ↓                                     ↓
┌─────────────────────────────┐       ┌──────────────────────────────┐
│ Joshua is feeling stuck.    │       │ Depression leads to more     │
│                             │       │ alcohol consumption.         │
└──────────────┬──────────────┘       └──────────────────────────────┘
               ↓
┌─────────────────────────────┐
│ He is immobilized.          │
└──────────────┬──────────────┘
               ↘
            ┌──────────────────────────────────────┐
            │ He does not contribute to his community.│
            └──────────────┬───────────────────────┘
                           ↘
               ┌──────────────────────────────────────────────┐
               │ He becomes a burden on his family and community.│
               └──────────────────────────────────────────────┘
```

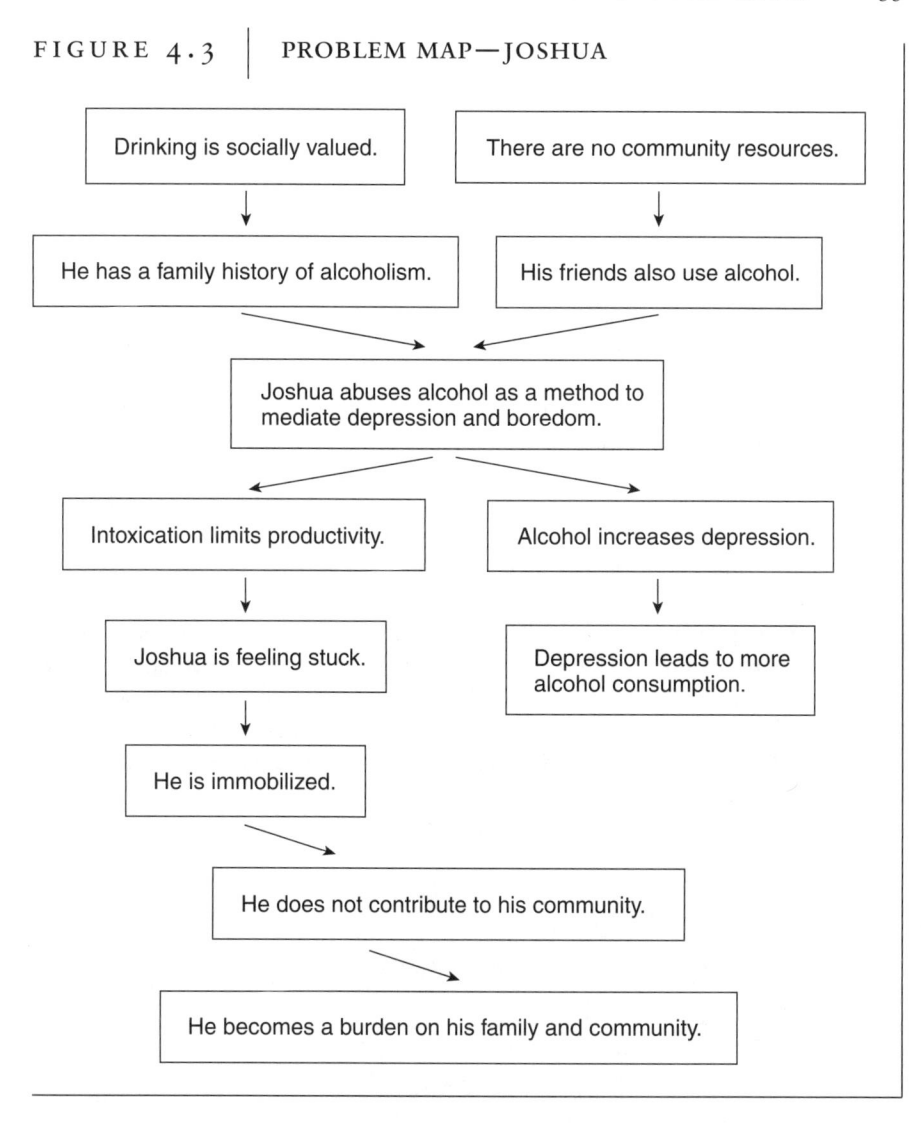

Following the steps in our model, a force field analysis for each point is presented.

RESTRAINING FORCES (WHAT KEEPS HIM IMMOBILIZED?)

No idea of what to do
No support from vocational counselor

Social norms
No observable options
Immobilization

DRIVING FORCES

Counseling
Desire for education
Desire for sobriety

With the construction of our problem map and force field analysis, we can see several directions for intervention. For example, the social worker might provide intensive counseling to address depression or refer Joshua to Alcoholics Anonymous. Assistance in securing a loan for college might be an option as well. How will the social worker decide on which directions are most likely to produce a resolution to the problem? The answer to this question is twofold.

The social worker has a grasp of research and literature that provide the systematic knowledge and theory underpinning professional decision making. However, without knowing what is needed from the many options, the social worker may make a nonproductive intervention choice. Needs assessment, which will be discussed in Chapter 8, is a crucial process in our evaluation practice model to assure that decisions are based on sound and systematically anchored reasoning.

Now let us create a force field analysis for limited community resources.

RESTRAINING FORCES

No community leadership
Limited money
Limited community awareness

DRIVING FORCES

Burdensome youth
Schools
Parents
Youth

Based on this force field analysis, the social worker would most likely take a community organization approach to facilitate the mobilization of the community for fund-raising and the establishment of a community center. Again, in this example, professional knowledge and research would inform action, *and needs assessment would be conducted to increase the likelihood of successful outcome.*

MAIN POINTS

1. Social problems are statements of value.
2. What is considered to be a problem may differ among diverse groups and individuals.
3. Problem mapping is a thinking process to locate an initial problem statement within an expanded context of its causes and consequences. This systematic process is important to obtain an understanding of the complexity of problems and to identify potential areas for intervention.
4. Force field analysis is a thinking process to further clarify the influences on problems and to identify correlates of it that can be acted upon.
5. Including the client system in the process will help formulate the problem in a way that is meaningful and relevant to those who are affected by the problem.
6. Clarifying the problem will lead you to ascertain what is needed to resolve the part of the problem that you will address.

EXERCISES

1. Identify a problem that you believe is within the domain of social work practice, and analyze its explicit and implicit values.
2. Create a problem map using your problem statement from Exercise 1.
3. From your problem map, select one point from causes and one from consequences for intervention, and conduct force field analysis on each.

CHAPTER 5

OBTAINING AND ORGANIZING INFORMATION

Diverse Purposes of Information in Evaluation Practice

When to Review Information in Evaluation

Mechanics of Information Review

Main Points

Exercises

DIVERSE PURPOSES OF INFORMATION IN EVALUATION PRACTICE

In the previous chapter, we discussed and illustrated the critical concepts related to social problems. We proposed a thinking process to expand and clarify social problems and differentiated need from problem. In this chapter, we look at the purpose of information in evaluation practice; sources of information, including traditional and electronic sources (Internet, intranet, and Web based); and methods through which to select, retrieve, organize, critically analyze, and use information throughout the evaluation practice process. We look first at the nature and roles of information in evaluation practice.

Historically, credible information in any inquiry has been derived from research literature. However, over the past several decades, multiple ways of knowing have been encouraged by scholars and researchers (Hartman, 1990). Acceptable sources of knowing can include developed practice wisdom and information gleaned from social work practice assessment, popular culture, intuition, experiences with arts, and fiction.

Building on the work done by DePoy and Gitlin (1998), we suggest that reviewing information is a thinking process in which the social worker critically delimits relevant information and then uses that body of knowledge to inform the content and process of the problem and subsequent steps of evaluation practice. Also, finding out what others know and how they come to know it helps determine how each evaluation effort and element contribute to existing problem definition and resulting practice.

Unfortunately, the need to review information as an essential part of evaluation practice is often a misconceived and undervalued activity. In reviewing many evaluation texts, we noted that few direct the reader to the literature and other information as a basic step. It is not uncommon to find that the authoritative source of information is the service participant. Because we find the information review an essential thinking and action process, we present an extensive section on how to review scholarly literature and other sources of information to inform evaluation practice and to contribute to the body of practice knowledge in social work.

Purpose of Information Review

Reviewing information in evaluation practice serves a slightly different purpose than reviewing conducted for other types of activity. Nonetheless, it is equally as rigorous and important. For example, part of the traditional distinction between the two roles in the continuum of scientist—practitioner, which we addressed in Chapter 3, is in diverse use of sources of information. In direct practice, the social worker typically consults the sources of professional information for practice guidance, often without examining the method through which the knowledge was developed and asserted. In research, the scientist critically reviews a large scope of knowledge that is directly or indirectly related to both the

> **BOX 5.1 | THINKING PURPOSES**
>
> 1. To ascertain what knowledge has been generated previously that informed the problem, indicated whether or not there was need for intervention, and gave rise to the intervention
> 2. To examine the social, cultural, political, economic, and theoretical context of the intervention
> 3. To obtain knowledge of competing interventions
> 4. To identify resource issues
> 5. To identify potential uses and misuses of the evaluation findings

topic and the proposed strategy of conducting the research, with a particular focus on method, data, and data interpretation. The purpose of doing a review is to obtain direction and rationale for the focus of an inquiry and an investigatory strategy and to position one's work within a theoretical body of knowledge. In evaluation practice, the social worker combines the purposes of information review from the viewpoints of both the scientist and the practitioner.

In addition to scholarly literature, numerous sources of information are important to consider. Among these are practice wisdom; political, economic, and service-based information such as mission statements, organizational charts, agency policies, and procedures; news; and anecdotes. Art, popular culture, and Web-based information have also been recognized as important sources in informing the context of social work and evaluation practice.

Look at Box 5.1 for a summary of the "thinking" purposes of information review in evaluation practice.

In addition to the thinking purposes of information review presented in Box 5.1, we consider practical and professional reasons for consulting and/or using information in evaluation practice. As you have seen, many evaluations are developed merely for one-time, limited inquiries about a program or intervention effort. These types of evaluations tend to be developed without a sound theoretical or methodological basis, and as such, they may provide limited information about an effort but will not contribute to the general knowledge base informing social work practice. In our view, evaluation practice is an organizing meta-framework for social work activity in which knowledge is generated to inform multiple scopes of practice beyond the direct target of the intervention. Thus, we believe that it is critical to ground any evaluation project in sound systematically generated and organized information.

In addition, many evaluation designs are developed to meet the needs of a specific intervention. Reviewing multiple sources of information helps social workers select a method based on the successes and lessons learned from previous evaluation practice.

Finally, given the role of systematically and rigorously generated evidence as a basis for credibility and rationale for practice, and our assertion that evaluation practice can and should become an overarching framework for social work, evaluation practice provides the structure for positioning knowledge gained from practice in contemporary peer-reviewed literature and/or other valued venues of information. Thus, the summative effect of using and disseminating evaluation practice is the growth of well-conceptualized and well-developed social work knowledge.

WHEN TO REVIEW INFORMATION IN EVALUATION

Use of the information can occur at any point in the evaluation practice process, following the initial identification of a social problem. Keep in mind, however, that the use of information, in concert with the political nature of evaluation is purposive.

Problem

Because the problem statement is fundamentally a value assertion, the potential exists for multiple, and sometimes competing, values to differentially shape the nature of problem statements for diverse stakeholder groups. What some may not consider a problem, others may see as an imminent deficit to be addressed. What evidence would one need in order to assert that resources ought to be directed to eliminate what we do not value and to produce what we do value? In our culture, authority and empirical evidence provide the most credible support for a position or value statement, and these sources are extracted from the corpus of information that is peer reviewed or generated by respected thinkers and experienced practitioners.

Those of you who have read and/or conducted naturalistic research may be familiar with the term **audit trail**. In the naturalistic tradition, an audit trail is the clear explication of both thinking and action processes (DePoy & Gitlin, 1998). That is, the naturalistic researcher provides the details of how method was conceptualized and implemented along with a clear explanation of what evidence was used and how it was used to support and verify an inductive claim. Applying this concept to the information review element of evaluation practice means that the social work evaluator clearly identifies the nature of information reviewed and details of how the information was organized, as well as demonstrates how knowledge was used to support a problem statement.

Let us consider Joshua's youth. The vocational counselor has identified Joshua's problem as alcoholism. Literature support for this problem statement would emerge from medical-diagnostic sources in which substance abuse is considered to be a biological disease that must be addressed through abstinence. On the other hand, the social worker who has identified Joshua's problem as a social phenomenon has empirical support from social learning and systems theory for social pressures as the cause of substance abuse. Practice wisdom factored into this problem statement as well, as the social worker used anecdotal information from previous experience to support the "social" perspective on Joshua's problem. The most compelling problem statement is the one backed by multiple, comprehensive, and credible sources of information. The social worker, using literature and anecdotal knowledge from practice experience, provides a sound and experienced rationale for looking beyond alcoholism to the causes and consequences of problem drinking behavior.

Need

In the needs assessment phase, information can be used fully, partially, or not at all to substantiate what is needed to resolve a problem. Moreover, the research literature can provide model evaluation methods for needs assessment and subsequent thinking and action evaluation processes.

Consider each of the stated views of Joshua's problem. A medical-diagnostic view supports the need to first treat the alcoholism before considering any future education and career. Thus, inpatient treatment and total abstinence would be necessary before any further support for education would be indicated. However, if Joshua's problem were seen through a social-cultural lens, changing Joshua's cultural reference group and advancing his social value through education would be primary intervention needs.

In Jennifer's case, a medical approach to her limited access would lead to the need for intervention focusing on individual accommodations and/or rehabilitation. On the other hand, intervention focusing on universal access and social justice would emerge from a problem statement grounded in social constructivist literature.

However, if a social worker is not knowledgeable about the community in which Jennifer's access is limited, a review of existing sources of related knowledge might be delayed until an inductive needs assessment is done. Obtaining knowledge of need directly from members of a community provides essential information that may not be available through other venues and which could inform important issues such as attitudes toward and treatment of disability.

Goals and Objectives

Information can provide guidance and rationale on why particular goals to structure interventions were specified and others not addressed.

In our example of Joshua, information supporting the need to treat the "disease" of alcoholism would provide an absolute rationale for goals and objectives related to recovering from disease over any other approach to intervention. Expected outcomes, success criteria, and specific indicators of these identified in the literature and in practice would form the basis for intervention goals and the objectives.

In our example of Jennifer, from the perspective of the social worker who sees access as an individual problem related to a medical condition, literature and practice wisdom from the field of individual rehabilitation and accommodation would guide the development of goals and objectives to "fix" Jennifer;

social constructivist literature would elicit support for goals and objectives to advance community change and movement to universal design.

Reflexive Intervention

Intervention can be fully, partially, or not informed by existing knowledge. In the presence of sound knowledge that describes successful interventions in a particular problem area, replication of such interventions may be indicated. *If Jennifer's community were similar to others in which access had already been successfully addressed, then information detailing previous relevant efforts would inform intervention to improve access in her community as well.*

If there is disagreement with or absence of formal knowledge on interventions, the gap in knowledge calls for innovation. In such cases, reflexive intervention and assessment of outcome would follow more exploratory strategies. *If Jennifer's community were unique or different from those described in literature, analogous bodies of literature on social change could be used to inform intervention strategies, or new strategies could be developed, implemented, and tested.*

When a previously tested intervention is implemented, practice experience and literature can identify what outcomes the practitioner can expect from which parts of an intervention. Moreover, this assessment inquiry may move beyond previously tested process and outcome to incrementally add to the practice knowledge.

Consider Joshua's issue regarding low test scores in his state. Literature describing the process and outcome of teacher initiatives to raise test scores could be used to structure similar approaches in Joshua's low-scoring school districts. Publication of evaluation assessment results examining why this approach did or didn't accomplish its stated goals would add to the body of literature on changing student performance through effecting change in teacher behavior.

MECHANICS OF INFORMATION REVIEW

With the explosion of available sources of knowledge, working to determine how best to access this information can be daunting. However, there are tricks of the trade, so to speak, to facilitate a systematic and comprehensive review process that is purposive, manageable, and even enjoyable. We begin with strategies to identify, delimit, critically examine, and use sources of knowledge in the evaluation practice process. Box 5.2 (on page 64) presents steps to lead you through a well-executed and useful review of information.

Step 1: Determine the Purpose of the Review

Attention to purpose and clear acknowledgement of the influence of purpose on the evaluation design, conduct, and use are hallmarks of evaluation practice. Thus, the purpose or purposes must be clearly identified to guide the social

> ### BOX 5.2 | STEPS IN REVIEWING KNOWLEDGE IN EVALUATION PRACTICE
>
> Step 1: Determine the purpose of the review
>
> Step 2: Delimit the scope of the search
>
> Step 3: Access databases, Web sites, and other comprehensive lists of relevant information
>
> Step 4: Obtain relevant information
>
> Step 5: Organize the information
>
> Step 6: Critically evaluate the information
>
> Step 7: Prepare a report of the information review

worker in searching for and using sources of knowledge. Consider the potential purposes of the following example.

Suppose the social worker who Jennifer contacts about her limited access to her work environment is approaching the problem and need as a social justice issue. Literature in the fields of civil rights legislation and related action would provide a compelling rationale for intervention focusing on community organization and large-systems change. Rather than consult rehabilitation or universal design sources, the social worker would focus on the oppression of disabled groups and the need for social change as a basis for the elimination of that oppression.

Once the purpose is clarified, the social worker will be able to delimit the search to guide when, and how to approach the vast amount of literature and other important sources of information. Critical review of all sources is essential to maintain rigor in the evaluation practice process as we discuss below.

Step 2: Delimit the Scope of the Search

Once you have made a decision about the purpose and timing of the review, you then need to set parameters on what is relevant to search. After all, it is not feasible or reasonable to review every single topic that is somewhat related to your problem statement. Delimiting or setting boundaries for the search is an important yet difficult step. The boundaries you set must assure a purposive and rigorous review, but one that is practical and not overwhelming.

Delimiting the search begins with knowing what sources are available and what each source is likely to provide. Consideration of time, use, and audience must be factors in determining what sources to search and ultimately use in the thinking processes.

Of course, the library is the most traditional location of sources. The library at our university lists 13 search options, which are presented in Box 5.3.

> **BOX 5.3** | **FOGLER LIBRARY: RESOURCES**
>
> URSUS (online catalog)
> Indexes and Databases
> Electronic Journals
> Electronic Books
> Virtual Reference
> Internet Search Engines
> Course Guides for Library Instruction
> Internet Subject Guides
> Research Guides
> Maine's Science, Technology, and Business Library
> Maine InfoNet and Other Library Catalogs
> Site Map
> What's New

Seventeen electronic databases are listed under "Indexes and Databases," each with a content or structural focus.

The contents of "Virtual Reference" (Fogler, 2000) are presented in Box 5.4 to illustrate the state-of-the-art "virtual reference" librarian and the scope of resources available through this one venue.

If you are not acquainted with the multiple browsers and search engines on the Internet, refer to Box 5.5 for those that we find most useful and comprehensive.

Box 5.6 identifies specific Web sites that we have used frequently in our own evaluation practice. They are general sites of interest to social workers, and each has links to many other sites.

To limit your search to a reasonable time frame, you might want to use a search engine or browser that both provides content direction and rates sites for their quality on the parameters that you find important to your search. The list in Box 5.6 only begins to scratch the surface of databases that you may find of general use. We acknowledge the important strengths of virtual references, but we also want to call your attention to the lack of a universal review process for online material. Be cautious in your selection and use of electronic information.

We also want to call your attention to *Dissertation Abstracts,* a compendium in book and electronic form of annotations of dissertations, as an excellent resource in uncovering comprehensive treatment of topics. Because the dissertation process requires a substantive coverage of knowledge and includes a comprehensive selection of sources, the author of the dissertation has already done much of the work that you would find necessary to locate such extensive information.

BOX 5.4 | FOGLER LIBRARY: VIRTUAL REFERENCE

Ask-a-Librarian: E-mail Reference Service
You Can Look It Up! Reference Sources on the Web

- News! Maine, U.S., and International News on the Web
- Almanac: An Electronic Mariner Omnium Gatherum
- Books and Publishing
- Citation Guides
- College and University Information
- Consumer
- Copyright
- Dictionaries and Thesauri
- Directories: Who, What, Where
- Full Text Web Sites
- Genealogy
- Grants
- Health
- Language and Writing Resources
- Library Catalogs
- Maine
- Maps and Geographic Data
- Statistics Express
- Travel and Regional Information
- Weather
- Other Virtual Reference Desks

Internet Resources by Subject

- Arts & Humanities
- Social & Behavioral Sciences
- Science & Engineering
- Links to Other Subject Lists

Revised: 03/27/01

Copyright 2000, Raymond H. Fogler Library

> BOX 5.5 | INTERNET BROWSERS AND SEARCH ENGINES
>
> AltaVista—Web and newsgroup search engine
> Argus Clearinghouse—can help if you're interested in what the Net has to offer
> Explore the Internet—from the Library of Congress
> Google—uses text-matching techniques to find pages that are both important and relevant to your search
> Health Abstracts Online
> Netscape—Internet search engine
> Social Work Abstracts
> Study Web—comprehensive searchable, categorized index with reviews of over 17,000 educational and reference Web sites
> Yahoo!—category-based Web directory

> BOX 5.6 | RECOMMENDED WEB SITES
>
> Department of Health and Human Services, www.acf/dhhs.gov
> Information on federal activities, legislation, and so forth, www.whitehouse.gov-accesses
> State Health Statistics by Sex and Race
> SWAN—Social Work Access Network
> U.S. Census Bureau
> World Wide Web Resources for Social Workers

Step 3: Access Databases and Web Sites and Other Comprehensive Lists of Relevant Information

Even though so much information is currently available online, the majority of scholarly and professional information is still found in printed journals and books. Our students often omit these sources since the Internet is readily available. For us, the joy of being in the library is an important determinant in our use of library sources. However, as we move through the 21st century, the library expands far beyond the walls of a building, presenting sometimes too many options for reviewing information. To avoid or lessen confusion, trial and error, personal preference for style and presentation, and content are three factors that can guide your selection of search tools. Availability, of course, is the most important factor driving the choice you make for search venues, with time limitations also to be considered. We find it helpful and informative to take some time to use Web browsers and search multiple types of databases. Hands-on experience can help you learn efficient techniques as well as identify your preferred search venues.

Step 4: Obtain Relevant Information

This step seems self-evident. However, we include it to remind you that there are numerous ways to obtain information, each with differing time and access requirements. Many social workers identify specific sources in the search process and then find that they are difficult to obtain in a timely fashion. For example, if your library does not have the book you want to review, obtaining your resource through interlibrary loan can take up to two weeks. The most readily available information exists on the Internet. These instantaneous sources can be accessed and examined, downloaded to a computer, and/or printed. Whichever way you choose, be sure to record the full citation immediately. We have had too many experiences of losing a citation, in total or in part, and then spending hours searching for it.

For a speedy perusal of relevant information in scholarly journals, abstracts and reviews of the literature can often give you a good overview. Of course, you cannot derive specific and detailed knowledge for critical review from either of these sources, but each can provide a general idea of the information. Accessing articles from journals will require a library visit or a request to have reprints mailed. Some databases provide the opportunity for you to order articles online for a nominal fee.

Art, literature, journals, and so forth can be accessed on the Web, in the library, or in numerous other arenas, such as museums and stores.

Another source is practice wisdom. How to access practitioner experience, record what you have learned, and then use this knowledge in an organized fashion can take many forms. A few examples include consulting with colleagues, attending regular meetings and supervision, joining a Web-based discussion group or **listserv,** and interviewing social workers and related professionals who have the knowledge you are seeking. Again, carefully and completely record the source of information, no matter how you obtain it.

Step 5: Organize the Information

There are an infinite number of "correct" ways to organize information for use. Common to all, however, are five basic elements that provide guidelines: content, structure, author, venue, and date.

Content is the topical substance of the literature. *If we were organizing literature to support a medical problem statement for Joshua's condition, we* would include literature on the topical areas of adolescence, alcoholism, and substance abuse intervention.

Structure refers to the way in which the content is approached and addressed. Typical forms include research articles, theory papers, relevant narrative, practice articles, program and intervention descriptions, legislative briefs, and other government documents. *For example, we might compare maps or blueprints of schools to illustrate access limitations as environmental rather than individual.*

Author refers to who created and presented the knowledge. Typically, authors are researchers, academics, theoreticians, or practitioners. However, as evaluation expands its scope, authors may be service consumers, artists, or policymakers. Remember that these are not mutually exclusive author categories.

Venue refers to the vehicle through which the knowledge is made available to the public. As has been noted, these include scholarly journals and government documents, the Internet, personal communication, presentations at local and national conferences, newsletters, newspapers, plays, poetry, and so on. Structure is limited only by creativity and purpose.

Date includes not only when the source was made public, but also when the source was developed and finalized. It is important to consider that most articles appear in scholarly journals two years following their submission; thus, the work that is presented in these journals is retrospective.

Although there are an infinite number of ways to approach information, we suggest charting as one strategy that has been useful for many students, practitioners, and researchers. In this approach, you select pertinent information from each source you review and record it in an organized fashion. You first need to determine which element (content, author, structure, venue, and date) is your primary organizer, and then you can begin the action process of organizing your information for use. The approach you choose should reflect the nature and purposes of your evaluation practice project. Charting knowledge will allow you to reflect on your sources as a whole and critically evaluate and identify the important points that support your purpose, evaluation design, and use.

Table 5.1 illustrates a template chart in which topic is the primary organizer. Important concepts and constructs representing the primary topical areas are identified and labeled across the top column. What each source has to say about each of the important topical areas, how each is organized, date, venue, author, and critical comments are then recorded under each column. A concept/construct matrix therefore organizes information you have reviewed and evaluated by key concept/construct. *Table 5.1 displays an example of a concept matrix template for an information review that would be used by the social worker who is working with Jennifer to support disability and access limitation as social constructs.*

This structure can be used for one or more sources and modified for personal preference. It is also possible to keep information organized in this or a similar fashion in a computer word-processing program or a database.

TABLE 5.1 | TOPICAL TEMPLATE

	Traditional Views of Disability	Current Views	Access
Date			
Venue			
Author/s			
Critical comments			

Step 6: Critically Evaluate the Information

The questions in Box 5.7 are intended to assist you in critically approaching and using knowledge by guiding your reading of evaluation and research literature, theoretical literature, and practice literature. The questions in Box 5.8 are designed to prompt your evaluation of nonresearch literature. Using these questions to guide your thinking processes will provide an analytic structure through which to approach and judge the credibility and efficacy of diverse sources of knowledge.

As you can see, there are many questions to answer in order to critically review and use information. While this element of evaluation practice might seem overwhelming for novices, you will see that with experience and practice, critical review becomes natural and indispensable.

Step 7: Prepare a Report of the Information Review

You have now searched, obtained, read, and organized your sources of knowledge. Finally, it is time to prepare a report. What is reported and how the report is structured are dependent on the purposes of the evaluation. For example, if an evaluation is designed to examine the outcome of clinical clients on specified variables, the social worker needs to clarify which problems are related to desired outcomes as well as what is needed to resolve the problems and thus produce outcomes. Choice of measurement strategy, use of findings, and degree of dissemination all need to be considered.

Consider Joshua. A medical-diagnostic approach to Joshua's problem would most likely be documented with diagnostic literature such as the Diagnostic and Statistical Manual, Mental Disorders (DSM IV). Specific goals and objectives for recovery from alcoholism would be extracted from this body of literature and written to express desired outcomes. Let's say that one objective was the acknowledgment by Joshua of his own alcoholism. This objective would be measured not only by his articulation of the assertion but by behavioral indicators that are supported in the literature as evidence that a person has accepted his or her condition as "real" and is in need of intervention.

> BOX 5.7 | GUIDELINES FOR ANALYSIS OF RESEARCH AND EVALUATION SOURCES
>
> 1. What is the nature of the problem statement? Is it clearly stated? Can it be addressed? Is the problem stated too narrowly to be remediated? Is the problem statement realistic? What are the ethical dilemmas presented by the problem statement? Who owns the problem?
> 2. Does the need statement address the problem? Is there sufficient and believable evidence for the need statement? Is the evidence systematically ascertained and revealed? Is the need one that social workers should address? can address? Who is in need? What is the scope of the need?
> 3. Are the intervention goal statements clear and well defined? Do they address the need and the problem? Fully, or partially? Are they realistic? Are the goals consistent with social work values? Can the accomplishment of the goals be evaluated? How?
> 4. Is reflexive implementation presented? How detailed? To what extent are formative data used to improve the intervention?
> 5. Criticize the outcome assessment plan. Is the method appropriate to the assessment questions? Are the procedures ethical? What purpose for assessment does the method imply? Is the plan systematic and grounded in sound investigative procedures? What are the limitations of the method? How might these methodological limitations influence the findings? Has confidentiality been protected? Is the data collection plan valid? trustworthy? Is there any evidence that instrumentation or assessment procedures are discriminatory?
> 6. Criticize findings. Are the author's conclusions believable? Who do they benefit? Was the problem addressed? If a needs assessment was conducted, was it sufficient to define need and to form the basis for the stipulated program goals? Were the intervention goals met? Are there alternative explanations for the findings? What purpose can the findings serve?

If the purpose of the evaluation practice were to influence legislative change, then the report would take a different shape.

Consider Joshua's concern about low test scores. Information to support the need for legislation and policy change would most likely include census data to illustrate demographics, comparative statistics of test scores in diverse geographic locations, and anecdotes and program descriptions illuminating the varied methods used to influence change in scores in other similar geographic areas. It is possible that what you have learned from your information might even be reported in visual format, such as charts or videotapes of compelling testimonials from students and teachers.

Look closely at the evidence that provides a rationale for the intervention approach, as well as the structural implications of each for outcome measurement.

In our clinical example, Joshua must exhibit directional movement on specific measures to indicate intervention success. In the large-systems change

> **BOX 5.8 | QUESTIONS TO GUIDE ANALYSIS OF NONRESEARCH LITERATURE**
>
> 1. What types of claims are being made? How do these claims inform, or emerge from social work practice? Who made them and in what context?
> 2. What support is advanced for the claims? To what extent is the support credible?
> 3. How does this literature inform problem and need? What are its limitations? What degree of reflexive intervention is presented, and to what extent can it inform your practice?
> 4. How are desired outcomes examined or asserted?
> 5. How current is the source?
> 6. Who benefits by this information? Who does not benefit?
> 7. What ethical dilemmas are elicited? What values? How consistent is this work with social work values and ethics?

intervention, anecdotal information and monitoring have provided the rationale for intervention, and formative assessment is therefore supported in place of expected outcome. The actual implementation of an effort rather than the outcome of the effort is the implied success criterion in Joshua's effort to elicit an increase in test scores.

Each report reflects relevant literature and other resources and organizes them in a manner to meet the purposive needs and the rigor of evaluation practice.

MAIN POINTS

1. Although professional and research literature has historically been the primary credible information used to support evaluation, the use of multiple sources of knowledge is increasingly discussed and recommended by social work educators, researchers, and practitioners.
2. Review of information is purposive.
3. Review of information can occur at any time during evaluation practice.
4. Review of information can occur through many different approaches, depending on purpose, timing, and available information resources.
5. Delimiting the scope of information is a critical step as information continues to expand.
6. There are specific strategies and sources for conducting an information search, and specific methods for organizing sources and preparing a report for multiple purposes and audiences.

EXERCISES

1. Using a practice example, identify where a review of the literature would be most useful in the evaluation practice model. Why?
2. Select a practice scenario, and determine when and how literature should be used to inform the intervention.
3. From the information in Exercise 2, determine the nature and timing of and delimiting factors for literature review. Why have you selected these?
4. Select a topic, and conduct a literature review. Begin with a clarification of your professional purpose, and continue through the report of your literature to diverse interest groups.

CHAPTER 6
ASCERTAINING NEED

Distinction Between Problem and Need

Choosing Needs Assessment Action Strategies

Main Points

Exercises

DISTINCTION BETWEEN PROBLEM AND NEED

In this step of evaluation practice, one must clarify what is needed to resolve the problem. Before exploring need in detail, let us revisit the distinction between problem and need. A problem is a value statement about what is undesirable. For a problem to be relevant to social work, it must be within the boundaries and theoretical domains of social work concern. For example, even though we would need to be conversant with and knowledgeable about certain medical conditions to work with individuals who experience them, diagnosing a medical condition would not fit within our professional knowledge base. Thus, if presented with a medical "problem" within clinical practice, a social worker would refer that "problem" to a physician for diagnosis.

Related to but different from a problem, a need is a systematic, evidence-based claim linked to all or part of a problem, which specifies what conditions and actions are necessary to resolve the part of the problem to be addressed. Thus, the identification of need involves collecting and analyzing information such as assessment data, client interview, and so forth to ascertain what is necessary to resolve a problem.

What could happen if need is not clarified and the social worker moves from a problem immediately to an intervention? As providers, we might assume that we know the needs of a population, group, or individual. Consider the following example.

A study was initiated by two social work students to examine how adults with developmental disabilities wanted to be included in community recreation. The students had already worked with the local YMCA to develop fully inclusive events and programs. The students developed an interview schedule in which each respondent was presented with the community recreation options and asked to rate the degree of interest and likelihood of attendance. Not even one of the respondents was interested in the inclusive programming. What should have happened here? Perhaps before assuming that adults with developmental disabilities would naturally want to be included in community events, the researchers should have asked. The two students immediately realized that they had made an assumption about need that was not accurate for the respondents. They therefore redesigned their study by initiating a focus group series, at which time they found that to their respondents, inclusion was frightening and seemed unsafe. The respondents therefore developed activities to which they invited community members. They wanted to say who could and could not be included in their planned recreation (Ippoliti, Peppy, & DePoy, 1994).

It is not unusual for social workers to assume need and develop interventions without verifying that the need for those specific actions is perceived by others who are involved. The problem of limited community participation by individuals with developmental disabilities would therefore not have been resolved at all if the social work students had gone ahead with their efforts at the YMCA without empirical evidence supporting that approach.

At this stage of the evaluation practice sequence, one may already have information on which to formulate need or one may collect data in a systematic fashion to clearly delimit and identify need. A needs statement should specify who is (are) the target(s) of the problem, what changes are desired, what targets will change, what is the degree of change, and how one will recognize that the change occurred. Need must be based on systematically derived data that already are contained in the literature, in documentation, or in what is revealed in needs assessment inquiry. Why do we need empirical data in order to ascertain and support need? Can't we just ask without all the effort necessary to meet empirical standards? Not exactly. Besides making the error of assuming without verifying our hunches, as in the previous example, we must also acknowledge another important issue.

Once again we face the considerable disagreement in the field of evaluation regarding the extent to which empirical inquiry is or is not value neutral. Looking back to the diversity of evaluation theory presented in Chapter 1, you may remember the fact-value debate that not only underpins all research thinking, but poses dilemmas when multiple perspectives and stakeholders differ in their opinions of need. We do not purport to solve the philosophical dilemmas of the field. Rather, we suggest that empirical inquiry, no matter what position one takes in the fact-value argument, clarifies both the nature of evidence on which a claim is based and the logical-thinking trail, so to speak, of how evidence was used to support or determine a claim. Evidence and its interpretation are thus public. Given the clarity and capacity in empirical inquiry to follow knowledge derivation and use, can you see that an empirical need statement holds within it the evidence base for what it claims? Thus, from where the need emerged, who perceives it as a need and who does not are points that are clarified and on which informed intervention decisions can then be made.

Knowing why, how, who, what, and when about a need will help you determine if you think the evidence is compelling, convincing, and important enough to warrant intervention action. If you do believe that the need must be met, the empirical approach provides a structure through which you can develop goals and objectives that point to how you will know that the need has been successfully filled. Systematic inquiry may also reveal if planned intervention is what is needed to resolve the problem as stated.

Thinking about Jennifer provides us with an example. In response to the access barriers Jennifer encountered in her work environment, the administration turned to the literature for guidance. Following a successful effort in a similar geographic area, in which public access barriers were addressed by the construction of a mechanical lift to move a person up a few steps, the administration had a lift erected. As detailed in the literature, one of the unanticipated consequences of the lift was damage caused by unsupervised use. The administration therefore followed the recommendation to have a staff person keep a key and supervise the operation of the lift. In this example, the administration looked at what was needed to address a problem of general public access. In reviewing the systematic evidence used to develop the intervention, the social worker could clearly see why the intervention would be unsuccessful in addressing Jennifer's problem. The evidence of need sought from the literature addressed public access rather than individual access, and thus, the need statement was inaccurate.

In any needs assessment, formal inquiry strategies or previously well-conducted studies make up the knowledge base upon which practitioners, scholars, researchers, policymakers, and funders can communicate about and come to a well-documented consensus of need. That is not to say that empirical understanding is the only way to determine need. Rather, inquiry-based need provides the rigor, and through well-described, clear, logical steps, shows how a claim was derived and on what evidence the claim is anchored. The use of research thinking and action therefore allows funding, policy, and practice decisions to be made on values (as would be the case if the problem statement were used solely for allocation decisions), and also adds a set of evidence and thinking strategies to support the values as well as define a clear and rational direction for practice and expected outcome. Consider the following example.

Traditionally, to educate students with disabilities, educators have actualized the perceived need to segregate those students from students without disabilities, with belief, attitudinal, and value foundations as the basis for the decision. Attitudes toward students with disabilities clearly placed them in a position of deficit; the assumptions that they would not be able to keep up and would need special help and special teaching techniques were translated into separate educational systems. These beliefs and attitudes have given rise to the field of special education, with many benefits for students with disabilities; however, the assumption of segregation as a need was not empirically examined, and thus efficacy of segregation has emerged as a problem to be remediated rather than a needed educational strategy. Empirical evidence supporting school inclusion suggests that separate educational systems for students with disabilities result in serious academic, social, employment, and community disadvantage for these individuals. Moreover, the negative effects on these students ultimately expand to community, state, and national economic and quality-of-life costs (Coutinho & Repp, 1999). In the 21st century, educational practice is looking toward systematic evidence to revise and restructure what was considered to be a need (segregation) as educational reform moves toward the creation of a single system for all students (Mackelprang & Salsgiver, 1999).

Having discussed our conceptual approach to empirical needs statement, let us turn to needs assessment thinking and action. How do you develop and use empirically based need in evaluation practice? If you were in clinical practice, for example, you might identify a client's problem as depression and then proceed to gather evidence of what may be needed to alleviate the depression. You might acquire a social history, a medical history, and a current description of your client's living situation. You might interview family, conduct standardized assessments, observe your client, or choose from among a host of other knowledge sources with the potential to inform your practice.

Given the huge amount of information, how do you decide how to identify and delimit the evidence you are going to collect to examine or determine need? First, you would consider the practice context. If you were able to provide referral intervention only, you certainly would collect different evidence than if you were in an agency or practice where you could provide counseling along with referral. Your professional context and function would help you delimit what evidence to amass. Consider the factor of time as well. If you had only

> **BOX 6.1** | **QUESTIONS USED IN CHOOSING NEEDS ASSESSMENT ACTION STRATEGIES**
>
> 1. What is known about a need?
> 2. What else needs to be known, and how will it be ascertained?
> 3. What limitations are imposed on needs assessment by resources and time?

three sessions to work with a client, you would certainly not obtain the same amount of information that you would seek if you had unlimited counseling sessions. In the case of brief intervention, you might turn to secondary, descriptive data, such as medical and social history records; in long-term counseling, you would most likely engage in your own data-collection strategies. Third, the purpose of your intervention would certainly be a factor in your choice of evidence. If your purpose were evaluation for admission to short-term hospitalization, you would focus your evidence gathering on description of suicide risk and medical factors. In a long-term counseling session, you might look for causal evidence related to family constellation and relationships as a possible direction for intervention.

As asserted previously, evaluation practice thinking and action provide the logical meta-framework for professional decision making. Using this framework, we suggest that there are three important questions to answer in choosing needs assessment action strategies. Answers to each of the questions presented in Box 6.1 will be given specific attention and will lead the social worker to sound decisions about how to design and conduct needs assessment.

CHOOSING NEEDS ASSESSMENT ACTION STRATEGIES

What Is Known About a Need?

To ascertain what is already known about need, a comprehensive information review is indicated. As discussed in Chapter 5, reviewing information is a large task that must be approached both practically and systematically. Unlike in other forms of information review, this task in the needs assessment action step must be purposive and delimited to the scope of the problem identified in the thinking step of problem definition. The social worker not only needs to consider the general knowledge about need, but in this step, must look at the existing nature of knowledge about the specified need (including the level of theory development, explicit and implicit value base, and the methods used to generate the knowledge), the degree to which this knowledge is relevant to the purpose of the needs assessment, and the extent to which the knowledge is applicable to the target(s) of change. Each of these components will be examined in detail.

Nature of Knowledge   A major consideration in the nature of knowledge is the level of theory development explicated in literature. Consistent with the research literature (Anastas & MacDonald, 2000; Rubin & Babbie, 2000), we identify three primary levels of empirical knowledge: descriptive, relational, and causal/predictive. These levels are anchored on research thinking and action in both naturalistic and experimental-type inquiry (DePoy & Gitlin, 1998) and on a set of value-driven thinking and action processes. We have discussed values in detail in Chapters 1 and 2. At this point, however, we also highlight that values not only guide knowledge content, but also influence the methods that a social worker selects to assess and generate knowledge. As we discuss the action processes of needs assessment, be on the lookout for values that are implicit in each methodological approach. We turn now to levels of theory development to clarify their relevance to needs assessment.

Descriptive Knowledge   This level of knowledge provides an understanding, illumination, and detailing of a phenomenon. The essential characteristics, examples, nonexamples, and borderline cases of the phenomenon emerge from a descriptive process. From empirical description, what the phenomenon "is" and what it "is not" should be clear. What is needed and what is not needed, therefore, can be clarified and understood. As we will discuss in detail later in the chapter, descriptive knowledge can be produced by naturalistic and experimental-type inquiry or by a combination of both.

If we were to ask Jennifer about some of her mobility and teaching needs based upon her specific disability, we might come away with some substantive information that we might not otherwise gain. Experimental-type inquiry can provide us with height of seat of wheelchair (letting us know about height of desk), range of motion (providing information on how high on the chalkboard she might be able to write, if at all), and grip strength (helping us understand whether she needs adaptive equipment to write on the overhead projector). Of course, occupational therapists and physical therapists administer many other measures that are increasingly able to provide us with information necessary to intervene and minimize classroom barriers.

What naturalistic-type inquiry will give us that experimental-type inquiry may not is a sense of the unique needs of an individual. In Jennifer's case, through naturalistic inquiry, we might have found out that her unique needs for access related to her schedule and the need to be at her work site when other staff were not present. Thus, we would have known that a keyed lift would not have been needed to resolve Jennifer's individual access problems.

Relational Knowledge   Once a phenomenon is described, its relational context can be ascertained. What factors are present and/or change as the phenomenon appears and changes? How strongly are two or more factors associated? What is the direction of the association? What is the web of association?

This level of knowledge begins the process of expanding understanding beyond knowing "what" something is to knowing "how" something relates to or is embedded in something else. Thus, an understanding of need moves beyond a single lens to begin to construct how need is distributed, related to other needs, embedded in contextual factors, and ranked in priority. Moreover, understanding how phenomena relate to one another may shed light on how each will change as specific needs are met and addressed.

For example, let's revisit Joshua's work as a legislator in the area of the public school students' perceived "low scores" on standardized academic achievement tests. As discussed in Chapter 2, the initial problem to which Joshua directed his attention was poor performance by the public school students in his state on standardized testing. But in identifying the problem, there was a wide variation not only in the ideological interpretation of the meaning of the low scores, but of causative factors and solutions as well. As a legislator, Joshua understands and relies upon the importance of assuring the voices of his constituencies in formulating the problem statement and the needs to resolve it. Suppose legislation is directed only at improving teacher performance as a basis for increasing student test scores. This approach has resulted in teachers "teaching to the test." However, if multiple needs are identified, such as teacher performance, exceedingly large class size, and insufficient learning resources, the responsibility for the problem is expanded, as are the needs and expected outcomes. Legislation to cap class size while providing new books and learning materials may enhance student performance and improve teacher morale so that teacher training is enthusiastically supported and placed within a context of overall school improvement.

Typically, experimental-type research has been used to examine relationship, based on the epistemological notion that in order to relate something to something else, both "somethings" must be clearly understood. However, as naturalistic traditions become more widely valued in evaluation research, these methods, too, can reveal important and complex relationships that may be overlooked with deductive approaches. Of particular note is the value of naturalistic inquiry in explicating the natural setting, as is often the case in evaluation practice. One caution about relational knowledge is necessary: "Association is not causation" is a phrase often heard and too frequently not heeded. When we ascertain association and context, we cannot determine predictive or causal inferences without appropriate methodological action processes. We will examine the causal/predictive level of knowledge and strategies to elicit it more fully later in the text.

Let us think a little about Joshua's test performance dilemma. It may be possible that teacher training, class size, and learning resources are not causative in and of themselves, so addressing these issues may not necessarily resolve the problem of low test scores. What is at the root of these associated problems is the lack of financial support for education in the state, resulting in low wages for teachers, schools that are too small to accommodate the student population, and outdated and damaged books. Without better pay, teachers may take on other, part-time, jobs and thus will have no time for training. The classes cannot be decreased in size if there are no additional spaces for students. And the purchase of new materials, such as computers, cannot occur without first allocating additional resources to education within the state. If we address the indicators of insufficient finances as causative, we lose the larger picture of where change must happen so that smaller classes, teacher training, and new learning resources can be actualized.

Causal/Predictive Knowledge As explicated by our category name, this level of knowledge answers the question *why*. Once we accept that phenomena are related, we then may want to look at explanations for cause as a basis for further understanding need and positing intervention goals that address the "why" rather than the "what" or "how" of a need. If we look at the body of knowledge through which causal relationships are examined, we note that true experimental design is the most widely accepted and valued method of supporting causal claims. However, as will be discussed later, naturalistic strategies can be used to induce understandings of cause as well within natural settings.

Consider the previous example. It is not likely that an experimental design involving the distribution of money to one school district and the withholding from the control region would be planned. Rather, Joshua might choose to uncover cause by interviewing key stakeholders and informants in his state.

Scope of Knowledge Equally important as content is the relevance of knowledge to the specific part of the problem you have delimited. Does the existing knowledge describe your domain of concern; apply to the population who owns, identifies, or is concerned with the problem; and address policy, resource, and practice issues that you are addressing? The thinking strategy of identifying the boundaries of your evaluation and the extent to which existing knowledge informs need within those boundaries is a critical step in needs assessment. The following example clarifies this important point.

The federal government identified the difficulty of transition to adulthood for adolescents with special healthcare needs as a problem warranting attention. Specifically, the problem was narrowed to the disproportionate number of adolescents who leave secondary education unprepared to maintain their health and/or to earn a sufficient living. From a comprehensive review of the literature, it was clear that the existing knowledge about adolescents' transition, their experiences, and their service needs was generated primarily from the perspective of providers and educators. Given that the existing supports and services were developed on that knowledge base and were deemed to be fragmented and in need of significant revision, it became obvious that using the current body of literature would not be useful in informing systems-change efforts, with the exception of providing an example of what should not be done. Thus, while a large body of knowledge existed on adolescent transition, it was not relevant to the scope of the change effort. A comprehensive, mixed-method needs assessment was undertaken with particular emphasis on giving voice to adolescents. The findings of the needs assessment were so far afield from the needs identified in the professional literature that the dilemma on how to resolve the disparity continues to be debated.

This example not only demonstrates the principle of relevance, but also addresses the issue of who is the target population. If the target is the adolescent, then the existing literature was not useful in informing adolescent need; but it did inform us about provider perspective and could have been a useful rationale for provider-centered systems change. However, given that the identified problem related to adolescent capability and preparation for transition, suggesting that current services and supports were not achieving desirable outcomes, it made sense to ask adolescents themselves to articulate their needs as a basis for systems revision (DePoy & Gilmer, 2000).

This point leads us to the second thinking strategy guiding needs assessment.

What Else Needs to Be Known, and How Will It Be Ascertained?

As illustrated in the previous example, the literature does not always provide the empirical foundation on which to assess need. Based on what the literature does not tell us, we then formulate a strategy to determine what we must know and how we can come to know it.

Box 6.2 contains guiding questions whose answers will equip the social worker with the necessary information to move onto the next step in our evaluation practice model: setting goals and objectives.

The following example explains how answering each of these questions thoughtfully and systematically defines the direction and scope of the needs assessment.

Consider Jennifer and the assessment of her environmental needs. There are a variety of ADA assessment tools all explicated and supported in the literature. A very good one has been developed and is available from the Department of Justice. Additionally, there are building codes that can help create a fundamentally accessible building according to standard regulations. However, what the literature does not provide, and what is rarely spoken about, is the critical need to work with an individual such as Jennifer to modify and adapt her environment in accordance with her individual physical, social, and unique needs and limitations. It is clear that much more information is needed to inform an understanding of Jennifer's, as well as other interest groups', needs related to access, only some of which can be learned by reading literature in social work and other relevant disciplines. To inform need at multiple levels, the professional should read micro-, mezzo-, and macrowork, including public policy writings, to expand what is learned about the "private" to the public domain. The social worker will also need to be able to conduct or obtain experimental-type inquiry based on application of a standardized building structure evaluation, a naturalistic design study based on an interview or series of interviews with Jennifer, and perhaps a naturalistic study involving observation of Jennifer during her workday. Sources may also include online resources, which are typ-

| BOX 6.2 | GUIDING QUESTIONS FOR ASSESSING INFORMATION NEED |

1. What aspect of the existing literature is inadequate to inform need?
2. What level of information is needed?
3. What source(s) of information should be consulted?
4. How should these sources be approached?

---

ically more current than articles in scholarly journals. This multimethod approach is essential if Jennifer's needs, as well as access needs of all teachers, are to be examined and promoted.

What Limitations Are Imposed on Needs Assessment by Resources and Time?

We have just laid out a basic evaluation of only one individual. You may be thinking that the type of needs assessment we outlined seems time-consuming and perhaps expensive. An administrator may even wonder about the costs if many employees seek out evaluations and needed facility modification. Although all the questions addressed in the case example of *Jennifer* are warranted and essential to her individual functioning on the job, the financial, human, and time resources may not always be available to conduct in-depth needs assessment. What can you do when it is apparent that needs assessment will be cost-effective in the long run to reduce the likelihood of intervention failure, but immediate resources are limited? You may want to think about the types of inquiry that are least time-consuming but most productive. Several examples include survey, key informant interview, and group interview. These strategies will be examined later.

MAIN POINTS

1. There is a distinction between problem and need that is critical to acknowledge in evaluation practice.
2. Because inquiry-based need shows how a claim was derived and on what evidence the claim is anchored, this approach to asserting need supports value-based intervention development while defining a clear and rational direction for practice and expected outcome.
3. There are three critical questions to answer in order to examine need:

    What is known about a need?

    What else needs to be known, and how will it be ascertained?

    What limitations are imposed on needs assessment by resources and time?

EXERCISES

1. From the literature, select a "problem" that is clear and delimited as relevant to social work. Pose three different need statements and identify which part of your problem they address.
2. For each need statement, examine the literature and determine if there is sufficient empirical evidence to support the need as you have stated it.
3. Select two needs assessment articles from the social work literature: one conducted through experimental-type design and one through naturalistic inquiry. Compare and contrast the articles, based on the following questions:

   What scope of need is supported?

   Who defines the need?

   Who is the target?

   What needs to be changed and how?

EXAMINING NEED WITH PREVIOUSLY SUPPORTED APPROACHES: DESIGNING EXPERIMENTAL-TYPE INQUIRY

CHAPTER 7

Using Experimental-Type Design in Needs Assessment

True Experimental Design

Nonexperimental Designs

Thinking Process of Experimental-Type Design Selection in Needs Assessment

Main Points

Exercises

USING EXPERIMENTAL-TYPE DESIGN IN NEEDS ASSESSMENT

Now that we have conceptually analyzed the distinction between problem and need and have examined the thinking processes related to the nature of knowledge and planning, conducting, and reporting of need, let us turn our attention to the action processes for conducting a needs assessment. Selection of evaluation design is based on purpose, scope, and current knowledge related to the problem or domain of professional intervention. If existing and sound evidence does not provide the empirical foundation on which to develop a clear and comprehensive statement of need, social workers need to engage in the action process of data collection and analysis. On the other end of the spectrum, if sufficient theory and practice literature are available and relevant to the problem statement, then the social worker may choose action strategies that are founded on the truth value of previously supported intervention and outcomes. Each condition provides the rationale for methodological selection. Situations that fall between the two extremes direct our attention to needs assessment action processes that may make use of multiple research traditions, such as those that include both a naturalistic and an experimental-type component.

When to Use Experimental-Type Design in Needs Assessment

When sufficient literature exists to provide a theoretical direction for intervention, the social worker has several action choices. From the literature, goals and objectives for intervention can be developed directly without any active data collection and analysis. This action strategy is particularly useful when time and resources are limited and the literature provides a sound and comprehensive foundation for intervention development.

However, if an intervention has been successful in achieving its outcome in similar populations or domains, but the social worker needs additional evidence to ascertain the degree to which the current knowledge fully informs the scope of a specific problem, needs assessment research strategies relying on deductive, experimental-type traditions are indicated. You will note that we focus on "program interventions" rather than individual interventions in this chapter, since experimental-type strategies are intended to investigate commonalities. These designs, also called **nomothetic** and quantitative approaches (Babbie, 2001), reveal characteristics of groups, not uniqueness of individuals. These strategies are deductive in that they begin with existing theory and seek, through **measurement** (the attribution of numbers to denote observed phenomena), to verify or falsify the theory. Later in the text, we will examine needs assessment strategies that are most useful in intervention with individuals.

In the discussion of experimental-type design in the needs assessment phase of evaluation practice, we use the notation system developed by Campbell and Stanley (1963) because of its wide acceptance and ease in illustrating the structure of deductive approaches to research. Campbell and Stanley used the following symbols to diagram design (refer to Glossary for definitions of boldface terms): X for **independent variable,** O for **dependent variable,** and R for **random sample** selection.

We also find it very helpful to use the symbol *r* to refer to **random group assignment,** which will be addressed later in the discussion of outcome studies. Needs assessment usually does not involve random assignment because it is primarily an inquiry conducted at one interval with a single group. Moreover, because practice need is most frequently specific to a known group, random sample selection is used in needs assessment research only in the infrequent situations where a population that is too large to be fully included in inquiry is addressed. Even if random selection seems fitting, it is often very difficult and frequently inappropriate or unethical for health and human service professionals to select a sample from a larger predefined population based on random selection (referred to as R in Campbell and Stanley's format). In needs assessment, subjects typically participate on a volunteer basis or are selected purposively to illuminate a specific need.

To fully understand the logic of frequently used quantitative needs assessment approaches, we first must look at true experimental design as the "gold standard" of experimental-type inquiry. True experimentation typically does not serve needs assessment purposes, but quantitative designs that answer needs questions are founded on the rigorous criteria of true experimental design. True experimental designs are most likely to be used in outcome assessment and will be illustrated in a later discussion.

TRUE EXPERIMENTAL DESIGN

R   O   X   O
R   O   O

The true experimental design is perhaps the design best known by beginning researchers and laypersons. True experimental design refers to the classic two-group design in which subjects are randomly selected and randomly assigned (R) to either an experimental or control group condition. The experimental condition (also called the independent variable) is manipulated by the investigator, usually by being present or absent. The control condition is defined as the absence of the independent variable. Before the experimental condition, all subjects are pretested or observed on a measure of the dependent variable (O). A dependent variable is the phenomenon that is expected to change in response to the independent variable. In the experimental group, the independent variable or experimental condition is imposed (X), and it is withheld in the control group. Subjects are then posttested or observed on the dependent variable (O) after the experimental condition.

In this design, the investigator expects that all subjects will perform in an equivalent manner on the pretest, and thus no difference between the experimental and control groups on the dependent measure should be seen at the time of pretest. The rationale for this expectation lies in the reasoning of **probability sampling** and assignment in which subjects are chosen randomly from a larger pool of potential subjects and then assigned to a group on a chance-determined basis. Random in this sense does not mean haphazard. Rather, randomization means that all individuals in the population studied (or other units of analysis) have an equivalent chance of being selected for a study sample. It is also expected that the control group will perform on posttest similarly to both pretest groups because nothing has been done to change the group. However, the experimental group is expected to change on posttest as a result of the influence of the experimental condition.

Because of random assignment, control, and manipulation, the only possible cause of the change in the experimental group is the experimental condition (X). **Bias** (unplanned influence that confounds the outcome of a study) is therefore theoretically reduced and/or eliminated to the extent possible with true experimentation.

Note the important assumption that bias can be eliminated. Because probability theory is the basis for many statistical procedures, the violation of probability through nonrandom sampling that is characteristic of so many evaluation inquiries is one of the criticisms of evaluation research.

Let us look in more detail at the foundations of true experimentation and why this design is held as the ideal within experimental-type approaches to inquiry. There are three major characteristics of the true experiment: randomization, control, and manipulation. All are designed to reduce bias.

Randomization

Randomization is the process of selecting and/or assigning units of analysis based exclusively on chance. Theoretically, each unit of analysis not only has an equal chance to be selected in the case of random selection, and assigned in the case of random group assignment, but also has an equal chance of being exposed to all influences affecting all other units of analysis. An observed change in the experimental group at posttest can then be attributed with a reasonable degree of certainty to the experimental condition.

If random sample selection is accomplished, the design notation appears as it was presented earlier (R). If randomization occurs only at the group assignment phase, the notation looks like this:

$$\begin{array}{cccc} r & O & X & O \\ r & O & & O \end{array}$$

As indicated earlier, design using random assignment only does not allow for generalization of the results to a population from which a sample was selected, but it is very common in the outcome assessment of evaluation practice to reveal casual relationships within the sample itself.

Randomization is a powerful technique that is intended to increase control and eliminate bias by neutralizing the effects of extraneous influences on the outcome of a study. Without random assignment of subjects, you would not have a true experimental design and thus could not make a causal claim between the independent and dependent variable.

Consider this example. You have been given the task of determining strategies to meet the growing need for social workers in gerontology. You establish an innovative educational intervention to recruit high school students into the profession of social work. To assure that this strategy will produce recruits, you select two high schools, one that would serve as the experimental school and one as the control. You are surprised that over the next six months you are unable to recruit more than 10% of your experimental group, but 30% of the students in the control group decide to enroll in social work education. You conclude that your innovative recruitment program is a failure until you read that compared to national standards, 10% is a phenomenally high number. What could have happened to yield these results? Suppose that the control high school had just been approached by a human service scholarship agency and the students were offered full financial support for enrolling in social work education; or that there had been a lecturer at the school assembly who identified social work in gerontology as one of the most lucrative and growing careers of the future. Without random assignment, there is no way to ascertain if the experimental and control groups are equivalent and are theoretically exposed to identical conditions, such that the only cause for change could be the independent variable. If the two groups were assigned randomly to the innovative recruitment and control condition, the potential for sampling bias is eliminated.

Control

Control is a set of processes to eliminate sampling or experimental bias. In true experimentation, the investigator uses a control group, one that has not been subjected to the experimental change condition, to see what the sample would be like without the influence of the experimental condition or independent variable; and thus, the control group is expected, theoretically, to test the same throughout the experiment. Therefore, the control group represents the characteristics of the experimental group before being changed by participation in the experimental condition.

Manipulation

In the true experimental design, the independent variable is manipulated by either having it present (in the experimental group) or absent (in the control group). It is the ability to provide and withhold the independent variable that is unique to the true experiment.

True experimentation has been discussed so that you can understand the foundation thinking processes of all experimental-type inquiry. We remind you, however, that true experimental design is rarely appropriate for use in needs assessment inquiry. Let us now look at designs based on the logic of probability and the exemplary practice of true experimentation that serve needs assessment questions.

> **BOX 7.1** | **WHEN TO USE EXPERIMENTAL-TYPE DESIGN IN NEEDS ASSESSMENT**
>
> Use experimental-type design in needs assessment in these situations.
> 1. You are already comfortable with knowing the universe of need.
> 2. You are limited to interventions that fulfill delimited, predefined needs.
> 3. You are looking for selection preferences for interventions and outcomes.
> 4. You are attempting to provide the most compelling evidence of need in order to garner resources.
> 5. You have sufficient theory to predict the likelihood of success with given interventions.

In most needs assessment, the social worker is interested in answering the following important questions:

1. What is needed to resolve the scope of the problem?
2. According to whom is this needed?
3. What is expected to occur as a result of needs being met?

The social worker using experimental-type design is therefore looking for descriptive through predictive, value-based information that empirically points to specific interventions and their desired outcomes. The social worker may expect that the responses to needs assessment questioning may differ according to who provides the empirical information.

Why use experimental-type design here rather than open-ended questioning? Indications for using experimental-type needs assessment inquiry are presented in Box 7.1 and will then be discussed.

Experimental-type designs are based on the notion that there is a single truth and that preexisting knowledge and theory developed and verified through these methods provide that truth. If the social worker already thinks that he or she knows the full scope of successful interventions for a problem, then needs assessment actually becomes a selection process. Of the scope of known options, which is preferred by respondents, who prefers which intervention, and what are the expected or predicted results of intervention? Using experimental-type needs assessment therefore assumes that the professional already knows the nature of need but is looking for verification, clarity, delimitation, and expected outcomes from the universe of interventions that have already been theoretically and empirically verified in other situations.

Experimental-type needs assessment is also used in situations where even if the need might expand beyond the options given, these interventions could not be provided. Moreover, the use of quantitative verification of need and outcome is well accepted as evidence and can be compelling in obtaining resources to implement interventions.

Finally, experimental-type needs assessment clearly creates an empirical path to the development, possible prediction, and ultimate measurement of expected outcomes.

To illustrate, we revisit our example of the substance-abuse intervention for professionals. The social worker was asked to develop an evaluation to determine if the program outcomes were met. He selected sobriety as the only measure of outcome, thereby implying that his program could produce sobriety in clients. It was likely that the social worker already knew the universe of current interventions, as well as outcomes, and also knew that sobriety was not an outcome that could be assured. Why did he select this outcome as a measure of program success? Many social workers select a long-term goal as an outcome measure even though they know that intervention can advance toward but not cause the attainment of that goal. A conscientious needs assessment design might therefore have included the intermediate, as well as long-term, expectations and intervention preferences of diverse interest groups and stakeholders. Let us say that the social worker, instead of selecting interventions to assure sobriety as the only need, developed a survey to ask about what might be needed to produce outcomes that were possible and that are highly associated with sobriety, such as development of social skills, development of support networks, relaxation training, and so forth. Such a needs assessment would not only have provided a direction for the program among possible choices, but would have served to delimit the scope of possible outcomes to those that were achievable and associated with long-term sobriety. The intervention would therefore have a chance to advance clients toward sobriety even if they did not achieve that outcome after their initial completion of the intervention. Moreover, the intervention need could be reexamined and refined as the evaluation of intermediate outcomes proceeded.

In most cases, experimental-type needs assessment designs fall into Campbell and Stanley's (1963) category of **nonexperimental designs**. The survey discussed would be an example of a nonexperimental survey design. Let us look at some nonexperimental designs that are frequently used in needs assessment.

NONEXPERIMENTAL DESIGNS

These designs, based on the logic of probability, are those in which the criteria for true experimental design (random selection, control, and manipulation) cannot be met. Nonexperimental approaches can be used from exploration to prediction but are most useful when measuring a concept, construct, or relationship among constructs. For the most part, nonexperimental designs examine naturally occurring phenomena and describe or examine relationships. Any manipulation of variables is done *post hoc* (after the occurrence of the phenomenon) through statistical analysis (see Appendix for a review of data analysis techniques).

There are three designs used most frequently in needs assessment: surveys, passive observation, and ex post facto.

Survey Designs

Survey designs are used primarily to measure characteristics of a population, including their knowledge, opinions, and attitudes (DePoy & Gitlin, 1998). Through survey design it is possible not only to describe population parameters but also to predict relationships among those characteristics. Questions are posed through either mailed questionnaires or telephone or face-to-face interviews.

Joshua's concern with low test scores can provide an example of using surveys for needs assessment. Because Joshua expected that low scores were caused by complex phenomena, he developed a teacher survey to answer the following research questions:

1. *What are teachers' beliefs about the causes of low test scores?*
2. *What methods would teachers suggest to promote an increase in test scores?*
3. *To what extent do teachers in school districts with high test scores differ from those in districts with low test scores on responses to questions 1 and 2.*

Surveys sent to a large sample of teachers revealed that the teachers in schools with low test scores believed that low scores were caused by family disinterest in and lack of support for the education of their children. These teachers also indicated that large classes and their own lack of knowledge about what was going to be tested were two other factors to be considered. Those from the schools with high test scores held the opinion that teaching style and content were critical factors in promoting student learning, which was then exhibited on standardized tests. Both groups of teachers suggested that teacher training be implemented as a means to improve test scores.

Passive Observation Designs

Passive observation designs are used to examine phenomena as they naturally occur and to discern the relationship between two or more variables. Often referred to as "correlational designs," passive observation designs can be as simple as examining the relationship between two variables, for example, height and weight; or can be as complex as predicting scores on one or more variables from knowledge of scores on other variables. As in survey designs, variables are not manipulated but are measured and then examined for relationships and patterns of prediction.

For example, let us revisit Joshua. Besides the survey, another way to decipher the cause of students' low test scores would be to use multiple methods of assessment of academic competence as a basis for comparison to performance on the standardized tests. If an observer noted that children in one school district had difficulty reading English but did well in French, it might be concluded that English was a second language; thus, poor test scores in reading compre-

hension in English depicted a language barrier rather than lack of competence in reading skill and literacy. Knowing that a language barrier existed, further needs assessment might examine the predictive potential of French reading comprehension on future capacity to learn and read English.

Based on the survey and the passive observation, Joshua begins to define a direction for intervention. Teacher training and intensive student education in English as a Second Language (ESL) are the two directions that may be cogent.

Ex Post Facto Designs

Ex post facto designs are considered to be one type of passive observation design. However, in ex post facto design (literally translated as "after the fact"), the phenomena of interest have already occurred and cannot be manipulated in any way. Ex post facto designs are frequently used to examine relationships between naturally occurring population parameters and specific variables. Within this group of designs are needs assessment action processes relying on secondary data analysis.

For an example, we revisit the professional substance-abuse intervention project in which the social worker is concerned about why professionals begin to abuse substances. A retrospective examination of job demands might shed light on the job stresses that are associated with substance use. This type of information can be used as a basis to explore the need to reduce job stress, to prepare professionals to cope with stress as a means to prevent substance abuse, and/or to promote sobriety in those who have experienced an abuse problem.

THINKING PROCESS OF EXPERIMENTAL-TYPE DESIGN SELECTION IN NEEDS ASSESSMENT

As you can see, needs assessment findings generated from experimental-type designs provide the numeric data on which to describe a need, to compare perceived needs among diverse populations, and to provide a clear empirical foundation for expected and/or predicted outcomes of an intervention.

You are now aware of experimental-type design structures and techniques typically used in needs assessment but may still wonder how to select a design to fit your particular purpose and questions. Begin by asking yourself the important guiding questions presented in Box 7.2.

If you are able to answer each of the questions comprehensively and thoughtfully, you can begin to have confidence in your needs assessment approach and its capacity to meet its purpose. However, one critical question remains: Does the design answer the needs assessment question(s)? This question gets to the heart of rigor in inquiry. Within experimental-type design, **validity** and **reliability** are the two criteria on which the soundness of your design can be judged.

> **BOX 7.2** | **GUIDING QUESTIONS IN THE SELECTION OF EXPERIMENTAL-TYPE NEEDS ASSESSMENT DESIGN**
>
> 1. What purpose does the needs assessment serve? Why am I doing it? What is (are) my question(s)?
> 2. Is the design consistent with the limitations of the practice arena?
> 3. Does the design yield information sufficient for articulating goals, objectives, and expected outcomes of an intervention?
> 4. What are some of the ethical and field limitations that influence the design?

Validity refers in general to the extent to which the action processes of an inquiry are consistent with the conceptual thinking processes. In other words, does the design answer the needs assessment question? To be able to judge validity, you must have clear questions in which you specify the concepts to be investigated and the scope of the investigation. Consider this example.

The social worker working with access issues raised by Jennifer is looking at what is needed to improve school access. The first needs assessment question is posed: What barriers to physical access for mobility-impaired individuals need to be removed from the school environment? As stated, this needs assessment question is vague. What does the school environment mean? What about mobility-impaired individuals? What types of impairments? Who is being asked? The social worker develops a mailed survey to be answered by all teaching, administrative, and support personnel in the school. The survey is specific in addressing the barriers to entering and then navigating the school building for teaching, meeting, and self-care for individuals who use wheelchairs. Does this approach answer the needs assessment question? It is impossible to know because the question is too broad.

Consider the wording of the second (revised) question: What do the educational, administrative, and support personnel currently employed in the school articulate as barriers to accessing work and self-care spaces in the school building for employees who use wheelchairs? The revised question includes two important changes: the clarification of exactly what knowledge is being sought and who is providing it.

Two validity concerns are resolved: **internal** and **external validity**. Internal validity assesses the extent to which the planned approach to collecting and analyzing information answers the needs assessment question.

In this example, one would look at the instrumentation to see if it measures the construct of articulated "barriers to accessing work and self-care spaces in the school building for employees who use wheelchairs" as stated in the question. How the information was sought and what might interfere with accurate responses would also be considered. Suppose that the day before receiving the survey, all school employees were told that any improvements to the building could be made only if employee salaries were reduced? Administering the survey under these conditions would certainly create a challenge to the validity of the responses.

Now consider clinical practice. What if an individual sought help from you for feeling lethargic? You choose to assess the client with a depression inventory and find that he scores within the range of clinical depression. Knowing that the client is depressed, you focus on the depression. But what if the client is actually presenting with chronic fatigue syndrome and is depressed because he is tired? Your failure to look at the whole construct of "lethargy" and use a depression inventory to uncover the cause of the lethargy would be clinically "invalid."

External validity, as suggested by the term, is concerned with the extent to which the findings of an inquiry are relevant beyond the inquiry itself. Specifically, the relationship between the **population** and the **sample** is addressed. By population, we mean the group of people (or other units of analysis) that are delimited by the investigator. A sample refers to a smaller number of people or units of analysis than those in the population named by the inquirer.

To ascertain external validity or extent to which what has been found in the sample is accurate for the population from which the sample was selected, the population must be specified in the question. *In the first question we posed, there was no population specified, and thus external validity cannot be judged. However, in the second question, the population was named as "educational, administrative, and support personnel currently employed in the school." What if the survey were sent only to teachers, the principal, and the assistant principal? This sample does not include all the characteristics (also called parameters) of the population in the question, and thus external validity would be challenged. However, if the survey were administered to all individuals who met the criteria stated in the question, then the inquiry would be externally valid.*

The second criterion for rigor is reliability. Reliability is defined as the stability of an inquiry approach. Clearly developing, following, and articulating procedures for the inquiry enhance reliability, along with using measures that provide stable and consistent data. If you read a study that you can easily replicate, the likelihood is that the investigators were concerned with reliability. *To improve the reliability of the needs assessment inquiry related to access, carefully detailed procedures in the administration of the survey would be indicated in a survey that was well constructed.* We address survey construction in Chapter 8.

Validity and reliability are essential in needs assessment. The field of evaluation has been severely criticized for lack of attention to these criteria. In our opinion, attention to rigor not only is important but is the only way to conduct ethical inquiry. If social workers do not attend to excellence in revealing need for intervention, they may implement practices that do not remediate the problems with which they are concerned.

MAIN POINTS

1. Experimental-type design is indicated for needs assessment when looking at the needs of a group rather than the needs of an individual.
2. Deductive logic underpins all experimental-type inquiry.
3. Experimental-type designs are based on probability theory.
4. True experimental design, while not appropriate for needs assessment, is the standard of excellence for experimental-type design and therefore must be understood if other experimental-type approaches are to be rigorously implemented.
5. Measurement is the foundation of experimental-type tradition.
6. Validity and reliability are the two primary criteria on which to judge the rigor of experimental-type inquiry.

EXERCISES

Select an experimental-type needs assessment journal article and answer the following questions about it.

1. What type of needs assessment questions are being answered: descriptive, relational, and/or causal/predictive?
2. To what extent does the literature support the use of experimental-type design? Give evidence for your answer.
3. Discuss the rigor of the design approach (validity and reliability).
4. You are a social worker in a rural community in which most buildings are over 50 years old. A new business with the potential to bring resources that can decrease poverty is considering relocation to your town but will only do so if the town will consider improving environmental access. As a community organizer, you are enthusiastic about this opportunity, but you first want to examine how favorable community members are to universal design as a basis for improving access. Consider how you would go about designing an experimental-type needs assessment to examine attitudes toward universal design in your home community. Who would you include in your population, and why? How would you design your inquiry, and why?

CHAPTER 8

OBTAINING INFORMATION IN EXPERIMENTAL-TYPE NEEDS ASSESSMENT

Introduction to Measurement

Instrumentation Structures That Are Useful in Experimental-Type Needs Assessment

Main Points

Exercises

> **BOX 8.1** | **GUIDING QUESTIONS TO DELIMIT CONTENT**
>
> 1. What theoretical frame of reference provides the foundation for the concept(s)?
> 2. How shall I define the concept(s) in words?
> 3. What are the essential characteristics of the concept(s), without which it would not be the same concept(s)?
> 4. What characteristics are nonexamples of the concept(s)?
> 5. What do I want to know about the concept(s)?

INTRODUCTION TO MEASUREMENT

The primary method of obtaining information in experimental-type design is measurement. As a reminder, in Chapter 7, we defined measurement as the translation of observations into numbers. This action process creates variables from lexical concepts (operationalization) that then are ordered and examined. Through measurement, **concepts** (abstractions of observed or experienced phenomena) can be reduced into their basic elements or **indicators**, quantified, and empirically examined. Thus, measurement involves both conceptual and operational or empirical considerations. These considerations fall into two basic categories: content and structure.

Content

By content, we mean the lexical definitions, the limits of concepts to be measured, and the relationships to be examined. The purpose and practical constraints are important determinants of the content of instrumentation. The thinking process of delimiting content involves a careful, clear analysis of what concept(s) is to be measured and what one wants to know about the concept. The questions in Box 8.1, extracted from philosophical language-analysis techniques (Wilson, 1971), should be answered in order to accomplish this initial process.

To illustrate this, suppose that young Joshua's social worker wants to assess Joshua's likelihood of sobriety before making a full commitment to support Joshua's request for help in higher education. From the literature and practice wisdom, the social worker selects a cognitive behavioral approach for this task (question 1). Within that framework, there is evidence to suggest that beliefs about alcohol are important determinants in how one uses alcohol (Connors & Maisto, 1994). The social worker therefore defines the prediction of problem drinking as beliefs about alcohol (question 2). Essential characteristics of the construct include one's belief about the effect of alcohol on an individual's behavior, capabilities and feelings, beliefs about the degree of control that one has over his or her judgment and behavior after ingesting alcohol, and the reasons that an individual believes that alcohol is used (question 3). Nonexamples of the construct are self-report of intended future alcohol use (question 4). The social worker is looking for description of the magnitude of a single variable: the likelihood of sobriety.

It is possible that the social worker would also be interested in a relationship among several variables, such as self-esteem and likelihood of sobriety. In this case, both concepts would be conceptually defined and the structure of the instrumentation would be designed so that a relationship could be determined.

Structure

Structure addresses the question of "How can we know the extent to which the concept exists, relates to, and/or predicts another concept?" There are two elements of structure: the *nature of the instrument* and the *level of measurement*.

Nature of the instrument refers to the way in which data are obtained. There are many types of methods used in inquiry, from complex surveys to structured observation. For the most part, experimental-type needs assessment in evaluation practice relies on questionnaires, interviews, and observations. We will look in more detail at these approaches later in the chapter. *In the previous example, the social worker used a scale (a series of items that total to measure a construct) the ABS (Alcohol Beliefs Scale), as the structure for instrumentation.*

The second element of structure is the level of measurement, which is defined as the properties and meaning of the numbers assigned to an observation and the type of mathematical manipulations that can be performed with those numbers. Determining how a variable is measured directly shapes the type of statistical analysis that can be performed and is an important part of the structure of instrumentation.

Variables can be formatted as discrete or continuous. Discrete variables have a finite number of values, each of which is mutually exclusive. These values comprise all of the potential observations of the concept. For example, if we conceptualize gender as "male" and "female," then the total concept of gender has two possible options. Each is denoted with a number (1 = male, and 2 = female). There is no in-between category.

Continuous variables have an infinite number of values. Age measured in years and height measured in inches are good examples. We now turn to the four categories of numbers that are assigned to discrete and continuous variables.

Nominal The simplest level of measurement is nominal, which involves classifying observations into mutually exclusive categories. The word *nominal* refers to "name"; therefore, nominal numbers provide numeric names for attributes of a variable. These numbers cannot be subjected to mathematical manipulation. Examples are your telephone number, the number on a soccer jersey, or your driver's license number. If you possess one of these numbers, you are a person who has a telephone, is a soccer player, or is a driver, respectively. No one else has your number, so you are a mutually exclusive member of the variable with a unique numerical name. Nominal numbers are used primarily to **code** (to assign a number) variables with discrete categories.

For example, we might classify individuals according to their political or religious affiliation, gender, or ethnicity. In each of these examples, membership in one category excludes membership in another. Another example of mutually exclusive categories is male (1) or female (2). *Thus, in the space for gender on Joshua's ABS, you would enter a 1 to denote his gender.*

The assignment of numbers is purely arbitrary, and no mathematical functions or assumptions of magnitude or ranking are implied or can be performed.

Ordinal Ordinal numbers give "order" to a set of numbers and thus provide ranking. Consider, for example, the following ranking: Suppose that you ranked individuals according to their scores on the ABS as 1 = not likely to reach sobriety, 2 = somewhat likely to reach sobriety, and 3 = very likely to reach sobriety.

We can say that the middle condition is ranked higher than the lower condition, but we can say nothing about the extent to which the conditions differ. The assignment of a numeric value is arbitrary, as in the case of nominal variables, because the distance or spacing between each category is not numerically equivalent. However, the numbers do imply magnitude; that is, one is greater than the other. Because there are no equal intervals between ordinal numbers, mathematical functions such as adding, subtracting, dividing, and multiplying cannot be performed.

Interval/Ratio Although these are two distinct types of numbers, we address them together here because of their similar use in social science inquiry. These numbers are both continuous and available for mathematical calculation because there are equal intervals between them. Height in inches is an example. If you are 51 inches tall and I am 53 inches tall, I am exactly 2 inches taller than you. If we were measured ordinally, I would know only that I was taller than you, but not by how much. The difference between ratio and interval numbers is that ratio numbers have an absolute zero, which allows you to compute a true ratio between numbers.

In social work literature, we often see considerable debate about whether behavioral scales represent interval levels of measurement. Such scales typically have a **Likert-type response format** in which a study participant responds to one of five or seven categories, such as "strongly agree," "agree," "uncertain," "disagree," or "strongly disagree." Some assign interval-level numbers to each response, asserting that the distance between "strongly agree" and "agree" is equivalent to the distance between "disagree" and "strongly disagree." However, because there is no empirical justification for making this assumption, others suggest that ordinal numbers are the appropriate level of measurement.

We suggest that based on purpose, you determine what level of data to assign. With interval-level data, more statistical options are available, so first determine what type of analysis you require and then make your decision about what level of data to assign.

As indicated earlier, answering the guiding questions for instrument selection lead the social worker toward administering the ABS (Connors & Maisto, 1994) to Joshua and lead away from asking Joshua about his intentions regarding future alcohol use. Thus, the social worker chose to observe the construct through an indicator that has been supported in the literature as accurate. The ABS is a complex instrument in which several subscales of beliefs about alcohol are included. All are scored on a scale of 1–11. Joshua's high score on the ABS regarding future sobriety provided the social worker with empirical evidence to support Joshua's articulated need to go to college. The social worker had to make decisions about both the content and structure of instrumentation. A time efficient structure, and one that was considered by the literature to be accurate in content, was therefore chosen.

INSTRUMENTATION STRUCTURES THAT ARE USEFUL IN EXPERIMENTAL-TYPE NEEDS ASSESSMENT

As discussed in Chapter 7, instrumentation structures typically used in experimental-type needs assessment include survey, structured observation, and interview.

Surveys are questionnaires that are administered through paper and pencil, Internet, computer-typed response to oral questions, face-to-face and/or telephone formats, recorded response to American Sign Language questions, and video-delivered questions to ascertain the characteristics of a population or phenomenon. Because need is a characteristic, surveys are often used to obtain information to define need.

Unlike surveys, in which the rater is a member of the group being investigated, structured observations are rated by the investigator, who looks at a phenomenon such as child play behavior and then rates it according to a specific scheme. For example, if you were looking for adequacy in motor skill in toddlers, you might have a checklist of activities and movements that are expected, and you would check each of these when you observed its performance.

Structured interviews are similar to surveys. The investigator uses a scripted list of questions with codes for the answers already developed to obtain data from an informant either face to face, on the telephone, or online. The interviewer usually completes the rating depending on the responses obtained in the interview. Box 8.2 highlights the survey instrument to illustrate instrument thinking and action processes. All the principles that we discuss related to survey also apply to the other frequently used needs assessment instrument structures described earlier.

Three types of questions can be included in surveys: **closed ended, semi-structured,** and **open ended.** Closed-ended questions pose a limited range of responses from which the respondent chooses; all responses are posited by the researcher. Thinking of the social worker involved in substance-abuse treatment in our example, a survey such as the one presented in Box 8.2 could answer the following evaluation questions:

1. What are the service and outcome preferences and expectations for substance-abuse intervention with professionals?
2. What differences in preferences and outcomes exist among diverse interest groups?

Box 8.2 presents some possible items that could be included in the survey. In this example, the social worker is interested in knowing about the knowledge and opinions held by four populations: healthcare professionals, social service administrators, program funders, and family members of a healthcare professional with substance-abuse problems.

As you can see, responses to the first question on the survey are nominal. Responses denote group belonging. The remainder of the questions could have ordinal or interval-level responses.

Adding an open-response category to a closed-ended item creates a semistructured item. For example, suppose the social worker included an "other" category in items 2 and 3 in Box 8.2. What rationale would support the addition of this open-ended response?

Open-ended questions are those in which the respondent is asked to offer his or her comment on a topic without being directed to specific answers. These types of items are included when the social worker is interested in obtaining responses that may not have been considered or known. It might be possible that respondents in our example might suggest a different intervention than those mentioned, such as wilderness therapy, Internet intervention, and so forth. If you make a choice to include open-ended responses on a needs survey, you must at least be willing to consider them as options. Otherwise, you are wasting your time and misleading the respondents.

Analysis of the closed-ended responses would first occur as descriptive. The social worker had 100 respondents. Counting the number of people who checked each category created the frequency and percentage chart in Table 8.1. A frequency is a count of how many times a value was checked. In this instance, the frequency could have exceeded the number of respondents if anyone had checked more than one category. However, the social worker found that each respondent checked only one. The percentage refers to the percent of total responses to the question for each category.

As you can see, the largest groups are providers and family members. This information is important when we consider how the responses and opinions differ according to groups.

To analyze the responses to questions 2 and 3, the social worker decided to compute **mean** scores for each option. A mean is an average. Table 8.2 presents the mean responses for question 2.

Table 8.3 presents the preferred methods of intervention.

What do these mean scores tell you? The mean scores on expectations are high in all the stated areas except sobriety. To obtain those outcomes, the sample has produced mean scores indicating that weekly counseling is most

BOX 8.2 | SAMPLE SURVEY

1. Are you a (please check all that apply to you):
   a. healthcare professional (1)
   b. social service administrator (2)
   c. program funder (3)
   d. family member of a healthcare professional with a substance-abuse problem (4)
2. On the list below, please rate each outcome to indicate the degree to which you believe each should result from substance-abuse treatment for healthcare professionals. Indicate your rating by circling the *one* response that best depicts your opinion:

Social Skills Acquisition
Must occur   (3)   Should occur   (2)   Not necessary to occur   (1)

Insight into Substance-Abuse Behavior
Must occur   (3)   Should occur   (2)   Not necessary to occur   (1)

Awareness of Strategies to Deter Substance Abuse
Must occur   (3)   Should occur   (2)   Not necessary to occur   (1)

A Support Network for the Substance Abuser
Must occur   (3)   Should occur   (2)   Not necessary to occur   (1)

Sobriety
Must occur   (3)   Should occur   (2)   Not necessary to occur   (1)

3. Please rate each service option below for the degree to which you believe it will meet your expected outcomes in the most efficacious manner.

Weekly Individual Counseling
Very likely   (3)   Somewhat likely   (2)   Not likely   (1)

Residential Treatment
Very likely   (3)   Somewhat likely   (2)   Not likely   (1)

Group Therapy
Very likely   (3)   Somewhat likely   (2)   Not likely   (1)

Aversive Medications
Very likely   (3)   Somewhat likely   (2)   Not likely   (1)

TABLE 8.1 | CHARACTERISTICS OF SURVEY PARTICIPANTS

Type of Respondent	Frequency	Percentage
Healthcare professional	43	43
Social service administrator	10	10
Program funder	7	7
Family member	40	40

TABLE 8.2 | MEAN RATINGS OF EXPECTED OUTCOMES OF SUBSTANCE-ABUSE INTERVENTION

Item	Mean
Social skills acquisition	2.7
Insight into substance-abuse behavior	2.8
Awareness of strategies to deter substance abuse	2.6
A support network for the substance abuser	2.6
Sobriety	1.5

TABLE 8.3 | MEAN RATINGS OF SERVICE OPTIONS

Item	Mean
Weekly individual counseling	2.5
Residential treatment	1.3
Group therapy	2.2
Aversive medications	1.3

preferred. These statistics can tell you the average, but don't be fooled. What if a score of 2.5 were an average of very high and very low scores rather than an agreement among the respondents? The standard deviation, another statistic, can be computed. The standard deviation tells you how widely dispersed scores are from the mean score, so you can look at the distribution of all scores and know more about the actual opinions of the group. (See Appendix for information about these basic statistics, called measures of central tendency.) Note that the social worker decided to treat the scores as interval in order to compute them. Remember that ordinal and nominal numbers cannot be mathematically manipulated.

TABLE 8.4 | OPEN-ENDED RESPONSES

Suggestion	Numbers of respondents who made the suggestion (frequency)
1 Horticultural therapy	21
2 Wilderness therapy	19
3 Adventure therapy	17
4 Herbal treatment	7
5 Antabuse	12
6 Professional sanction	10
7 Forced leave of absence from work	14

To know how each group differed from the others, the social worker then computed a statistic that reveals the extent to which the differences in scores were likely to be significant (not caused by chance). Because the dependent variable data are interval and there are four groups in the independent variable, a one-way analysis of variance (ANOVA) was the statistic selected. No significant differences were noted. If there had been differences, the ANOVA would indicate only that differences existed but would not decipher which groups differed. A *post hoc* test would then be computed to see which groups were significantly different from others.

To analyze open-ended responses within the experimental-type approach, you would first read all the surveys, list each of the open-ended answers, and then decide how to code each response. You would then record this analytic scheme in a **codebook,** a list of directions denoting how you have assigned labels and/or numbers to the survey responses. We suggest that you assign numbers to each response, although some investigators choose to assign names in text. Suppose that in the survey example, 100 individuals each wrote the responses depicted in Table 8.4.

There are seven distinct suggestions to which you would assign categorical numbers as names. The assignment of numbers allows you to enter numeric data into your statistical software package and to conduct statistical analysis. Although the assignment of categorical numbers is arbitrary, pick a numbering scheme that makes sense. In Table 8.4, we selected the numeric codes of 1–7. The frequencies can tell you quite a bit about the opinions of your respondents. You can ascertain the strength of a suggestion by looking at how many individuals took the time to write it.

To simplify your findings and put the data to use, you might also want to reduce the categories into nature-based (1) and aversive interventions (2). These categories were arrived at inductively by examining the commonalities that emerged. It may not always be possible to reduce responses into broader cate-

TABLE 8.5 | NATURE-BASED AND AVERSIVE INTERVENTIONS

Intervention Category	Frequency
1 Nature-based	64
2 Aversive	36

gories. If patterns do not emerge, don't impose them. In our example, you would code horticultural therapy, wilderness therapy, adventure therapy, and herbal treatment as "1" and antabuse, professional sanction, and forced leave of absence from work as "2." See Table 8.5.

You would report the frequency of each response. How you code depends on the purpose of the open-ended items and the feasibility of their implementation.

If you were most interested in the breadth of responses, you would leave the responses as expansive as possible. However, if you were interested in supporting a particular suggestion, such as nature-based therapies, you might reduce the categories to demonstrate the frequency with which respondents suggested this genre of intervention.

From this simple survey, the social worker has learned quite a bit about perceived need for group therapy to produce the expected outcomes of social skills, insight, and support. The social worker also learned that nature-based interventions were highly thought of by this sample.

Perhaps the most well-known survey is the U.S. census, in which the government administers mailed surveys and conducts selected face-to-face interviews to develop a descriptive picture of the characteristics of the population of the United States. You might want to look at this survey structure for a model of sound survey construction.

The advantages of survey design are that the investigator can reach a large number of respondents with relatively minimal expenditure, numerous variables can be measured by a single instrument, and statistical manipulation during the data analytic phase can permit multiple uses of the data set.

Disadvantages may include the limitations of each design action process. For example, the use of mailed questionnaires, while cost-effective, may yield a low response rate and thus not provide a broad enough understanding of need. Face-to-face interviews, while substantive, are time-consuming and may differ according to how the interviewer and respondent interact. Mailed surveys may also exclude respondents who cannot access the instruments because of sensory, cognitive, physical, or other barriers.

When deciding on survey design, the social worker must be adept at survey construction or have the resources for consultation. Developing a survey instrument is not as easy as it may seem. Many people develop and send out surveys that yield equivocal and confusing results, not because of the respondents but because of the difficulty of developing a clear and statistically sound instrument. Survey development is beyond the scope of this text, and there are many excellent sources that can guide you (Fink, 1995a, 1995b, 1995c, 1995d). However, we mention three important considerations in measurement that must be taken into account in survey development and/or selection: **validity, reliability,** and **accessible design.**

Validity

In general, as discussed in Chapter 7, validity assesses the relationship between concept and evidence. Instrument validity addresses the relationship between a concept and its measurement. It answers the question "To what extent does the instrument measure what it is supposed to measure?" Put another way, instrument validity is concerned with the link between a lexical definition and an operational definition. A lexical definition is one in which concepts are explained in words (other concepts), and an operational definition is the translation of the lexical definition into a method of measurement.

Look back at Box 8.1 to remind yourself of the questions that you answer to select instrumentation. These questions are in essence "validity guidelines." They assure that your thinking processes consider the concept and its operationalization in your choice of measurement strategy.

Consider the construct of family stress. How one would measure this complex construct depends on its conceptual definition. In Fischer and Corcoran's (2000) compendium, looking at just two measures of family stress illuminates the importance of how one measures a phenomenon. McCubbin et al. (in Fischer & Corcoran, 2000) define family stress as the accumulation of key life events that have been shown to cause discomfort. The extent to which families experience these events is considered to be an indicator of family stress, regardless of how the family members behave, interact, and express feelings of discomfort.

Unlike McCubbin et al., Hudson (in Fischer & Corcoran, 2000) approaches family stress from the standpoint of family relationships and interaction. Behavior within the family rather than factors that impact family interaction defines family stress. Although both approaches measure stress, the construct is both lexically and operationally different in each. Measuring stress as a series of events would not fit with the lexical definition of stress as exhibited behavior and interactions.

Joshua's legislative dilemma provides an excellent example of instrument validity in needs assessment. He is confronted with the problem of "low test scores." Validity is the fit between the construct being measured and the measure itself. In this situation, however, what the instrument measures is not clear, and the validity of the measure cannot be determined. Joshua is confronted with uncertainty about the nature of the problem to be addressed and how to intervene. What if the test measures test-taking ability rather than competency in academic skills? What if there is a cultural or racial bias that obfuscates how academic achievement is being assessed?

Instrument validity is shown to be a very important concern. Too many times, vagueness and/or misinterpretations of what is being measured lead to serious dilemmas. A classic example is the measurement of intelligence. In his classic book, Gould (1974) gives a historical account of the definition and measure of intelligence. Throughout his book, he illuminates how measurement of intelligence, selected by dominant cultural groups, discriminates against and oppresses marginal populations. Murray and Hernstein (1994) have been severely criticized for their assertion of difference in innate intelligence based on race. Instrument validity is being called into question in these examples.

There are many types of instrument validity, such as those that examine comprehensiveness and accuracy. The techniques to examine and assert validity are equally as varied and numerous. It is beyond the scope of this text to examine validity in detail. However, many methodology textbooks provide an excellent and comprehensive discussion of validity (Anastas & MacDonald, 1999; DePoy & Gitlin, 1998; Rubin & Babbie, 2000; Thyer, 2001). In evaluation practice, because instrumentation is often developed to ascertain need in unique contexts and because there are time constraints, extensive validation of measures is often prohibitive. If the social worker cannot use an already-validated measure or cannot validate a measure, it is important to follow rigorous instrument construction steps. Following these steps, which were presented in Box 8.1, will increase the likelihood that the instrument will obtain the desired information.

Reliability

Reliability is the other primary criterion for rigor in experimental-type inquiry. Reliability refers to the extent to which you can "rely" on the accuracy and stability of results obtained from a study. Instrument reliability focuses on the stability of instruments used in the study; that is, if you were to measure the same variable in a similar or identical situation, would your result be the same? The reliability of an instrument or indicator is important to assess in order to be assured that variations in the variable under study represent observable variations and not those resulting from the measurement process itself. If your survey yielded different scores each time it was administered, you would not get a sound and stable picture of need.

Suppose you ask the following question in your needs assessment survey:

1. From the list below, what topic is most needed in continuing social work education:
   ___ clinical skills
   ___ ethics
   ___ fund-raising

What are the reliability problems with this question? Because of its vague wording, lack of instructions regarding how to respond, and lack of context, an individual might answer differently from one administration to another. Ambiguity increases the likelihood of misinterpretation and thus of error. Suppose that during the two weeks between sending and receiving the survey, a clinical agency was closed because of lack of funding. Those who answered prior to closing might want clinical skills in continuing education, but the same individuals responding after the agency closing might prefer fund-raising. Clarity and careful instructions and construction of items about who would participate in continuing education, when it should be offered, and why it should be offered would enhance the reliability because you would be measuring what you knew to be a context-embedded phenomenon rather than a static preference, as implied in the original wording of the item.

The longer the test or more information collected to represent the underlying concept (that is, service preference), the more reliable the instrument is likely to become (Sullivan, 2001). However, there is always some error in measurement, for example, a tape measure that is not held precisely at the same place for each measure. This random error may vary with each measurement, and the investigator must account for error in all measurement action processes.

To assert reliability, experimental-type researchers frequently conduct statistical tests. These tests of reliability focus on two elements: **stability** and **equivalence** (Sullivan, 2001). Stability refers to the longitudinal accuracy of a measure; that is, if repeated under similar circumstances, will the findings be the same? If I stand on my scale today, tomorrow, and the next day at the same time of day, without varying my eating habits, a stable scale will give me a consistent weight.

Equivalence refers to the extent to which all of the indicators on an instrument aggregate to measure the construct to be tested. Suppose you are measuring depression defined as internalized anger by posing 10 questions to respondents. Each of the 10 questions measures one element of depression, and all 10 aggregate to yield a single score. If an individual is depressed, he or she should score as depressed on all of the items as all are indicators of the construct. Similarly, the degree to which a respondent is not depressed should be consistent on all indicators. If, however, you are trying to measure depression and the scores on items are divergent, then the scale may be measuring something different than depression.

The choice of instrumentation depends on the nature and intended purpose of the instrument. In evaluation practice, instruments are often developed for single administrations and unique situations under time-limited conditions. Establishing reliability through statistical analysis is therefore not always an option in needs assessment. In any case, action processes such as consistent conditions in administering instrumentation and training interviewers to ask questions in the same way, should be implemented to increase the reliability of measurement.

Accessible Design

In designing and/or selecting instrumentation, the social worker should ensure that the respondents can competently complete the measure. Such factors as level of education, socioeconomic background, verbal ability, access to American Sign Language or language-of-origin interpreters, sensory status, cognitive status, socioemotional environment of the administration of the instrument, and participant receptivity influence the selection and design of a data collection method. For example, college students are very familiar with a fixed-format type of self-administered questionnaire. However, this format may not be appropriate for people with visual impairments or cognitive challenges. Methods such as interviewing, reading questions and responses to visually impaired respondents, using screen readers on computers, using pictures to supplement or replace text-based items for respondents with reading challenges, and using proxy respondents are just a few of the strategies that can enhance accessibility.

In needs assessment, accessibility is critical if the social worker is to obtain a full and accurate understanding of need from the perspective of diverse groups who are involved in a problem.

The development of new instrumentation is, in itself, a specialty within the experimental-type research world. We have introduced you to the basic components of measurements and have given you some principles for ensuring that your items are reliable. However, constructing an instrument and its components is a major research task, and it is best to seek consultation.

MAIN POINTS

1. Measurement involves consideration of the content and the structure of instrumentation.
2. Content refers to the lexical definitions, the limits of concepts to be measured, and the relationships to be examined.
3. Structure refers to the nature of the instrumentation and the scoring.
4. Experimental-type needs assessment in evaluation practice relies most frequently on questionnaires, interviews, and observations.
5. Variables can be discrete or continuous.
6. Questions can be asked in varied formats, including closed ended, semi-structured, and open ended.
7. In experimental-type needs assessment, analysis of data is statistical, even with open-ended questions.
8. The criteria for rigor in experimental-type needs assessment are instrument validity and reliability.
9. Constructing instrumentation is a difficult skill that requires much practice.

EXERCISES

1. Read a needs assessment article, and select the important concepts that are being measured. List them, and then try to find lexical definitions of each.
2. From the article, critically evaluate the fit between the lexical definition and the instrument that measures the concept.
3. Describe the content and structure of the instruments in the article.
4. Critically discuss the instruments for rigor. To what extent are they reliable and valid?

5. Look at the statistical analysis. What types of numbers (nominal, ordinal, interval/ratio) are used and how?
6. Think of a concept that you want to measure. Define it by answering the questions in Box 8.1. Then try to develop a simple survey, interview, or observation to measure your concept.
7. Have a peer critically examine your instrument for rigor.

CHAPTER 9

ASCERTAINING NEED IN UNEXAMINED CONTEXTS: DESIGNING QUALITATIVE INQUIRY

Underlying Tenets of Naturalistic Inquiry
Selecting a Design in Naturalistic Needs Assessment
Mixed-Method Designs
Main Points
Exercises

UNDERLYING TENETS OF NATURALISTIC INQUIRY

We now turn to the action processes that social workers can use when empirical evidence does not seem to fit the problem or when insufficient empirical study of need has been conducted to inform an intervention. In both instances, we suggest that naturalistic strategies are indicated either on their own or in concert with experimental-type needs assessment. In Chapter 8, we addressed only "program evaluation" because experimental-type approaches, which we know as nomothetic, aim to investigate commonalities in groups.

Naturalistic inquiry can be used not only for program development but for ascertainment of individual and subgroup needs related to problem resolution. Naturalistic designs are therefore **idiographic**, in that they are concerned with context and yield textured meaning and findings rather than commonalities. Before examining specific action processes, we present a brief review of the underlying tenets of naturalistic inquiry. We then look at designs that can be used to ascertain need.

Naturalistic inquiry is a category of research that relies on multiple epistemological perspectives (Anastas & MacDonald, 2000; DePoy & Gitlin, 1998). All, however, share to a greater or lesser extent the construct of pluralism, the limited knowledge that the investigator has about the phenomenon of interest, and an inductive approach to revealing principles. Yet, because of the multiple philosophical frameworks on which naturalistic thinking and action processes are based, there is no agreement in the literature on the exact nature and criteria for rigor in this research tradition. Several authors have attempted to define the commonalities of naturalistic designs. Among them, DePoy and Gitlin (1998) have suggested that there are nine attributes of naturalistic inquiry.

1. Range of Purpose: Naturalistic strategies vary in purpose from developing descriptive knowledge to revealing complex theoretical frameworks.
2. Context Specificity: All naturalistic inquiry is conducted in the context in which the object or subject of inquiry occurs. Naturalistic action processes are therefore context-specific.
3. Complexity and Pluralistic Perspective of Reality: Because of its underlying epistemology and its inductive approach to knowing, naturalistic research assumes a pluralistic perspective of "reality" that seeks to articulate rather than reduce complexity.
4. Transferability of Findings: Because naturalistic inquiry is context-specific, the aim of generalizability is not relevant to this form of study. Rather, principles and theory derived from naturalistic study can be considered for their relevance to and further tested in alternative contexts.
5. Flexibility: Unlike experimental-type inquiry in which initial and careful planning of the design determines all subsequent action processes, naturalistic designs are flexible and changeable in response to incremental learning that occurs within the time frame of the inquiry. It is not only acceptable but expected that procedures, the nature of the research query, the

scope of the study, and the manner by which information is obtained are constantly reformulated and realigned to fit the emerging "truths" as they are ascertained.
6. Centrality of Language: Language is central to naturalistic inquiry. That is, a major shared concern in naturalistic inquiry is understanding the language and its meanings for diverse people. Through language, symbols, and ways of expression, the investigator comes to understand and derive meaning within each context.
7. The Importance of Perspective: Naturalistic designs vary in their "emic" or "etic" orientation. An "emic" perspective refers to the "insider's" or informant's way of understanding and interpreting experience. An "etic" orientation refers to an outsider's perspective where the investigator brings understandings and processes external to the domain of concern to bear on the investigation.
8. Shift in Knowing Power: Because the investigator enters an inquiry with the aim of openness to new and unfamiliar ideas, the naturalistic researcher defers to the informant or "experiencer" as the knower. This abrogation of power by the "investigator" to the "investigated" is characteristic, to a greater or lesser degree, of all naturalistic designs.
9. Interspersion of Gathering Information and Analysis: Finally, analysis in naturalistic designs relies heavily on qualitative data and is an ongoing process that is interspersed throughout data-gathering activities. Data gathering and analysis are interdependent and simultaneous and/or interactive processes.

As you can see, naturalistic inquiry differs from experimental-type designs not only in method, but in philosophical foundation, and thus provides another important set of thinking and action processes through which to understand need. In the naturalistic tradition, there are many approaches to inquiry. The five approaches that we believe best serve needs assessment aims and purposes are listed in Box 9.1.

Interview

Interview is a method in which the investigator obtains information through direct interchange with an individual or group who are known or expected to possess knowledge. Interview technique varies in structure and in the degree of control maintained by the investigator in the interview process. As discussed in experimental-type design, interview can be fully controlled and coded deductively. In naturalistic design, however, interview serves an inductive purpose and is a primary method used in needs assessment. There are numerous types of interview, including, but not limited to, long interview (McCraken, 1988), key informant interview, small unit interview (that is, family interview), and focus group (Denzin & Lincoln, 2000; Patton, 1997). For the most part, investigators conducting needs assessment rely on key informant interview and focus group.

BOX 9.1 | SIX APPROACHES

Interview
> Individual
> Focus group

Life history

Open-ended survey

Ethnography

Inductive secondary data analysis

Individual: Key Informant Interview In key informant interview, the key informants are individuals who possess a body of knowledge and a perspective that are needed to purposively inform the development of an intervention and specification of desired outcomes. Key informants are identified and asked to meet with the interviewer to discuss the topic for the inquiry. It is not unusual for key informants who represent diverse and competing points of view to be asked to participate in the interview process, especially when the problem being addressed is complex and requires the commitment of resources. It is critical to remember that informants are therefore chosen both for knowledge and for political purpose. We urge social workers to be inclusive and expansive in informant selection so that informants with a range of perspectives, from those who are seen as "having the problem" to those who have the resources to commit to problem resolution, can have voice in shaping the intervention and desired outcomes.

The degree of structure and investigator control in key informant interview vary and are dependent on purpose, knowledge of interviewer and informant, and needed structure of knowledge.

To illustrate, in Jennifer's case, a social worker without disabilities might want to select key individuals with and without mobility challenges to reflect the diverse needs of multiple interest groups. The assumption that a keyed mechanical lift was sufficient for Jennifer's access to the building would not have been supported if Jennifer or another individual with similar experiences had been included as a key informant in the needs assessment inquiry.

Focus Group A focus group is a group interview in which the moderator or moderators pose topics and/or questions for group discussion. Recordings of the focus group discussions and/or interactions comprise the data set. Although originated for marketing purposes, focus group inquiry has become one of the most frequently used methods for naturalistic needs assessment. In focus groups, social workers can choose the degree of control and direction that they introduce into the process. Box 9.2 lists the advantages and disadvantages of focus group methodology.

BOX 9.2 | FOCUS GROUP METHODOLOGY

Advantages
1. Qualitative data
2. Group process—group think
3. Time-efficient
4. Directive

Disadvantages
1. Possibility of group pressure limiting individual responses
2. Time-consuming to organize

Although there are many variations, focus groups generally contain the following essential elements and action processes.

The first step in any inquiry is the clarification of the question or query. What should be known in order to understand need? A question or series of questions requiring knowledge that is not sufficiently developed in current literature or practice wisdom will often provide the rationale for a focus group. However, why conduct a group interview instead of individual interviews?

Focus groups rely on the principle of group process. You would choose a focus group when looking for group cohesion or dissent, seeking data that capture interaction in the discourse among several individuals who are knowledgeable, attempting to obtain consensus with shades of difference, exploring and understanding a complex whole, and working with resources that limit the time that can be devoted to interview. For example, *Joshua could organize focus groups to ascertain what is needed in his state to remediate low student scores on national standardized tests. To obtain the perspectives of multiple groups with specific attention to obtaining a complex understanding of need, Joshua decides to convene focus groups with parents of school-age children, teachers, and faculty in the state university school of education who focus their teaching, research, and service on standardized testing.*

The second step is the selection of focus group design. In this stage, social workers determine the degree of control they will have over the process, the specificity of the questions to be posed to group participants, the role of facilitators and participants in the process, and the method of data collection, analysis, and reporting. The questions presented in Box 9.3 will help you plan a design to meet your purpose.

Returning to our example, because each group holds a different position relative to education, Joshua structures four separately conducted focus group sessions, three of which are homogeneous for each group and one of which includes representatives from each of the three groups. The homogeneous groups are intended to yield consensus regarding perspectives of individual interest groups without influence from other potentially conflicting views. Mixing the

> BOX 9.3 | FOCUS GROUP GUIDELINES
>
> 1. Begin with your questions, and delimit the scope of the focus group in informing those questions.
> 2. Based on what you want to know from the focus group, determine the participation and facilitation structure. How many moderators will you have? How directive should facilitators be?
> 3. Select an interview format. Especially with new focus group participants, try to use topic or question guides. Visual props (in accessible formats) help focus discussion.
> 4. Questions and topics must be clear and mutually exclusive.
> 5. Questions and topics must be internally consistent and sequential.
> 6. Begin with general questions, and then pose more specific queries if answers to your queries are not embedded within the general answers.
> 7. Begin with positive questions, and then proceed to negative and/or sensitive ones.

four groups in a single session was planned to stimulate interchange that would reveal potential areas of disagreement.

These are the primary needs assessment questions posed to each group:

1. *What causes of low test scores need to be addressed? can be addressed?*
2. *What outcomes related to each cause should be sought?*
3. *What action strategies would attain these desired outcomes?*

Because of the specific focus of the needs assessment inquiry, Joshua decides to have two facilitators conduct the groups in a structured fashion, asking each question sequentially, recording the common responses on a large white board (with accessible formats as needed), and redirecting any tangential dialogue to the question being posed.

In Box 9.4, we suggest principles that will help you choose a structure and sequence that best fit your questions and purposes.

We have also found that several structural and process elements, such as the following, may be helpful in guiding the focus group:

1. Vignettes to provoke thinking and discourse
2. Debate about specific issues
3. Closed-ended questioning (for example, lists, ratings, or fill in the blanks) to obtain targeted information
4. Role-playing activity to reveal attitudes and cultural role expectations

There are numerous additional strategies to catalyze a focus group and introduce ideas for reflection, analysis, and discussion. Focus groups provide the opportunity for imagination as long as rigorous criteria are upheld throughout the process.

> **BOX 9.4** | **FOCUS GROUP GUIDELINES**
>
> Assemble room, including props and equipment.
> Decide on roles for cofacilitators.
> Welcome participants and thank them.
> Introduce participants to one another.
> State purpose and rules.
> Ask the opening question.
> Moderate discussion (moderate, but don't participate!).
> Give a summary, and member-check (clarify facilitator impressions of meaning with focus group participants) periodically.
> End with overall summary, next steps, and use of data.

Returning to the example, one strategy that Joshua decides to use is the presentation of a vignette in which two schools with disparate fourth-grade standardized test scores are presented. One school is well supported with tax dollars, and the other is not. Specific questions are posed to ascertain what can be done in the school with limited tax support to improve test scores.

Focus group data most frequently are recorded transcripts of the discourse. Analysis of the data is qualitative and inductive, revealing themes and perspectives of group members (see Appendix for more information on inductive data analysis).

Joshua's focus groups engage in a substantive discussion of methods to prepare students for test taking. One theme is teacher training. Venues for teacher training included graduate school, online courses, and workshops supported by extramural funding. Based on these descriptive data, a grant was planned by a nonprofit community training agency.

Life History

Life history is a method whereby the investigator focuses an inquiry on individual lives in the context of the social environment. This design can answer important needs assessment questions related both to the present and to the history that led to the current needs as articulated by individuals.

In conducting the action processes of life history methodology, the sequence of life events and the meaning of those events to the unfolding of a life are examined from the perspective of the informant and his or her significant others. Specific events, termed *marker events* or *turnings* (Denzin & Lincoln, 2000), are used as the anchor on which a narrative life history is built. To elicit life history data, social workers frequently conduct unstructured interviews, which may begin with statements such as "Tell me about your life history." Once the narrative of historical events is obtained, an investigator may look for the meaning of specific events in shaping the lives of the individual informants. Life history studies can be retrospective or prospective. In needs assessment, the majority of life history studies are retrospective in their approach. Informants are asked to reconstruct their lives and to reflect on meaning. Among the additional data sources to construct a life history are personal artifacts, photographs, and personal records. Because prospective longitudinal studies can be costly and extremely time-consuming, they are often beyond the resources of the social worker who is examining need.

Consider this example. In the recent study of the transition service and support needs of adolescents with special healthcare needs (Hartman, DePoy, Francis, & Gilmer, 2000), the evaluation team wanted to examine the way in which services were initially accessed and then obtained over time. They wanted this information because the team felt that needs assessment based on a single, current point in time did not illuminate how those needs arose and how previous services and supports influenced transition needs for diverse groups.

Three individuals, each with different diagnoses and transition issues, were interviewed in depth along with family members who could shed light on services and supports received from birth. The life histories revealed that how an infant was initially diagnosed and classified were critical determinants in what services were received over time.

One informant, who was diagnosed with Down's syndrome at birth, was immediately introduced into the rehabilitation and special education systems; another child, who demonstrated "aberrant behaviors" following his experiences of physical abuse, was placed in the juvenile justice system until he sustained a closed head injury. He then entered the physical rehabilitation system. The third informant was a young woman born with a seizure disorder that was not formally diagnosed until she entered elementary education. Although she was having extensive difficulty in her environments, no service system accepted her until the formal diagnosis was made. She then was introduced into the medical and special education systems.

The needs assessment therefore revealed the essential role that early classification and intervention took in the lives and transition experiences of individuals.

If we look again at Joshua's youth, life history would be an excellent method to reveal specific events or turnings in his life that influenced his substance abuse. What if, for example, the social worker could identify a pattern of substance abuse that was exacerbated when Joshua spent time on the weekends with other youth who drank, and abated when Joshua was actively engaged in physical activity with some element of competition. Such information would be extremely valuable in developing a comprehensive understanding of need to guide intervention.

Open-Ended Survey

Similar to interview, open-ended survey poses broad questions to informants for their responses. The survey can be structured in several ways, but the majority are administered through the mail or by telephone.

Although there is some overlap in survey and interview, survey is designed primarily to examine multiple and delimited phenomena through the advancement of topical, targeted questions to a respondent. Moreover, different from interview, discussion or written responses beyond the scope of the specified items are not desirable in survey. In naturalistic open-ended survey designs, data are primarily narrative and analyzed using inductive strategies (see Appendix).

Open-ended survey could be used in Joshua's case. Suppose that Joshua finds in the focus groups that parents express the need for more structured homework for their children, with specific attention to the academic skills of reading, writing, and arithmetic. Teachers suggest that parents need to become more involved in their children's education through assisting them with homework assignments and restricting television and other distractions from academic work. Administrators identify the need to increase the funding for teacher training to prepare students for testing. To further detail the needs, Joshua decides to conduct an open-ended survey with each group, posing the suggestions and asking each group to define specific strategies on how the needs can be filled. A range of responses, from disagreement with the identified needs to methods to implement after-school homework programs led by both teachers and parents, might emerge from such a survey. Additional needs beyond those identified in the focus group might also be revealed as data are analyzed for themes.

Ethnography

Ethnography is the primary inquiry method in anthropology, but it also plays an important role in social work research, as well as in other disciplines. Although there are many schools of thought that present theories and action processes of ethnography, we suggest the following elements in Box 9.5 as most useful to needs assessment inquiry.

Ethnography is a naturalistic design that reveals and characterizes the underlying patterns of behavior and meaning of a **culture**. Synthesizing numerous definitions, we define culture as the set of explicit and tacit rules, symbols, and rituals that guide patterns of human behavior within a group.

Most typically in needs assessment, ethnographic techniques rather than a complete ethnographic study are used to understand the experience and needs of an unfamiliar group. The investigator is etic (an outsider to the cultural group) and is aiming to obtain perception of needs from the "insider" perspective (Creswell, 1997). The notion of research subjects, in which those being observed do not participate in the methods of inquiry or analysis, is turned around in ethnography. Subjects do not exist, but rather, the members of the group are

| BOX 9.5 | ETHNOGRAPHY |

Naturalistic
Etic perspective
Cultures are those with a common social problem
Slice-in-time approach
Time constraints

considered to be informants or participants in the inquiry process. This ideological shift locates the "knowing power" within the group that is the subject of the inquiry and gives an important voice to individuals and groups who are silent in more traditional research (Denzin & Lincoln, 2000).

Classical ethnography relies heavily on extended observation, immersion, and participation in the culture where data are collected through several primary methods: (a) interview and observation of those who are willing to inform the outsider about behavioral norms and their meanings, (b) the investigator's participation in the culture, and (c) examination of meaning of cultural objects and symbols (Atkinson, Coffey, & Delamont, 2001). Insiders who willingly engage with the investigator are called "informants" and "participants" (DePoy & Gitlin, 1998). Informants are distinguished from participants by their more integral role in the inquiry.

In needs assessment inquiry, ethnographic strategies must be selected based on purpose, resources, and the way data will be applied to informing intervention. The cultures that social workers seek to identify and characterize are not exotic peoples but groups who are identified as having a "social problem in common." Thus, principles from ethnography frame the inquiry, but classical techniques, such as full and prolonged immersion, are often truncated and modified to fit the needs assessment context.

Any inquiry relying on ethnographic principles begins with gaining access to a culture. The social worker then explores the context in which the culture operates by observing the environment. Equipped with an understanding of the cultural context, the inquirer uses participant observation, informant interview, and examination of materials or artifact review to obtain data. Although materials and artifacts may be in any form, social workers frequently use existing records, narratives, and policies as important and illuminative data sources. Social workers using a "slice in time approach" may enter the culture at random times throughout the week or weeks in the field to obtain a comprehensive picture of the culture at different times and intervals and aggregate these data to form a chronicle of need. Thus, in needs assessment, targeted use of ethnographic techniques in a purposive manner is a reasonable and cost-efficient action process to obtain a sense of cultural or group need.

> **BOX 9.6** | **SEQUENCE OF ETHNOGRAPHIC TECHNIQUES IN NEEDS ASSESSMENT**
>
> Gain entrance into the culture.
> Identify several key informants.
> Conduct slice-in-time broad observations (recording observations).
> Analyze data for initial themes.
> Interview informants for additional data, and member-check initial impressions.
> Continue to collect and analyze data until needs assessment questions are answered (saturation or time limit is reached).

Ethnographic techniques lead the social worker from a broad understanding of a culture to the roles, rituals, language, and patterns of the members and subgroups who belong to the culture. Notes, tape recordings, and video recordings provide a rich set of data through which themes emerge inductively as the investigator and/or cultural members analyze the findings. Member-checking, a technique in which an etic investigator checks for the accuracy of his or her interpretation of the data, is a hallmark of rigor in ethnography (Agar, 1996) and provides the vehicle for the social worker to verify impressions with members of a culture. Analysis of ethnographic data proceeds inductively and is an iterative process that co-occurs with data collection. Corrections in interpretation are made as new data reveal new and revised understandings. The end point of the ethnography occurs when saturation has been reached, the point at which new data do not provide any new insights. Time constraints, however, may prevent saturation as an end point in needs assessment. If so, the investigator should keep in mind that a full picture of need as experienced by cultural members may not have been obtained.

Box 9.6 suggests a sequence of ethnographic techniques in needs assessment. Of course, because naturalistic inquiry is characteristically dynamic and changing, the sequence is not prescriptive. Thus, we only provide guidelines for the social worker who is thinking of using these techniques for needs assessment.

Looking at our example of low test scores to illustrate the use of ethnographic action processes in needs assessment, suppose that Joshua decided to use ethnographic techniques, in which an outsider would observe classroom activity to ascertain what is being taught, which methods of teaching-learning are being used, and how the tested focus areas are being integrated into the classroom activity. Attitudes and expectations of teaching staff might also be revealed as important influences on testing performance. He would begin by requesting access to a classroom as an observer. Initial observations would be broad, looking at the environment and how individuals and groups behave within it. Patterns of behavior, rules, and tacit understandings would emerge from analyzing the field notes and videotape recordings obtained during his participation in the classroom. Analysis of recordings would provide an initial set of interpretations and themes to be checked out for accuracy with members of the culture. Over time, Joshua would interview key informants, conduct focused observations, examine artifacts of the culture (for example, student assignments or classroom resources), and inductively analyze the data concurrent with obtaining additional data. Data collection would end when Joshua reaches saturation. From this type of inquiry, Joshua is able to uncover that negative attitudes and low performance expectations of teachers, parents, and students toward testing are primary influences on how students approach the testing situation. Furthermore, he finds that the crowded classroom provides an environment in which students can remain distracted from the learning activities that address test content.

Inductive Secondary Data Analysis

Inductive analysis of existing data sets is a frequently used strategy in naturalistic needs assessment. There are many data sources that are illuminating and lend themselves to inductive analysis. Typically, social workers use materials such as social histories, agency records, policy and legislative documents, agency mission statements and bylaws, existing narratives generated through previous naturalistic studies, and analysis of media products (for example, newspapers, TV shows, and advertising). These secondary sources are approached with specific needs assessment questions, and analysis is inductive.

In our access example with Jennifer, systematic blueprints and photographs of accessible and nonaccessible school environments might reveal needed changes not only to physical structures but to additional aspects of environments, such as their human elements, their emotional climates, and so on.

SELECTING A DESIGN IN NATURALISTIC NEEDS ASSESSMENT

Design and methodological elements of naturalistic inquiry have been discussed, but given the complexity of this tradition, how can you select a design to answer your queries? Remember that naturalistic design is flexible and dynamic. Unlike in experimental-type design, once you begin your naturalistic inquiry, it is expected that initial methods will change as the process of the study unfolds.

The following questions in Box 9.7 will guide your selection of initial inquiry. However, as you proceed, be prepared to change and shift methods to respond to your inductive findings.

124   THINKING PROCESSES OF EVALUATION PRACTICE

> **BOX 9.7** | **QUESTIONS TO GUIDE CHOICE OF A DESIGN**
>
> 1. What purpose does the needs assessment serve?
> 2. Why am I doing it?
> 3. How informed am I about my domain of concern?
> 4. Who best can inform me of need?
> 5. Where will I conduct the inquiry?
> 6. What degree of participation will I seek from my informant(s)?
> 7. What resource and time constraints must I consider?
> 8. Is the design consistent with the limitations of the practice arena?
> 9. Can the design lead to the discovery of information sufficient for articulating goals, objectives, and expected outcomes of an intervention?
> 10. What are some of the ethical and field limitations that influence the design?

MIXED-METHOD DESIGNS

In this chapter, we have discussed a broad range of material related to needs assessment design. We have covered both experimental-type and naturalistic inquiry, examining the basic foundation of each, typical designs used in each approach to needs assessment, basic design techniques, and guidelines for selecting a needs assessment approach. As you can see, each tradition offers a range of diverse options for design structure. In this section, we suggest that mixing naturalistic and experimental-type design in needs assessment is a powerful strategy for examining preexisting principles and unearthing changes in need over time. There are too many ways to mix methods to discuss here. Mixing methods in needs assessment is dependent on one's ontology, purpose in conducting the study, potential for comprehensive coverage of complex problems, and limitations in resources to conduct the inquiry.

The following example illustrates the use of mixed methods in needs assessment. Attend to how the use of these strategies leads to the generation of multiple perspectives that yield diverse and sometimes competing expectations for successful outcome.

Consider how need related to the problem of limited access in educational environments might be approached. Suppose that a focus group of disabled teachers and an ethnographic inquiry were conducted. Revealed in those elements of the needs assessment are the following:

1. *The problem of access to educational environments expands beyond compliance to federal requirements for physical access.*
2. *Diverse time schedules require physical access to school buildings to fit individual needs.*

3. *Physical access is affected by the number of people in an environment and the weather (for example, wet floors inside doorways on rainy days pose barriers).*
4. *Access is affected by attitudes of those who function within environments regardless of physical design. Negative or paternalistic attitudes toward disabled individuals may limit the degree to which the environment is welcoming and user-friendly.*

These findings are important in defining need, but suppose that the school district had only minimal resources and finances to make changes in the school environment and there was little support from the community for this effort. The social worker decides to conduct a survey of community members to examine attitudes and their correlates. In the survey, the social worker finds that nonsupport for increasing access is related to beliefs that individuals with disabilities cannot work. The need to debunk myths about disability, therefore, would be essential before the community would be supportive of and advocate for the allocation of resources to increasing access to the school environment.

As we will see when we look at case study approaches, ascertaining need for individual intervention with mixed methods can provide multisource, broad, longitudinal data. As we continue to look at *Joshua*'s youth throughout the text, consider how mixing naturalistic interview data, life history, and standardized testing of academic achievement with vocational interest and talent might create a comprehensive picture of need and potential methods to fulfill need.

MAIN POINTS

1. The basic elements and philosophical foundations of naturalistic inquiry include pluralism, dynamic process, and inductive analysis.
2. Interview, life history, open-ended survey, ethnography, and inductive secondary data analysis are frequently used designs in naturalistic needs assessment.
3. Interviews can be conducted with individuals or with groups.
4. Multiple, creative approaches to individual and group interview can be implemented providing that systematic and rigorous methods are followed.
5. Life history is a method that provides a retrospective longitudinal understanding of need.
6. Within the naturalistic tradition, open-ended needs assessment surveys are delimited by topic and analyzed inductively.
7. Ethnographic techniques provide a flexible, dynamic, and complex approach to need through examination of social and cultural settings.
8. Inductive analyses of secondary data sets are an efficient method of revealing patterns of need.
9. Mixed-method designs are powerful in identifying and describing complex need.

EXERCISES

1. Locate an area in your neighborhood where adults engage in recreation (tennis court, park, movie theater, and so on). Observe the patterns of behavior among the individuals with specific attention to who is included and who is not. Through systematic observation, develop impressions about the factors that influence access to recreation.
2. Interview one or more key informants about who has access and how decisions are made about who can and who cannot participate. Ask each about what, if anything, is needed to expand recreation to those who are not included.
3. Based on data, suggest needs to address change in recreational access.
4. Based on data, suggest how you would work with a single individual who is unable to access the community.

SETTING GOALS AND OBJECTIVES

CHAPTER 10

Introduction and Definitions

Objectives

Deriving Goals from Need Statements

Action Process of Writing Process Objectives

Action Process of Writing Outcome Objectives

Main Points

Exercises

INTRODUCTION AND DEFINITIONS

Once you have a clear and well-documented statement of need, the action process of setting goals and objectives can be initiated. In this chapter, we begin by defining **goals** and **objectives** and then examine how needs are translated into goals and objectives. Goals and objectives provide the structure for interventions and posit desired intervention outcomes at one or more time intervals. The action process of goal and objective formulation is critical in our evaluation practice model because it is the first step in which specific accountability criteria are set.

Goals are broad statements about the ideal or "hoped for" (Coley & Scheinberg, 2001). They look forward in time to specific "desirables." In evaluation practice, goals emerge directly from the need statement and thus reflect the value set of the problem statement in what should be accomplished through an intervention. Because evaluation practice is purposive throughout its entire thinking and action processes, goals are purposive as well. Expected goal attainment can range from immediate to the long-term and can be simple or complex.

Let us look at some goals and their relationship to both need and problem statements to examine these important links and time expectations for goal achievement. We begin with an example from a project that is currently being conducted by DePoy et al. (2000) in a New England state.

In efforts to improve the transition of adolescents with disabilities to adulthood, a comprehensive needs assessment was conducted. For this example, let us consider one of the problem statements to which the project was directed: "Adolescents with disabilities frequently move into adulthood without the vocational skills to be competitive on the job market." Given this complex problem, a needs assessment was conducted in which the adolescents clearly identified their need for equal opportunity and full inclusion in the same vocational preparation opportunities available for youth without disabilities. Further inquiry revealed that disabled youth were systematically excluded from vocational experience and training opportunities in large part due to negative attitudes held by teachers and employers regarding the cost of accommodation and skepticism about the capacity of these youths to compete adequately in the job market (DePoy et al., 2000). Based on this understanding of need, a number of goals were developed including the overall intermediate goal of educating teachers and employers about typical accommodation costs and about the capacity of disabled youth to work. Education was an intermediate goal leading to the long-term goals of attitudinal change and an increase in vocational preparation of youth with disabilities.

In the example above, the direct relationship between need and goal is seen in the intermediate goal of education of teachers and employers. The long-term goals of enhancing favorable attitudes of teachers and employers and increasing vocational preparation of disabled youth are linked directly to the part of the problem statement that addresses underemployment of these youth. Note that increasing employment of disabled adolescents is not a goal. We return to this important point later in this chapter.

Now let us apply the previous example and its principles to one of our familiar characters.

As we saw earlier, multiple needs emerged from Jennifer's initial problem of limited access to work. We will work with the need for universal access to the educational environment that could accommodate the diverse schedules and roles of each participant in the "culture." From this need, a long-term goal for intervention could be stated: "Render the educational environment universally accessible."

This goal is broad and most likely will be incrementally approached over time, so the intermediate goal "to educate the community about universal design and its benefits for all, including individuals with disabilities" would be stipulated.

Because goals are broad statements of what is desired, how the goal will be attained and how you will know that it has been attained must be articulated. These two elements are the purpose of objectives and frame the nomenclature for two types of objectives: process and outcome. Objectives are therefore operationalized goal statements. If you apply the concept of operationalization, as described in Chapter 8, to goals and objectives, you can see how we arrived at this definition. Goals are abstractions of what is desirable. Objectives provide the action steps on how, when, and who will do what to achieve the stated goals and how you will know that you have achieved them. Because a goal is a broad statement, one of the challenges in establishing objectives is to make sure that the goal will be achieved when the objectives are met. Objectives that specify actions are process objectives, and those that specify outcomes are outcome objectives.

Working with Joshua again, consider two scenarios illustrating goals and objectives in evaluation practice with individuals. In the first scenario, the social worker sets the goal of sobriety. In the second scenario, the social worker specifies two intermediate goals: Joshua's awareness and acknowledgment of his problematic substance use, and college entrance. A long-term goal of elimination of substance abuse is also set. Both goal statements target the elimination of problematic substance use, but each sets a different conceptual and practice direction.

OBJECTIVES

Process (also called formative or monitoring) objectives state what will be done when, sometimes how, and by whom, while outcome (also termed summative) objectives delineate how you will know that you were successful in producing a desired result from what was done. Both types of objectives are derived from goals statements.

Using the example of preparation for employment by adolescents with disabilities, let us see what objectives we might frame from the goal statements. Look first in Box 10.1 at the adolescent needs assessment previously discussed.

There are several important points to note in these objectives. First, they are time sequenced. Second, some are process objectives and some are summative

> **BOX 10.1** | **INTERMEDIATE GOAL**
>
> Goal Statement: "Educate teachers and employers about typical accommodation costs and about the capacity of disabled youth to work."
>
> **Objectives**
> 1. Assemble youth who will participate.
> 2. Train youth in curriculum planning.
> 3. Work with youth to specify content and structure of training curriculum.
> 4. Complete materials and formal curriculum.
> 5. Work with youth to develop adult education skills.
> 6. Conduct mock training with an audience.
> 7. As assessed by the audience, youth will demonstrate beginning competence in training skills.
> 8. Revise and complete necessary youth training according to feedback from mock-training evaluation.
> 9. Assist youth in scheduling education and training sessions with teachers and employers.
> 10. Conduct two education and training sessions for educators and two sessions for employers.
> 11. As a result of attending training sessions, employers and teachers will obtain knowledge about employment opportunities and issues for adolescents with disabilities.
> 12. As a result of attending training sessions, employers and teachers will specify uses of their knowledge to enhance the employment preparation of youth with disabilities.
> 13. Obtain feedback from educators and employers suggesting improvements to the curriculum structure and content.
> 14. Revise curriculum content and structure, based on session feedback and assessments.
> 15. Develop and implement long-term plan for education and training of teachers and employers.

objectives. Can you select which objectives fit into each category? Third, each objective can be assessed according to the degree of its completion. We will return to these points and to objectives related to the long-term goals later in this chapter.

If you selected objectives 7, 11, and 12 as outcome and the remainder as process, you are correct. The process objectives specify what will be done and how. They structure the sequence of activity for an intervention and provide the mechanism to specify the source of evidence to be used to assess objective completion. Similarly, outcome or summative objectives delineate what is expected if the intervention is successful and provide the foundation for determining what evidence will be used to assess success. Process objectives are those that will be used to guide monitoring and formative evaluation. Outcome objectives are used to determine summative value of an intervention. The objectives as stated in this example are not "measurable" until the source of evidence and the way the evidence will be used to assess objective completion are articulated. Some definitions of objectives specify that they must be measurable as stated; however, we do not agree. First, not all objectives will be measured. All will be assessed, but some may be assessed in ways that do not use measurement. Second, in our model, objectives provide a structure for reflexive intervention. Until we examine these points in more detail, suffice it to say that objectives are critical statements of action processes that provide the foundation for reflexive intervention and outcome assessment.

Let us turn to *Jennifer* and *Joshua* to look at process objectives related to intermediate goals in two domains of social work practice.

A long-term goal for Jennifer was the establishment of universal access to educational environments. Because this goal is so complex, we specified an intermediate goal of educating the community about universal design and its benefits for all, including individuals with disabilities.

Table 10.1 presents process and outcome objectives that structure the action processes of reflexive implementation of and success criteria for the intermediate goal. If you look at these objectives closely, you will see that they present a structure for the action processes and outcomes necessary to attain the goal. But how are these objectives "ascertainable"? As stated, you can't know. However, Table 10.1 shows you how each objective is conceptualized and translated into a format so that attainment can be assessed.

As you can see by examining the table, linking each objective to one or more success criteria, evidence on which to assess the criteria, and a time line, the structure is set for the intervention, the determination of which action process addresses each objective, and the determination of when and the extent to which objectives are successfully achieved. The thinking process of specifying objectives begins to illustrate how distinct parts of the intervention can be monitored and linked to outcome.

In the example of Jennifer, suppose that the steering committee omitted school administration personnel from its target list. The failure of full community support for universal design in the future could be traced back to the action process and attributed to its being only partially completed. Thus you can see that it is critical to specify objectives for both monitoring and outcome. If process objectives were not included in the monitoring system, there would be no way to examine why support for universal design was not obtained. However, if monitoring occurs, then small programmatic changes may be all that is necessary to achieve long-term goals. Knowing that educational administrators may not be educated about universal design could be the key to revision and intervention success.

The specification of process objectives thus provides the structure to reflect on intervention. Our term reflexive intervention was therefore coined to denote our ideal approach to social work intervention as one in which careful and informed scrutiny is not only possible but inherent in all social work practice.

Let us now return to the project regarding adolescents with disabilities to illustrate the thinking process of establishing objectives to accomplish a long-term goal. Derived from the needs assessment in Box 10.1, a long-term goal was specified: "Employers and teachers will demonstrate increasingly favorable

TABLE 10.1 | PROCESS AND OUTCOME OBJECTIVES FOR REFLEXIVE IMPLEMENTATION OF INTERMEDIATE GOAL

	Success criterion	Evidence	Time line
Select a steering committee to represent community diversity	Complete steering committee representing the full diversity of the community	Fit of representation with diversity statistics of the community	Month 1
Work with the steering committee to delimit the boundaries of the community (i.e., who will be targeted for education?)	Specific list of target groups and numbers for education and training	Invitations to education and training sessions	Months 2–4
Develop curriculum for the diverse target groups	Completed curriculum for each target group, with learning objectives and specific activities	Education and training curricula and materials in fully accessible formats	Month 6
Establish educational protocol and procedures	Trainers hired/identified and prepared for educational sessions	Trainer names and schedules	Months 6–7
Train all "trainers" to deliver the universal access curriculum to target groups	Trainers prepared for educational sessions	Self- and peer evaluation of mock educational sessions	Month 7
Target-group participants will learn basic principles of universal access and suggest a plan to integrate universal design into the community.	Tested knowledge and articulated plans from each target group	Scores on knowledge assessment and written plans	Months 7–24
Target-group participants will identify the specific benefits of their suggested plan to all community members	Benefit statements of plans illustrate consideration of full community	Trainer evaluation of written statements of trainees	Months 7–24

attitudes about the capacity for and value of youth with disabilities to be prepared for competitive employment." Box 10.2 lists the objectives related to this goal.

Can you select the outcome and process objectives? If you said that both are outcome objectives, you are correct. Common sense tells us that, as time passes, we become increasingly focused on outcome rather than process. Be

BOX 10.2 — OBJECTIVES TO REACH THE GOAL OF INCREASING FAVORABLE ATTITUDES OF EMPLOYERS AND TEACHERS

1. Employers and teachers participating in training will improve on attitudinal assessments at yearly time intervals.
2. Employers and teachers will behaviorally demonstrate increasingly favorable attitudes by participating in efforts to improve employment preparation for adolescents with disabilities.

BOX 10.3 — PROCESS AND OUTCOME OBJECTIVES TO MOVE JOSHUA TOWARD THE GOAL OF SOBRIETY

1. Joshua will state that he is an alcoholic.
2. Joshua will attend a twelve-step program weekly.
3. Joshua will permanently abstain from ingesting any intoxicant.

aware that as you move from short- to long-term activity, the objectives will reflect an increasing concern with outcome and a decreasing focus on process.

Let us look at the domain of intervention with individuals to illustrate intermediate goals and objectives.

Earlier we discussed two approaches to working with Joshua in his youth. The first goal was set as sobriety. Box 10.3 presents process and outcome objectives that might be formulated to move toward achievement of this goal.

Objectives 1 and 3 are summative, and objective 2 is formative. Using this approach, can you set success criteria, evidence to assess the attainment of the criteria, and time lines for each objective? It is difficult to do so when the objectives address a long-term goal without setting intermediate goals. In Joshua's case, we prefer the second approach to goal setting: Joshua's awareness and acknowledgment of his problematic substance use; and college entrance. A long-term goal of elimination of substance abuse is also set.

To achieve the goal of awareness and acknowledgment, the social worker establishes the objectives in Box 10.4.

Establishing success criteria, evidence, and time lines for these objectives is still complex but can be done in a meaningful way. The two process objectives (1 and 2) lead temporally to the outcome objective (3).

Now, let us look at Joshua's second intermediate goal: college entrance. Objectives to achieve this goal are presented in Box 10.5.

> **BOX 10.4** | **OBJECTIVES TO ACHIEVE THE GOAL OF AWARENESS AND ACKNOWLEDGMENT**
>
> 1. Joshua will attend weekly group therapy with other youth with substance abuse problems.
> 2. Joshua will work with a peer mentor to identify his future life goals and current barriers that he experiences in achieving these goals.
> 3. Joshua will identify how substance use has been problematic for him in advancing toward his personal goals.

> **BOX 10.5** | **OBJECTIVES TO ACHIEVE THE GOAL OF COLLEGE ENTRANCE**
>
> 1. Joshua will seek information about colleges, acceptance criteria, and college application procedures.
> 2. Joshua will identify three colleges to which he will apply and will indicate why he selected these institutions.
> 3. Joshua will complete and submit applications to three colleges.

As you can see by these process objectives, the intermediate goal of college acceptance, because it is not something that is under the control of the social worker or Joshua, is approached through objectives. If Joshua were not accepted to any institution, the objectives might be repeated or reexamined and revised.

So far, we have discussed the thinking process of relating goals and objectives. However, many different goals and objectives can be formulated to achieve the same need. We now move to the action processes of translating needs into goals and objectives.

DERIVING GOALS FROM NEED STATEMENTS

As has been illustrated, even though a needs statement is clear, many goals can be gleaned from the same needs statement. Consider the following example.

Let's revisit the adolescent transition project in New England. This problem statement was initially posed: "Adolescents with disabilities frequently move into adulthood without the vocational skills to be competitive on the job market." Based on the needs assessment, we presented several goals. But were they the only goals that could have been derived from that needs statement? What if the goals did not address attitudes and training, but rather directed intervention to policy reform mandating full inclusion of disabled youth in vocational preparation? Such an approach was responsible for affirmative action, which was a social change effort and not aimed at education and attitudinal change. Perhaps the goal would provide economic incentives for employers to provide work opportunities and on-the-job training for disabled youth. This type of approach was used in the tax incentive for employment of individuals with disabilities. Each of the approaches addresses the same needs statement but from differing perspectives. Each approach has its advantages and limitations, and none is the "correct" or "incorrect" way to structure the aim of an intervention.

How do you translate needs statements into goals? There is no simple answer or formula, but there are action processes and principles that can guide you.

First, it is important to identify who will be formulating goals for intervention. Will a collaborative model be used? If so, who is involved? How will decisions be made?

Second, what are your values and the values of collaborators if you are working with others? In which direction would they take you for goal setting? Using the previous example, would you work directly with educators to elicit attitude change, or would you go to the policy level to mandate cooperation? This decision would depend on your own values, the willingness of the educators to collaborate, and the investment that you want them to have in the process.

Third, the literature or previous practice experience may provide clues to your direction. If you are engaging in a need that has been addressed previously, what were the process and outcome? How consistent were process and outcome with your vision of meeting the stated need?

Fourth, what limitations and advantages are provided by your resources? In the example of disabled adolescents if you did not have access to the individuals or spaces to train adolescents to speak on their own behalf, you could not set the education and training goals discussed. On the other hand, if you did not have knowledge of or access to policy change, you would not be able to set goals to move in that direction.

How long can you concern yourself with the need? What fiscal resources do you have? Who is funding you, and what are the values of the funder?

Finally, purpose must be the overriding factor in translating needs into goals. This is a critical point to remember. The action processes of goal and objective setting are thus embedded within purpose and are in essence a delimitation of time, interaction, audience, and approach.

ACTION PROCESS OF WRITING PROCESS OBJECTIVES

Objectives structure activity (process) and provide the foundation for identifying evidence and criteria for successful completion of each objective (outcome). To develop sound process objectives, the program goals should be clear, and the financial, time, material, and human resources must be known. Objectives and their success criteria are then specified to guide the intervention and illuminate how you will know if the objective has been accomplished in a timely

> **BOX 10.6** | **ACTION PROCESS GUIDELINES FOR WRITING PROCESS OBJECTIVES**
>
> 1. Each objective must be derived directly from one or more goals.
> 2. Process objectives must be time sequenced.
> 3. Only one activity per objective should be described.
> 4. The objective should answer the questions what, who, when, and sometimes how.
> 5. Statements must be unambiguous.
> 6. Process objectives must be written such that the expected time of completion can be specified in assessment of the objective.
> 7. Process objectives are purposive.
> 8. Process objectives must consider resource limitations.
> 9. Process objective completion must be assessable by collection and analysis of empirical evidence without looking at outcome.
> 10. Accountability (who does what) is specified by process objectives.

fashion. Box 10.6 provides guidelines for the action process of writing process objectives.

ACTION PROCESS OF WRITING OUTCOME OBJECTIVES

Outcome or summative objectives specify successful outcome criteria and provide the structure for how success will be conceptualized and ascertained. Similar to process objectives, outcome objectives are clear, with each addressing a single desired outcome of an intervention. Outcome objectives also provide the structure for timing of outcomes. That is, outcome objectives indicate when an outcome should occur and at what level. As you can see, the outcome objectives depicted in the examples can refer to one or multiple targets and issues. Thus, in writing outcomes, you must be sure that what you expect is reasonable, is not impossible due to factors outside your control, meets the purposes of the intervention, and is within the value set of your problem statement. Revisit the outcome objectives in the previous examples. Can you see that they specify who will do what or what will happen as a result of an intervention? Note that outcome objectives do not specify how the intervention will be organized, but rather what will occur from an intervention and for whom. In our evaluation practice model, we reiterate that objective statements do not need to contain the specific measurement and success criterion but must provide the structure for that information to be articulated. In our discussion of outcome assessment in Chapter 15, we will examine how objectives structure outcome assessment and analysis.

> **BOX 10.7** | **ACTION PROCESS GUIDELINES FOR WRITING OUTCOME OBJECTIVES**
>
> 1. Articulate the desired results of your project and translate into objectives that detail one result each.
> 2. Link outcome objectives to one or more goals.
> 3. Clarify the desired impact by including what, who, when, and where in your objective statement.
> 4. Delimit both the scope and the nature of the impact so that it is assessable with empirical evidence.
> 5. Write your objective so that it provides the structure and rationale for the selection of data and analytic techniques that can best let you know the degree of desired impact that has occurred.

There are some important considerations in writing outcome objectives. Box 10.7 presents action process guidelines for writing outcome objectives.

As we will see later in the text, outcome is not easy to assess. The causal links between intervention and outcome are challenging to investigate due to the limitations of research designs with which social science has to work. Keep this point in mind when writing outcome objectives so that you do not create a set of expectations that are unattainable or unable to be assessed. Sound outcome objectives are those that make sense for the intervention, are within the scope of what social services can do, are purposive, and provide the structure to examine the links between project and outcome.

MAIN POINTS

1. The action process of goal and objective formulation is critical in our evaluation practice model because it is the first step in which specific accountability criteria are set.
2. Goals and objectives provide the structure for interventions and posit desired intervention outcomes at one or more time intervals.
3. Goals are broad statements about the ideal or "hoped for."
4. How the goal will be attained and how you will know that it has been attained are the purposes of objectives and frame the nomenclature for two types of objectives: process and outcome.
5. Process (also called formative or monitoring) objectives state what will be done when, sometimes how, and by whom.
6. Outcome (also termed summative) objectives delineate how you will know that you were successful in producing a desired result from what was done.
7. There is a set of action process guidelines for extracting goals from needs statements and for writing objectives to address goals. In doing this task, one must consider purpose, resources, constraints, and values.

EXERCISES

1. Based on *Joshua*'s case study, establish one intermediate goal that has not been advanced in the text to guide him in improving student test scores in low-scoring districts.
2. Link your goal to the needs statement, and state why you selected this goal.
3. Establish process and outcome objectives for your goal, and develop a table indicating the success criteria, evidence, and time line for the accomplishment of each.

REFLEXIVE
INTERVENTION

PART 5

INTERVENTION SELECTION AND REFLEXIVE INTERVENTION

CHAPTER 11

Translating Goals and Objectives into Interventions
Selection of an Intervention Approach
Reflexive Intervention
Main Points
Exercises

TRANSLATING GOALS AND OBJECTIVES INTO INTERVENTIONS

During the implementation of interventions, systematic thinking does not cease. As practice proceeds, the social worker makes practice decisions based on feedback from the actual intervention itself, as well as from examination of use of self in and other influences on the intervention process. We have developed the term *reflexive intervention* to denote the role of evaluation practice thinking and action during the intervention phase of social work practice. Unlike the social worker whose practice is skill-based and intuitive, the social worker who applies the principles of reflexive intervention carefully scrutinizes the implementation of goals and objectives through systematically monitoring intervention. That is not to say that practice wisdom and intuition do not occur. They do, but in evaluation practice, the social worker makes it a point to be well aware of the evidentiary basis from which he or she is making decisions and carefully looks at all practice to obtain clarity about what was done and feedback from engaging in practice action processes. Knowing what was done provides important information that contributes not only to the immediate practice situation but also to future intervention. Let us look at an example.

Return to Joshua and his issue of low test scores. One of the needs that was revealed was teacher training. A short-term goal was established to introduce a bill in the legislature to support teacher training. To accomplish the objective of crafting and introducing the bill, Joshua met the objective of obtaining and organizing the research literature for presentation to the state legislature as a basis for garnering support for and participation of coauthors for the bill. Joshua presented compelling data and was surprised when he received a cool and unenthusiastic response. Without reflexive intervention strategies, Joshua might have concluded that the problem of low test scores was not a priority for the legislature. However, Joshua systematically compared his strategies to those of others who had successfully garnered interest and support for their priorities. In examining how and what he presented to his colleagues, Joshua realized that in each of the successful efforts, the presenters were prepared with videotapes of individuals, testimony, and executive summaries of research. What Joshua realized through reflecting on his intervention approach was that he had selected an approach that was irrelevant and inaccessible to those he wanted to recruit. With these data, Joshua was able to revise his strategies and successfully engage several of his colleagues.

Each year in our evaluation classes, we send our students out to interview clinical social workers about how they evaluate their practices. The students ask practitioners a series of questions that follows the sequence of our model, beginning with the social problem addressed through asking about how practitioners assess outcome. It is not unusual for practitioners to pause before answering the questions and to express uncertainty about the actual social problems that they address or how they systematically examine outcome. The majority of practitioners, however, do articulate their understanding of the need for empirical support for social work practice in this fiscally oriented climate of service delivery.

In concert with the perspectives of practitioners and with new educational standards being developed by the Council on Social Work Education (Educational Policy and Evaluation Standards, 2001), social work needs to expand empirical methods to structure intervention. This chapter focuses on translating systematic evidence from the previous steps into well-conceptualized, goal-oriented intervention that can be monitored and assessed for the extent to which the intervention addressed the initial problem statement. The intervention process presented here is one of application of systematic thinking and action processes to intervention action. Please note that we are not favoring a substantive practice theory but rather are suggesting that our model serve as a framework for organization and application of theory, knowledge, and skill to all aspects of practice.

SELECTION OF AN INTERVENTION APPROACH

This point in the evaluation practice model is a clear illustration of the intersection of the evaluation practice meta-framework and substantive practice reasoning; however, we do not see a "correct" or singular intervention approach to a problem. The steps of problem definition, needs statement, and setting goals and objectives all inform the direction of intervention and identify the constraints, resources, and purposes that bear on intervention decisions and choices. By the time a practitioner has reached the intervention phase of evaluation practice, it is likely that he or she will have a good idea of what action processes should occur. Most important, the theoretical approach and skills basis for intervention that are held by the social worker will define the practice process. However, it is not uncommon for social workers to move to action without articulating a systematically thought-out rationale. We believe that if social workers examine their practice, they will see the implicit assumptions about problem and need that are being addressed. In our model, we assert that implicit assumptions are problematic in that they do not provide the clarity necessary to ascertain and demonstrate the efficacy of practice. Rather, intervention should be anchored on the thinking and action processes of problem identification, needs assessment, and establishment of goals and objectives; and it should clearly indicate how substantive social work theory, knowledge, value, and skill fit within this framework.

Look again at the discussion of force field analysis presented in Chapter 2. This thinking tool provides an excellent strategy through which to further clarify and specify intervention actions that will accomplish objectives and attain goals. We looked at the application of force field analysis in clarifying intervention points to resolve social problems. The initial step involved stating a problem, estimating its severity, and then looking at the forces (driving [positive] or restraining [negative]) that influence the extent to which a problem remains the same, increases, or decreases in severity.

At this point in the evaluation practice model, force field analysis serves another function: identifying specific intervention actions to achieve goals and objectives. To use force field analysis to plan specific intervention strategies, the thinking processes presented in Chapter 2 are applied to a specific objective rather than a broad problem statement. Even if you don't use force field analysis, we suggest that you engage in a similar systematic thinking process that helps you be specific and clear in why you are selecting intervention actions and what you expect each to elicit in terms of process and outcome. By using a systematic approach to intervention planning, the link between objectives and intervention action processes becomes clarified and allows for process and outcome assessment to examine specific parts of intervention. As we will see in the chapters on intervention assessment, it is not an easy task to attribute outcome to intervention in total or to its parts. Therefore, the more clarity and specificity in how interventions are conceptualized to actualize goals and objectives, the easier and more useful your intervention assessment will become. Let us look at an example.

In our last encounter with Jennifer, as part of a long-term goal to achieve universal access in educational environments, the following intermediate goal was set: "Educate the community about universal design and its benefits for all, including individuals with disabilities." The following seven objectives were asserted in Box 10.2:

1. Select a steering committee to represent community diversity.
2. Work with the steering committee to delimit the boundaries of the community (that is, who will be targeted for education?).
3. Develop curriculum for the diverse target groups.
4. Establish educational protocol and procedures.
5. Train all "trainers" to deliver the universal access curriculum to target groups.
6. Target group participants will learn basic principles of universal access and suggest a plan to integrate universal design into the community.
7. Target group participants will identify the specific benefits of their suggested plan to all community members.

First, as a basis for comparison, let us look at an intervention plan that is not systematic. In this scenario, the social worker uses theoretical knowledge that defines diversity as ethnic difference, identifies the ethnic diversity of the community, and selects a steering committee of six providers and educators (three of each) who are interested in access issues and who represent the community ethnicity. The committee makes a decision to target the initial education on universal design concepts to administrative educational personnel. These individuals will then be asked to educate teachers, teacher assistants, and student teachers about universal design concepts. The rationale for this approach is the steering committee's belief that educational administrators are familiar with the important district issues that can impact access and can consider these factors in educating teaching personnel. The curriculum selected by the steering committee is an existing informational approach to definitions of universal design in which experts in the field are brought in to lecture and answer questions. A group of 10 school principals is recruited to attend a two-day workshop in which they are educated about universal design and trained in how to deliver this information to others. Each administrator conducts three sessions with teaching personnel. To assess the process and outcome of the intervention, the six participating administrators are asked to report the following:

1. The number of teaching staff who attend the seminars
2. The scores of attendees on a simple posttest of universal design concepts
3. Plans for integrating universal design concepts into the community developed by teaching personnel
4. A list of benefits of universal design to all community members

The results showed that process objectives were met in a timely manner and the outcome objective of knowledge of universal design concepts was met. However, intervention assessment revealed that the plans for applying universal design to school access and then articulating the benefit of these plans for all community members were not developed beyond the level of vague ideas.

In the second scenario, the social worker begins with a force field analysis process to identify steering committee members because the theoretical approach to "diversity" is too vague to select a diversity variable with no further inquiry. Driving forces impacting the attainment of this process objective included a large group of individuals interested in the problem of access and their desire to learn how to expand access. Restraining forces included not knowing which aspects of community diversity were important to consider. Based on empirical information in the literature on planning and operationalizing universal design, the social worker finds evidence that diversity in age and disability are most critical to address in access issues. The steering committee is therefore selected to represent these areas of diversity.

The steering committee subsequently engaged in a force field analysis to complete objective 2. They identified restraining forces as time constraints of individuals who are employed full time or caring for young children and fear of the cost of environmental modifications to expand access on the part of community members. Driving forces included interest expressed by parents of children with disabilities in the issue of school access and increasing news coverage about disability issues, including access. Based on the force field analysis, the steering committee decided to educate and work with disabled adults and parents of disabled children to learn and apply universal design principles to resolve access issues in the schools. A group of six core individuals worked online and within workshops throughout a three-month period to learn universal design techniques. As part of the committee work, each member was asked to develop a universal design for his or her ideal school environment and present it to the work group. The most viable ideas were selected by the work group, *synthesized into a plan, and sent to all adult taxpayers in the community. The group also developed public service announcements for radio and television media on the project. An important part of the program of public service announcements was a short vignette about how limited access to schools affects all community members, not only those with mobility impairments. The committee wanted to disseminate information about how specialized, segregated environments increased the costs of education. Moreover, committee members wanted to raise awareness of how segregation violated student civil rights and deprived the community of the potential contributions of those who are excluded. The evaluation was conducted through these means:*

1. *Assessing the work group members on their knowledge of universal design through evaluating their plans*
2. *Reporting the number of public service announcements that were disseminated over radio and television*
3. *Randomly polling taxpayers to ascertain their exposure to the public service announcements*
4. *Polling public attitudes toward improving school access*

The social worker noted a large increase in community awareness of access issues as a result of the public access campaign. The degree to which the universal design plans suggested by the work group was supported was unknown. The social worker used the evaluation information to establish a new goal of increasing community support for universal design in the public schools in the community.

As you can see by comparing the two scenarios, both social workers were committed to the goal, both developed interventions to complete process and outcome objectives, and both evaluated process and outcome with viable assessment strategies. However, the systematic force field analysis thinking process in scenario 2 was instrumental in identifying a critical element in outcome success that was missed in scenario 1: the element of selecting relevant diversity variables to be represented on the steering committee. In scenario 1, it was assumed that diversity was equivalent to ethnic difference, and thus the age and ability perspectives so frequently associated with physical conditions that challenge sensory and mobility access were not obtained. In scenario 2, the social worker went to empirically established knowledge as a basis for the rationale for intervention and thus was able to judge the application of previous work to the current challenge.

We present guidelines for intervention planning in Box 11.1. These guidelines show you how to systematically identify and select interventions that resolve the social problems to which the intervention is directed.

The detail with which you address the guidelines in Box 11.1 will be an important determinant in the degree to which you can ultimately attribute changes in outcome to the intervention. We will examine this point in greater detail later in the text. Now let us turn to what we consider a critical part of all social work practice, reflexive intervention.

> **BOX 11.1** | **INTERVENTION PLANNING GUIDELINES**
>
> 1. Be clear on the problem statement. To whom does the problem belong, whose values are represented in the statement, which part of the problem is to be addressed, and which stakeholder groups are concerned with the problem?
> 2. Consult and keep the needs assessment in mind as you are planning your intervention. What is needed by whom and why, what is the scope of need, what disagreements exist among stakeholder groups about what is needed, and who can fill the need as articulated?
> 3. Be sure that goals and objectives clearly emerge from and respond to the full scope of need.
> 4. Use a systematic thinking process to plan implementation strategies, based on a sound, empirically and theoretically informed rationale that will be conducted to achieve goals and objectives.
>   Consider the purposive, organizational, and resources context of the intervention.
> 5. Clearly articulate the action processes of the intervention, being sure to detail the temporal sequence, distinct intervention action processes, and outcomes expected from each aspect of intervention.
> 6. Clearly link each action process of the intervention to one or more objectives that it is designed to accomplish.

REFLEXIVE INTERVENTION

As we indicated in Chapters 1 and 2, reflexive intervention is our newly coined term for what we believe all social work intervention should be. **Reflexivity** is a term used in naturalistic method to indicate the thinking process in which investigators identify the influences that they bring to an inquiry and to the interpretive process that shapes the knowledge derived therefrom (Steier, 1991). We extrapolate the meaning of the term and apply it to evaluation practice to describe intervention in which the social worker is engaged in a systematic examination of practice, resources, and use of self and other influences that impact practice process and outcome.

Reflexive intervention consists of three important evaluative processes: monitoring, cost analysis, and analysis of external influences on the intervention process and outcome.

Monitoring

Monitoring is the set of actions used by practitioners to regularly examine their actions and record information about the intervention that will be used to assess process outcome of the intervention to clearly document what was done and the resources that were used. Answering *who, what, when, where,* *why,* and *how* questions is a good way to monitor intervention action processes. Chapters 12 and 13 discuss specific methods of monitoring intervention process.

Cost Analysis

In the 21st century, the global economy and concern for cost-efficiency are becoming hegemenous. Cost of providing social work services has not been a popular topic in our profession except for those whose jobs focus primarily on administration. Practitioners are constantly asking how an intervention and its value to humans can be reduced to actual dollars. Two ethical questions continue to be debated in the literature (Reamer, 1999), in our educational institutions, and in social work agencies: Should human services be subjected to fiscal measurement? and if so, how? We know that we cannot sidestep the concern for the economics of social work practice in a managed-payment system, in which the paradigm of economic scarcity is accepted as true and in which, for the most part, social work services function. We therefore include cost analysis in reflexive intervention because the cost of providing services must be considered in any thinking process about intervention.

Analysis of External Influences on the Intervention Process and Outcome

There are numerous influences on social work intervention. However, as part of the reflexive intervention process, it is essential that we be as expansive and analytic as possible in examining all the factors we can find that may impact both the outcome of our practices and the way in which we conceptualize and deliver interventions.

MAIN POINTS

1. Reflexive intervention is the term we created to describe the systematic process of scrutinizing.
2. Intervention selection is a systematic process in which the practice decisions are based on the steps of problem identification, needs assessment, and establishment of goals and objectives.
3. Actualizing goals and objectives is a systematic process in which multiple factors and evidence must be considered to make decisions.
4. Once the intervention is specified, reflexive intervention should be a consistent practice.
5. Reflexive intervention comprises process assessment, cost analysis, and analysis of the external influences on intervention process and outcome.

EXERCISES

1. Examine the processes that your agency or a social work agency to which you have access uses in order to monitor its intervention practice, cost, and influences that affect its operation and outcome.
2. Assess the extent to which systematic data are used/generated to elaborate the intervention. Are these processes sufficiently detailed so that you have a good picture of the intervention processes? Can you answer who, what, when, where, why, and how about intervention activity? If so, what are the processes? If not, what is missing?
3. What cost analysis systems are in place? Who conducts these analyses?
4. How does the agency account for external influences on the process and outcome of intervention?

CHAPTER 12

THINKING PROCESSES OF REFLEXIVE INTERVENTION

Elements of Reflexive Intervention

Main Points

Exercises

ELEMENTS OF REFLEXIVE INTERVENTION

In this chapter, we explore the thinking processes of reflexive intervention. We have posited three elements of this phase of evaluation practice: monitoring process, cost analysis, and examination of external influences on the process and outcome of intervention. In this chapter, we examine each in detail.

Monitoring

There are five basic questions to ask in monitoring process:

1. What happened during the intervention to accomplish the intervention goals and objectives?
2. How did it happen?
3. Who participated? Who did not?
4. What were the strengths and limitations of the approach?
5. What processes need to be changed?

Before discussing the thinking processes of each question in more detail, we advance a conceptual understanding of monitoring and how it fits with evaluation practice.

Definitions of Monitoring Processes **Intervention processes** denote the set of actions that occur in order to meet the goals and objectives of intervention. Processes fall into five categories:

Administration: policies, procedures, and activities that provide the structure through which to manage the internal and interactive functions of an intervention

Direct service (micropractice): processes to deliver interventions to the target population(s) identified in the problem statement and need

Indirect service (mezzo- and macropractice): processes that impact the target population but do not engage them in active participation

Staff development: educational processes to advance the knowledge and skill of staff

Systemic interaction: processes through which an agency, intervention structure, group, or individual articulate with systems that affect intervention planning, development, implementation, and outcome

Let us look at examples of each to clarify.

Think back to the intervention that was piloted as a result of the identified need to improve test scores in Joshua's state. The multimethod needs assessment identified as necessities teacher training, collaborative teacher-parent after-school academic support, and lobbying efforts to increase state financial support for technology in elementary education. The administration of the project was handled by the school principal's office. A social worker was hired to convene and oversee the collaborative teacher-parent academic support groups, to work with a lobbyist, and to organize teacher training.

Given the multiple domains of process, an important job of the social worker within the framework of evaluation practice is to decide on the scope and detail with which the reflection on process will be implemented.

Monitoring or process assessment (we use these terms interchangeably) is therefore a set of thinking and action processes to ascertain, characterize, and document the relationship between articulated objectives and what occurs during an intervention, what factors impact the intervention, who is involved, and what is the extent of the resources used.

Related to the need for teacher training in Joshua's example, one of the goals for a five-year period is for students in a pilot school district to increase their scores on standardized tests. To accomplish this, the following objectives have been established:

1. *Identify two elementary schools (grades 1–6) in similar parts of the district who will participate in the experimental program (to be done by the state department of education based on aggregate demographic and school resource data). Randomly select one school for the experimental program and one as a control.*
2. *In the month of August prior to each new school year, educate all head teachers (those who provide the supervision and oversight for academic work in each class) in both schools in how to implement a curriculum that focuses on the knowledge and skills contained within the test (teacher education to be delivered by state university faculty).*
3. *Administer the standardized state tests annually in April to children in grades 1–6.*
4. *Implement a financial incentive of $3,000 at the end of each academic year for teachers in the experimental school only if there is a significant increase in test scores (based on a formula that addresses differences in initial scores, demographics, number of students, and so forth).*

Each of these objectives is a process objective that guides the nature and sequence of action processes of the intervention.

In social work, most process assessment focuses on the examination of the extent to which interventions were conducted, who conducted them, and who participated. It is not unusual to see reports that measure process success by indicating the number of hours that the staff devoted to each project activity, the number of "clients" who participated, and the extent to which these data met expectations stated in the initial project. This information may provide utilization knowledge, but how the staff functioned, what was done in each activity, what was the process of recruitment and participation, and what was the context of the processes are critical pieces of knowledge that are not captured in a count of staff hours and clients served. Monitoring in evaluation practice is much broader in scope and involves the application of rigorous research design to an examination of how an intervention was enacted within cost, service, policy, and community contexts. Recognition of the context in which monitoring occurs eliminates the perfunctory nature of "counting" that so frequently occurs in many agencies and organizations. Unlike typical approaches to process assessment, the necessity to understand the context embeddedness of evaluation practice expands both the scope of inquiry, the methods that are acceptable, and the utility of the knowledge derived from monitoring.

A comprehensive reflexive approach to monitoring also serves to inform others who are not directly involved in the intervention about its performance. Moreover, sound monitoring, when linked with outcome assessment, can provide exponentially greater analysis and detail regarding how and why outcomes occurred, what differences in processes produced differential outcomes, and what future changes need to be made to optimize goal attainment.

In Joshua's example, the first objective to achieve the goal of increasing scores on standardized tests is the selection and assignment of schools for the experimental teacher training and incentive intervention. The objective specifies that the selected schools must be similar in demographics and resources. How this process occurs is critical to understanding the degree to which financial incentive was associated with improvement in scores. What if only the base budget was the resource criterion used for matching schools, but the control school received private resources from a community fund? There would be no way of knowing about resource differences unless the monitoring plan was expansive in its scope, extending beyond the selection criterion of base budget.

Process assessment, therefore, has numerous purposes and domains, again highlighting the importance of delimiting the scope to useful information for intended audiences and to resource-imposed boundaries.

Ideally, all monitoring is formative since these terms have been used interchangeably. This statement may seem redundant, but we suggest that it is not. Historically, evaluation has been divided into formative and summative elements. Formative evaluation provided systematically derived input about intervention process for the explicit purpose of service improvement. A mere count of hours and participants may provide some information about need for revision of service but cannot reveal what specific intervention activities need to change, how the change might occur, and who should participate in revision. Moreover, a cursory process evaluation cannot specify how one will know if the changes have occurred. There may be significant resource and time limitations on monitoring, given the focus of funding sources on outcomes, but we urge providers to consider how systematic, detailed process findings can save resources that might be spent on attempting to improve outcomes through uninformed revision or maintenance of the status quo.

Box 12.1 presents the essential elements of monitoring, no matter what the scope of the inquiry.

Monitoring Is Purposive Purpose not only underpins the scope of the intervention processes to be explored, but shapes how process assessment information is to be known. Thus, monitoring design as well as reporting is guided by purpose. We suggest that all monitoring be formative. In evaluation practice, the purpose of improving interventions is common to all process assessment. Unlike other approaches to process evaluation, this important tenet of monitoring

> BOX 12.1 | ESSENTIAL ELEMENTS OF MONITORING

1. Monitoring is purposive.
2. Monitoring uses systematic inquiry.
3. Monitoring has multiple audiences with differing information needs.
4. Monitoring describes an intervention.

in evaluation practice is a critical link between practice, research, and knowledge. Conceptualizing monitoring as a method to improve practice clearly locates evaluation practice within the domains of social work practice and knowledge generation.

However, there are many other purposes for monitoring, including, but not limited to, examining efficiency, assessing input, determining resource use, determining utilization, describing intervention similarities and differences, and examining contextual factors that should be considered in intervention delivery.

As we saw earlier in the example of Joshua, the manner in which the schools were selected was critical in assessing the outcome of the financial incentive. We found that the control school had received a large infusion of resources from a private source, thereby changing the nature of the funding and the potential for the control school to pay higher teacher salaries, as well as acquire additional resources. Knowing about these resources and how they have been used in the school are critical pieces of information for assessing the efficacy of incentives.

Monitoring Uses Systematic Inquiry This statement, too, may sound redundant, but it is not uncommon for evaluation efforts that are considered to be formative in nature to be inferior in their rigor to outcome assessment. Perhaps this laissez-faire approach to monitoring occurs because monitoring and description are not considered as important as understanding outcome. However, any compromise of systematic rigor weakens the evaluation practice aim to contribute to practice advancement and knowledge.

Suppose that scores in both schools improved but the scores on student tests in the control school increased more than those in the experimental condition. We might surmise that the incentive program was a failure. However, what if the infusion of money in the control school funded a "test-taking" curriculum in which students took mock tests on a monthly basis to become familiar with the testing strategy? Knowing this information would certainly be important in any explanation of the outcome assessment.

In the example relating to adolescents with disabilities, one of the goals was to improve attitudes of the teachers and employers toward these youth. The objectives delineated an intervention through which youth trained in public speaking would present their strengths, experiences, and needs to teachers and employers. Monitoring how youth prepare and deliver presentations would be critical in any understanding of attitudinal change.

Monitoring Has Multiple Audiences with Differing Information Needs Take another look at the adolescent program example. The audiences are diverse, and each has an agenda that differs in part or in total from that of the other. For the youth, being able to talk about all experiences could be liberating. However, the teachers, for example, might be concerned if youth presented their school experiences as limiting. That same information might help employers understand why youth with disabilities seem to lack the skills of youth without disabilities. Monitoring the content and process of presentations could be extremely valuable in providing feedback for formative purposes and illuminating differential outcomes for diverse audiences.

Consider the same point for intervention with individuals. If the intervention plan suggested by the vocational counselor had been implemented, Joshua would have been directed to participate in substance-abuse rehabilitation. Any failure on Joshua's part to meet the success criteria of full attendance and abstinence may have resulted in discontinuation of any future support. However, monitoring would have revealed that substance abuse was only part of Joshua's "problem." Monitoring Joshua's progress could therefore have provided the formative data to revise rather than curtail his intervention.

Box 12.2 lists audiences who are frequently involved in monitoring and typical questions that each might want to have answered in a process assessment.

Looking back to one of the previous examples, let's examine how these questions might be posed and answered and how responses that are satisfactory to one audience may not be to another.

In the experimental program to increase student scores, Joshua knows that he needs to anticipate the monitoring interests of school administrators, funders, and policymakers. He therefore uses the questions posed in Box 12.2 to help him identify areas for reflexive intervention.

Administrators most likely will want to know about the efficiency of the experimental intervention processes and the degree to which the staff were able to be productive in their typical work responsibilities. The funders, in this case the state government and outside funding sources for the experimental teacher-incentive program, are most likely concerned with the efficiency of resource use and the processes to assure full participation of all students who would have the potential to show an increase on test scores. Joshua might anticipate that policymakers would want to know about ongoing costs and resource use beyond the base budget as a basis for legislative and budgetary decisions relative to the continuation of the project.

Thus, as illustrated, the wise social worker considers audience before monitoring design is formulated. Preparedness for multiple audiences not only expands access of the process report, but can head off serious consequences that might occur.

In Joshua's work to increase standardized test scores, failing to monitor all resources, including those beyond base budget, would have been a serious error.

| BOX 12.2 | **TYPICAL QUESTIONS OF AUDIENCES FREQUENTLY INVOLVED IN MONITORING** |

Service User
> What parts of the intervention were satisfactory? Why?
> What parts of the intervention were unsatisfactory? Why?
> What parts were easy to access or use? Which parts were difficult?
> How was I treated by staff?
> Did the intervention include all services that I needed?
> What else might I need?
> What changes should be made to improve intervention access, participation, and termination?
> Were the facilities and resources satisfactory to me?

Direct-Care Providers
> How much intervention did I provide?
> What did I do that I would continue? Why?
> What did I do that I would not continue? Why?
> How satisfactory were the intervention context and resources for me? for intervention recipients?
> What activities helped me learn?
> What parts helped me advance my career?
> Did I feel valued?
> Were recording requirements reasonable?
> Was the workload appropriate to the time that I spent on the job?

Administrators
> Was my staff productive?
> Were the interventions efficient in goal attainment?

Monitoring Describes an Intervention This principle seems evident but is often violated in monitoring. How many times has evaluation practice focused on program usage without describing what intervention activities occurred, how they occurred, the context in which each occurred, and factors that influenced intervention processes? We assert that any process evaluation beyond a perfunctory, compliant one must provide a multidimensional vision of how interventions are formulated, publicized, and delivered. Moreover, it is critical to know the context of the intervention if monitoring is to serve a useful formative purpose. In our examples of *Joshua* and *Jennifer,* this concept is well illustrated.

Were the costs and resource inputs reasonable? sufficient?
Were staff meetings productive?
What are the agency policies, and do they need to be changed?
Was the flow of the intervention activities efficient relative to goals and objectives?
Were clients/groups informed, recruited, served, and terminated in a timely and useful manner?
Is staffing appropriate?

Funders
How was the money used? Was resource use efficient?
Who participated in the intervention?
What actually comprised all aspects of the intervention?
What processes should be changed?

Policymakers
What policy governs the intervention and how?
Does the policy need to be changed and how?
Did the intervention comply with current policy?

Community Members
What are the goals and objectives of this intervention?
For whom is this intervention planned?
Who does the intervention serve?
Whom should it serve?
Is the environmental context desirable?
Is the intervention accessible to all who can benefit?
Do I want to support this intervention in my community?

Given the definitions for monitoring that have been discussed, we also highlight in Box 12.3 what monitoring is not.

Because monitoring is intended to provide information about an intervention and its related contextual influences, the findings are not used to make final decisions about resources, performance, and worth. Rather, process evidence is intended to obtain detailed systematic knowledge of the elements of an intervention, their sequence, and their variation. Moreover, process assessment is not a means to verify or falsify the operationalization of practice theory. It is primarily designed to contribute to theory development and refinement by providing feedback that can be used for intervention revision. An essential element

> **BOX 12.3** | **WHAT MONITORING IS NOT**
>
> It is not punitive or final.
> It is not designed to be summative.
> It is not designed primarily to test the efficacy of theory.
> It is not designed to overlook unintended or unplanned results of an intervention.

of evaluation practice that differs from other evaluation approaches is that all monitoring is formative and should be used to improve the manner in which goals are attained and objectives are accomplished, and to contribute to the advancement and improvement of practice theory and methods.

Now we turn to the second important element of reflexive intervention, cost analysis.

Cost Analysis

Looking at cost is a part of social work practice that many social workers do not do or do not want to do. In an agency, direct-service providers often do not see cost analysis as part of their job. Unlike in other models of practice and evaluation, in evaluation practice, consideration of cost is regarded as part of all social work practice.

As an example, in looking at direct intervention with Joshua, the vocational counselor was proceeding with the notion that the cost of the intervention was restricted to immediate supports and services. Reducing costs therefore meant being frugal and addressing the most visible problem of alcoholism. The social worker's cost approach was more expansive in that the long-term risks of financial dependence were weighed against the costs of providing education to Joshua. According to the social worker, frugal use of resources meant future investment in education to head off a full life of financial dependence.

In Joshua's concern with low test scores, the direct intervention implemented was a monetary incentive system for teachers. Cost analysis here would at minimum look at the dollars spent per points of increase on standardized tests. Cost analysis is, therefore, a complex but essential part of evaluation practice.

This text addresses two important approaches to examining cost: measuring the cost of process and measuring the cost of expected and unexpected outcomes. Unlike many texts and models of evaluation that discuss cost analysis as a discrete part of evaluation, we present a conceptual approach because any analysis of costs must occur as a monitoring process of intervention inputs. We return to cost analysis in each of the remaining chapters as it applies to each subsequent area of evaluation practice being addressed.

> **BOX 12.4** | **QUESTIONS TO GUIDE THE THINKING PROCESS OF COST ANALYSIS**
>
> 1. What resources will be considered as costs?
> 2. What worth factors will be addressed?
> 3. How will resources be associated with worth?

Conceptual Approach to Examining Cost Some of the many names for various approaches to assessing cost are cost-benefit analysis, cost-efficiency, cost-utility, and cost-effectiveness. What all have in common is that they address resource allocation (cost) and worth (value of attainment of goals, objectives, and consequences) (Yates, 1996).

Box 12.4 presents the questions that you would answer in order to guide the thinking process of analyzing cost.

Question 1 is answered in the step of reflexive intervention. Questions 2 and 3 are a critical part of outcome assessment and will be addressed in Chapters 15 and 16.

The question of what resources will be considered as costs may seem simple, but it comprises several levels.

As an illustration, we saw as far back as identification of Joshua's problem that the vocational counselor was concerned with the question of which resources to use. According to the counselor, spending public money to support a college education for an individual who was considered an active alcohol abuser was unreasonable. Yet to the social worker, college not only was a reasonable expense, but was the choice that would cost the least in the long run.

Just as with any other step in evaluation practice, problem definition is a critical factor in deciding what resources will be utilized. The first level of cost, therefore, is the nature of resources that should be devoted to problem resolution. Second, once a decision is made on the nature of resources needed, the magnitude of the resources that are directly devoted to an intervention are defined. *Does Joshua get counseling once each week? For what duration? Over a year? For more than a year? While he is in college?*

Finally, what costs are considered to be part of the intervention? At this juncture, careful monitoring of resources expended is critical if questions about worth will be answered. This point will be addressed later in the discussion of outcomes.

As part of reflexive intervention, we are concerned with the costs of providing an intervention. What should be considered as costs? Certainly the cost of providing counseling would be specified. Would administrative expenses such as completing paperwork be considered as part of the cost? What about the cost of maintaining the facility in which the counseling occurs? There are many decisions to be made about what expenses should be included in cost. In a large-scale intervention, determining what is included in cost becomes even more complex. *Consider the example of teacher incentives that we advanced earlier. Are the costs limited to the incentives as this condition is the only factor being tested?*

There are no easy answers on what to include in costs. However, assessing costs must be consistent, rigorous, and purposive if this element of reflexive intervention is to be formative or useful in ascertaining the association between cost and worth.

External Influences on Intervention

As we have indicated, one of the strengths of monitoring is that the context embeddedness is basic to the inquiry. How far to expand your look at context is an important thinking process. Many approaches to monitoring examine the immediate action processes without examining the factors that influence the intervention. For example, we often see utilization statistics without any further information about recruitment, environmental, payment, or policy contexts. Consider this example. Day programs for senior citizens are established in two different parts of the same state. Each is based on a clear support for the need of such a program, and both are identical in their action processes. One program has high utilization, and one does not. The disparity in utilization is a concern that cannot be informed without a further examination of the context. Is it possible that the environments differ in transportation accessibility, literacy rate, and so forth? What if the center that has low utilization is placed adjacent to a noisy factory that impedes hearing and thus diminishes the benefits of program participation? Context needs to be a consideration in process evaluation. We have discussed the issue of external influences on intervention process, as the thinking process of what variables to monitor must include consideration of scope. We discuss external influences in subsequent chapters as they relate to outcome assessment.

MAIN POINTS

1. Reflection in evaluation practice is a careful examination of the intervention and influences that are external to it.
2. Monitoring is an action process in which data about intervention processes are systematically obtained and analyzed.
3. An essential element of evaluation practice is the use of monitoring for improving practice and advancing social work knowledge.
4. Cost analysis answers three questions that address the relative cost of an intervention.
5. Examining external influences on the intervention process is a critical part of reflexive intervention.

EXERCISES

1. In your agency, or an agency to which you have access, look at how monitoring occurs. What data are obtained? How are they obtained, and how are they used to assess process?
2. Critically analyze monitoring in the agency, and suggest how improvements can be made to ensure that the data are used for formative purposes.
3. In the agency, are costs assessed? What is included in cost? What factors are considered in worth, and how are the two related?

13 CHAPTER ACTION PROCESSES OF REFLEXIVE INTERVENTION

Introduction to Design Selection
in Reflexive Intervention

Experimental-Type Process Assessment Designs

Naturalistic Inquiry

Mixed-Method Design

Process Assessment Questions Posed
by Diverse Groups

Selecting a Method—Guiding Questions

Main Points

Exercises

INTRODUCTION TO DESIGN SELECTION IN REFLEXIVE INTERVENTION

In this chapter, we examine methods by which reflexive intervention can be actualized. As we discovered when looking at thinking processes, the purpose, scope, and practical constraints that you encounter, as well as the audiences who will receive and work with the findings, are important determinants in the design that is selected for any part of reflexive intervention. Reflexive intervention comprises three elements: monitoring, cost analysis, and examination of external influences. As we proceed through the action processes, you might want to think about how each approach to design would be relevant to each element.

EXPERIMENTAL-TYPE PROCESS ASSESSMENT DESIGNS

Although we often equate reflexive intervention with naturalistic inquiry, experimental-type designs are both useful and prevalent in process inquiry. Unlike outcome assessment, process assessment does not focus on cause-and-effect relationships between intervention and its results. Thus, true experimentation is rarely suggested as a viable design in reflexive intervention, unless it serves outcome purposes as well. Rather, it is most valuable to use descriptive designs that can identify resource input and use, and contextual and internal correlates of intervention process. Among these designs, nonexperimental, preexperimental, and quasi-experimental designs can numerically answer reflexive intervention questions. Experimental-type designs are nomothetic, in that they illuminate group phenomena. These designs are therefore indicated when the social worker wants to know something about groups of individuals, more than one group, and/or groups of other units of analysis.

In Table 13.1, we present nomothetic nonexperimental to quasi-experimental designs (using Campbell and Stanley [1963] notation) and the types of process questions that each can answer. X is the independent variable, which is most frequently the intervention; and O is the dependent variable, or measure of what is expected to occur.

For each experimental-type approach to reflexive inquiry, follow the steps in Box 13.1.

Joshua's substance-abuse problem can illustrate the use of experimental-type methods in reflexive intervention. In Chapter 9, two process objectives were established to achieve the goal of Joshua's awareness and acknowledgement of his problematic substance use:

1. *Joshua will attend weekly group therapy with other youth with substance-abuse problems.*
2. *Joshua will participate in a peer mentoring program.*

To achieve the goal, the social worker enters Joshua into a counseling and mentoring program. Monitoring using experimental-type design involves

TABLE 13.1 | FREQUENTLY USED NOMOTHETIC DESIGNS AND QUESTIONS THAT THEY CAN ANSWER

Design	Question
XO Passive observation design in which the observation follows the intervention or part of an intervention	How satisfactory was the intervention process? (X = intervention, O = satisfaction) What changes are suggested from among a fixed selection? (X = intervention, O = suggested changes to the intervention) What contextual and internal correlates relate to different intervention processes? (no distinction between dependent and independnet variables) What were the costs of conducting the intervention? (X = intervention, O = costs)
OXO Pretest, posttest	What changed over the course of intervention? What was expected to change as a result of the intervention? (X = intervention, O = change)
X_1 O X_2 O Comparative group design	What comparative changes were noted in different parts of the intervention? What was expected to change as a result of the intervention? ($X_{1,2}$ = intervention parts, O = change) How satisfactory were differential intervention processes? ($X_{1,2}$ = intervention parts, O = satisfaction) What comparative changes are suggested in different intervention processes from among a fixed selection? ($X_{1,2}$ = intervention parts, O = suggested changes) What comparative changes in costs occurred over the course of the intervention? ($X_{1,2}$ = intervention parts, O = costs)
OXOXOXO Time series design	What changes in intervention process and resource use were seen over time in response to formative feedback? (X = intervention, O = process, resource use, costs)

Joshua but is not directed to him as an individual. Using an OXOXO approach, the following monitoring questions are asked by the social work agency administrator and answered by measuring each program participant on the selected measures:

1. What degree of participation occurred in group therapy?
2. What degree of participation occurred in peer mentoring?
3. What are the changes in participant well-being over time?
4. What degree of sobriety is exhibited among participants?

> **BOX 13.1** | **GUIDELINES FOR DESIGN STRUCTURE IN EXPERIMENTAL-TYPE REFLEXIVE INTERVENTION**
>
> 1. Specify the questions to be answered.
> 2. Detail the structure of the approach by identifying the variables and the nature of the description or relationship that you are examining.
> 3. Determine the boundaries of your inquiry. Will you use a sample? a population? What will be the units of analysis (individuals, families, communities, etc.)?
> 4. Identify the constructs to be measured.
> 5. Articulate the lexical definitions (dictionary) and operational definitions (measurement) of the constructs.
> 6. Design the data analysis strategy to be used.
> 7. Specify how you will report your findings.
> 8. Specify how you will use the findings.

In this action process, the intervention (X) comprises the overall set of social work and related programs in which Joshua is participating. The observed phenomena (O) are

1. *Attendance in group therapy (measured in attendance through each entire scheduled session)*
2. *Monthly ratings of well-being (defined as self-reported sense of efficacy and health) on a numeric index (scaled 0–10, with ascending scores indicating greater well-being) and documented abstinence from alcohol (measured in total continuous days in which no intoxicating substance was discerned on urine testing)*
3. *Attendance at peer-mentoring sessions (full participation throughout each entire scheduled peer-mentoring session)*

Attendance records provide a record of what happened in group counseling, as well as a count of clients served. The numeric indicators provide an ongoing longitudinal description of client progress and activity. To assess how intervention processes occurred within the agency, data from attendance and client scores on indicator scales are also aggregated by the agency administrator. To assess costs of intervention processes, data are kept on counseling hours. As you can see, these data are all descriptive and follow client and counselor action processes over time within the context of specified costs. If these data were used to monitor Joshua as an individual, the strategy would be called single-case design. We look at this set of methods later in the text.

These same objectives are listed in Table 13.2, which presents the process objectives and specifies the success criteria, time line for completion, and the evidence used to examine the completion of each objective. This type of approach clearly explicates monitoring structure.

TABLE 13.2 | PROCESS OBJECTIVES AND MONITORING STRUCTURE

	Success criteria	Evidence	Time line
Joshua will attend weekly group therapy with other youth with substance-abuse problems	Regular, weekly attendance at group for all enrolled participants	Attendance recordings	Ongoing
	Significant improvement in weekly indicator scores	Scores on indicator tests	Weekly
Joshua will participate in a peer-mentoring program	Regular attendance for all program participants in peer-mentor program	Records of meetings documented by peer mentor	Ongoing

Note that in this table, the information is organized to assure that each objective delineates the action processes to be accomplished during the intervention, as well as the structure and content of monitoring. The use of non-experimental design allows the social worker and the agency administrator to quantify the completion of objectives. Attendance recordings, along with the numeric forms of evidence, provide the descriptive data through which the monitoring questions can be answered. Data analysis would be primarily descriptive. Frequency of attendance would be recorded for group therapy and the peer-mentoring program. To answer the questions regarding change in well-being over time, significance testing (looking at the extent to which an effect was likely to be a chance occurrence) would be conducted (see Appendix). The monitoring information obtained through these strategies would most likely be important to share within the agency. Participation statistics would certainly tell the agency administrator about utilization and client compliance. However, this method would not reveal the reason for the findings. Unexpected findings could be further investigated. Suppose, for example, we found that attendance was regular and consistent at group therapy but spotty in peer mentoring. This valuable information would indicate a need to explore why clients did not have regular attendance in the peer-mentoring aspect of the intervention.

For an example of reflexive intervention in a large-system intervention, look back at the process objectives in Table 10.1 to review the access intervention in Jennifer's case. The process objectives in the table were specified to meet the goal of educating the community about universal design and its benefits for all, including individuals with disabilities. Looking at the objectives and related criteria, you can see that the time line and the evidence for monitoring successful completion are specified and already point to an XO design in which X is the conduct of the activity and O is the observation of the degree of attainment of the success criterion through an examination of the specified evidence.

In this intervention, cost monitoring can be approached in multiple ways. A simple approach would be to examine the salaries and expenses of conducting the education and training. For example, the salaries of the project staff and the actual expenditures for supplies, telephone, travel, equipment, and materials could be documented as cost. However, this approach would omit resources such as time contributed by the steering committee members and trainers. What if steering committee members had to take time off from work to participate? Would those missed days at work be included in costs? Purpose of the cost analysis would be an important determinant in delimiting the scope of resources considered as cost. If the training effort were planned as a pilot to garner future resources, expanding the scope of costs to assure that future programs could be supported well enough to be successfully implemented would be important. On the other hand, if cost containment was a community value, then omitting in-kind (noncash) contributions to cost might be appropriate and purposive.

Although experimental-type reflexive intervention answers many questions, queries about context and uniqueness of process cannot be captured by quantification. We now turn to the naturalistic tradition to illustrate its use in reflexive intervention.

NATURALISTIC INQUIRY

Complexity, flexibility, narrative, and induction, to a greater or lesser extent, are essential elements of naturalistic inquiry. The naturalistic tradition is extremely valuable in formative processes, in that it provides a vehicle through which information can be garnered, even if this information has not been considered prior to the inquiry. The complexity of description in naturalistic inquiry also lends itself to specifying nuance, differential implementation, and context of intervention. Naturalistic methods are extremely valuable in process assessment both in describing the richness of the intervention and in providing data about the context of the intervention.

Review Chapter 9 for a complete discussion of naturalistic inquiry. We apply the nine essential elements of naturalistic design here, because inherent in these elements are the reasons that a social worker uses this tradition in process assessment.

Nine Elements of Naturalistic Inquiry

Range of Purpose Because naturalistic methods span the range of purposes from advancing descriptive knowledge to revealing complex theoretical frameworks, these methods can meet the multiple purposes and audiences of reflexive intervention. Description can reveal the complexity of "what happened." More complex purposes for process assessment can also be accomplished, such as exploration of unintended correlates and outcomes of intervention.

In the example of Joshua, process recordings of group therapy in which verbatim text is documented provides rich description of the content and group process. An examination of the narrative text can reveal important knowledge upon which to assess group process and the need for revision. If attendance was erratic in the peer-mentoring program, naturalistic inquiry relying on client interview and observation of mentoring sessions would yield important information about the reasons for this phenomenon.

Context Specificity Because all naturalistic inquiry is conducted in a context, methods within this tradition are invaluable for examining intervention action processes, both embedded within and influencing multiple system levels.

Consider Joshua again, but this time as an adult. Observation of teaching practices in each of the pilot schools participating in the experimental program to increase student test scores could reveal important information about teacher-student interaction. For example, what if the teachers in the experimental school saw a news program on a similar effort in which teachers received a $10,000 incentive. The observer/interviewer would be able to ascertain resentment and lackluster teaching stemming from the comparatively small sum of money being offered as an incentive. These data could be used to explain external factors, insufficient resource allocation, and unanticipated internal correlates that negatively influence process and outcome.

Complexity and Pluralistic Perspective of Reality This element of the naturalistic tradition is most valuable in revealing different perspectives about intervention process and areas for improvement.

Consider the issue of universal access in Jennifer's case. Observation and narrative recording of steering committee processes could yield critical information on conflicts that arise between members representing various interest groups. What if tension arose between the selection of a professional versus grassroots approach to community education? If not addressed, this tension could potentially halt the community education process. Implicit in this conflict would also be issues of cost.

Transferability of Findings Although naturalistic inquiry is context-specific, the rich description that is often conducted allows reflexive intervention findings to be applied to comparable interventions within analogous contexts.

Improvement in test scores resulting from teacher incentives in Joshua's district could inform similar school regions. If Joshua presents comprehensive information about intervention methods, monitoring, cost, and factors that are unique to his region, other school districts could extrapolate intervention components that seem applicable and discard those that are more specific to Joshua's region.

Flexibility The flexibility of naturalistic strategies allows the social worker to be responsive to incremental learning and need for method change throughout the intervention. The capacity to modify strategies and still maintain rigor is especially important in ongoing monitoring over a long period of time.

For example, knowing that the teachers in the experimental school resent the small incentive, a larger incentive, even if it were in release time from typical duties or another form, could be arranged.

Centrality of Language Because of the primacy of language and symbols in naturalistic inquiry, the meaning of what is communicated can be explored. This element is most valuable in understanding and improving communication within and among diverse groups involved in intervention action processes.

In Jennifer's case, the issue of access elicits diverse understandings and responses from interest groups. To individuals with disabilities, access means equal opportunity and civil rights (Charlton, 1998); but to small-business owners, access may denote exorbitant expense for a small and select group of people who may not spend sufficient dollars to warrant the cost. Understanding the differential interpretation of a term is critical in both planning and assessing process.

The Importance of Perspective The recognition of emic (insider) or etic (outsider) perspective of the social worker can enhance understanding and use of findings (Denzin & Lincoln, 2000).

Regarding Jennifer and access, the emic perspective might be held by numerous interest groups. As discussed, the intervention of a key-operated lift was planned by an individual without a mobility impairment. To the insider, an individual with a disability, this intervention process is one in which some barriers may be addressed, but full access is not possible. To the outsider, the intervention meets the ADA requirements for access. Reflexive implementation taking both perspectives into account provides rich discussion and direction for community education.

Shift in Knowing Power The element of "partnership" rather than top-down investigation in reflexive intervention is a valuable tool in recruiting wide participation and use of findings. If diverse groups feel that their knowledge and perspectives are important in informing change, it is likely that they will be increasingly invested in the process of assessment and revision.

In the teacher incentive intervention to improve test scores, we see that the curriculum and incentive action processes were developed without teacher input. Moreover, teacher input into reflexive intervention was not planned. Therefore, it would not be surprising to see resentment develop from the teachers, especially when they have learned that the incentive is comparatively small. A sound approach to monitoring would respect teachers as "knowers" and, perhaps through group interview, obtain their impressions and experiences of the intervention as well as methods for improvement. Having a voice in the intervention process is important, but even more critical is the understanding that the outcome success of the project is in large part a function of teacher cooperation and respect for the teachers as the experts in the classroom process.

Interspersion of Gathering Information and Analysis The capacity to use findings as the monitoring proceeds is a benefit in that changes can be made based on initial data, inquiry can be flexible and changeable in response to findings, and process evaluation can be responsive to diverse groups who would benefit from even minor revision during the course of the inquiry.

As we saw in the test score intervention, a change in incentives occurred in response to new data about external influences on the intervention process.

Naturalistic inquiry comprises multiple philosophical approaches and methodological strategies. Although we do not eschew any of these designs, we do suggest that some designs are more useful than others in process assessment. These three designs are recommended for specific purposes: interview—individual and group; passive observation; and inductive analysis of documents. Besides the discussion in Chapter 9, there are many excellent texts that detail naturalistic inquiry listed in our comprehensive bibliography.

Interview Individual interview elicits information from an individual perspective that might not be shared in a group or in writing. Individual interview can uncover information that the social worker may not have considered asking.

In the intervention to improve transition for adolescents with disabilities, youth who entered college and who participated in an experimental, comprehensive advising process were interviewed in a group about their advising experiences and needs. The findings did not reveal any need for change. However, in individual interview, the failure of the advising system became clearly evident after several students shared their resentment toward the invasion of the comprehensive advising strategies proposed in this model into their personal lives. As a result of this information, students with disabilities were asked to participate in a needs assessment halfway through the project to express their advising needs and expectations.

Group interviews are most useful in promoting "group think" and in expanding individual perspectives within a group context. Although group interview may silence uniqueness, it is designed to obtain consensus or to understand disagreement within homogeneous and/or heterogeneous groups. Members can support, stimulate, and/or silence others, allowing the evaluator to see a microcosm of group process within the intervention actions. Data collection usually occurs through audio and field-note recording, with analysis being inductive.

As the needs assessment on adolescent transition continued, the adolescents stated that the concern for them as individuals with atypical needs was not how they wanted to be perceived. As one youth said, "We want to be like others. . . . sex, drugs, and rock and roll." Thus, an important part of the monitoring process in systems change to support adolescent transition was consulting adolescents when there is uncertainty about what questions to ask. In the chapter on needs assessment, one area of need expressed by adolescents was having a voice and disseminating knowledge about their experiences and needs. Despite this articulated need, monitoring revealed that several public-speaking training sessions were poorly attended. Adolescents were therefore interviewed within a group format to seek an understanding of the poor attendance and to elicit their perspectives about increasing participation. Audio-taped transcripts revealed explicit recommendations, but the most important information was derived from the sub rosa conversations in which the adolescents talked about their resistance to participating in any activity in which the principals of their schools were involved. The action process of seeking nominations for leadership and public-speaking training from school principals was therefore changed.

Passive Observation Passive observation is a strategy frequently used to monitor clinical intervention. Through observation, discourse, as well as nonverbal interaction, can be used as data to assess action process and to provide important feedback to the clinician or the observed individual or group. Frequently, data are recorded from videotapes, audiotapes, and field notes and inductively analyzed. Passive observation is not limited to clinical assessment. There are numerous applications for this approach that range from assessing an individual to examining the efficacy of action processes in large systems.

Consider this example from Joshua's case. Observation of classroom teaching in the experimental school revealed that the teachers were choosing the time period just before lunch to implement the new curriculum to improve test scores. Students were anxious to get up from their seats and go to lunch. As a result of observation, a change in the curriculum was made, in which the teaching sessions were more interactive and delivered after students settled down in the morning.

Inductive Analysis of Documents You have probably been exposed to document review in many ways. Consider how you have been assessed on your fieldwork. A common method of process assessment is the use of process recordings or journals. An evaluator examines these documents to ascertain how your learning is unfolding. In agencies, process assessment using documentation is a convenient assessment method because they are required to document their actions and outcomes. Thus, the data set already exists. Naturalistic document review is particularly valuable when notes do not follow a systematic sequence. What is written, by whom, and in what context can yield important information for assessment and informed revision. The social worker can use many analytic strategies, including thematic analysis, content analysis, semiotic analysis, and so forth.

In the example of youth with disabilities, process recording of group therapy was one of the ways that the social worker monitored the content and processes within the group. Thematic analysis of the data revealed that the group members who had participated the longest functioned as the historians and transmitted the tacit rules for what behaviors would be tolerable within and outside the group. Thus, the process recording revealed the importance of the group process not only in producing articulated insight, but in functioning as a disciplinary structure as well.

Naturalistic inquiry is extremely valuable in reflexive intervention as a systematic process that can be inclusive, flexible, and rich with insights to improve interventions. However, we support mixed-method design in reflexive intervention whenever possible.

MIXED-METHOD DESIGN

Mixing methods, in our opinion, is most desirable in all evaluation practice but particularly in reflexive intervention. Integrating approaches allows for pluralism in data collection and analysis necessary to obtain complex and diverse knowledge upon which to yield formative suggestions. Moreover, mixed methods engage multiple interest groups and use of diverse strategies and epistemologies. Let us look at an example of how integrated design can produce a comprehensive process assessment.

In each of our cases and examples, we have illustrated how each tradition can be used to reveal information. Let us aggregate the material from Jennifer to illustrate. As we indicated, experimental-type monitoring was implemented to examine the timely completion of process objectives to achieve the goal of community education about universal access. Narrative recording and observation of the steering committee process was also implemented as a monitoring strategy. The integration of these traditions of inquiry was not only valuable in verifying that all objectives were accomplished in a timely manner, but in revealing a potential area of tension that needed to be addressed. If the grassroots-professional tension had not been uncovered, action processes, as well as planning for costs, would have been problematic despite the completion of all the process objectives.

PROCESS ASSESSMENT QUESTIONS POSED BY DIVERSE GROUPS

Now that we have looked at design traditions, let us examine how reflexive intervention may look to diverse groups. What questions can reflexive intervention answer for the multiple groups who participate in an intervention?

Using the example from Joshua's youth, we pose the questions that would be of importance to Joshua, the social worker, and the agency administrator.

Service User—Joshua
What parts of the intervention were satisfactory to me? Why?
What parts of the intervention were unsatisfactory? Why?
What parts of the intervention were easy to access or use? difficult?
How was I treated by staff?
Did the intervention include all services that I needed?
What else might I need?
What changes should be made to improve intervention access, participation, and termination?
Were the facilities and resources satisfactory to me?

Provider—Social Worker
How much service did I provide?
What did I do that I would continue? Why?
What did I do that I would not continue? Why?
How satisfactory are the intervention context and resources for me? for intervention recipients?
What activities helped me learn?
What parts helped me advance my career?
Did I feel valued?
Were recording requirements reasonable?
Was the workload appropriate?

Agency Administrator
Were the objectives of the intervention accomplished in a timely manner?
What was the cost?
What resources beyond what projected costs were needed? used?
How efficient was the intervention?
What changes should have been made in agency structure? Why?
How well did staff perform?
What external influences impacted the intervention? How?
What policy and procedural changes need to be made?
What other monitoring strategies are needed?

Ideally, process assessment will meet the needs of all interest groups involved directly or indirectly in intervention. Of course, purpose and practical considerations limit the scope, and questions asked by all groups may not be answered.

SELECTING A METHOD—GUIDING QUESTIONS

To select method, given the multitude of factors that you need to consider, look at the questions in Box 13.2. The answers to these questions will help you structure your reflexive intervention approach.

We illustrate how these questions can be used for guiding design selection in Jennifer's case. One of the interventions was the conduct of educational sessions to increase awareness of diverse community segments of the benefits of universal design. Box 13.3 provides the answers that led to the monitoring strategy.

A written registration form served as the data collection instrument. The form allowed a simple count of who was there, how each person learned of the education session, and what groups they represented.

BOX 13.2 | **GUIDING QUESTIONS FOR SELECTING A METHOD FOR REFLEXIVE INTERVENTION**

1. What is your evaluative question?
2. What are the purposive considerations?
3. What are the practical constraints—time, resources, context (acute, time-limited intervention, community-based inquiry, etc.)?
4. Which type of approach will be used—nomothetic, idiographic, or mixed method?
5. Are there multiple targets or a single target?
6. What is the scope of the inquiry?
7. Who are the audiences, and how will they best be able to consume and use the assessment knowledge to improve the intervention?

BOX 13.3 | **SAMPLE ANSWERS TO GUIDING QUESTIONS**

1. What is your evaluative question?
   How many community members attended, and what groups were represented?
2. What are the purposive considerations?
   The aim was to obtain as many people from diverse backgrounds as possible, with particular attention to recruitment of individuals who were not favorable toward spending money on improving accessibility.
3. What are the practical constraints—time, resources, context (acute, time-limited intervention, community-based inquiry, etc.)?
   The time constraint was that only a single education session could be conducted to examine if this method would meet with interest and participation from the community.
4. Which type of approach will be used—nomothetic, idiographic, or mixed method?
   Nomothetic design is appropriate for counting.
5. Are there multiple targets or a single target?
   Numerous targets included policymakers, business owners, and many other groups who were known opponents of spending money on access.
6. What is the scope of the inquiry?
   The scope is limited to a single session.
7. Who are the audiences, and how will they best be able to consume and use the assessment knowledge to improve the intervention?
   Audiences are providers, educators, disabled individuals, and those targeted as needing information on the benefits of universal design for all community members.

These guiding questions can be valuable tools to help you find a viable and reasonable strategy for reflexive intervention. You will see that each question simplifies the thinking and planning processes necessary to choose cogent and useful action processes.

MAIN POINTS

1. Experimental-type and naturalistic traditions of inquiry each have unique uses in reflexive intervention.
2. A full range of nonexperimental, preexperimental, and quasi-experimental designs can be useful in monitoring group action processes and cost analysis.
3. Naturalistic inquiry can be used in reflexive intervention to examine contextual and pluralistic factors that are inherent in all intervention processes.
4. Mixed-method design is the most complete and versatile approach to reflexive intervention.
5. Diverse participants are interested in the answers to different and varied questions in the intervention process.
6. Selecting an approach to reflexive intervention is dependent on purpose, resources, audience, and expected use of the data.

EXERCISES

1. Look at the mission of your agency or one to which you have access. Then, examine the goals and objectives for one specific intervention and the monitoring processes that are in place.
2. Critically evaluate the monitoring process to determine what methods are used to monitor implementation processes, costs, and external influences.
3. What are the strengths and limitations of the monitoring approach?
4. To what extent does the approach specify criteria for the successful completion of objectives? What is the scope of the inquiry?
5. What changes would you suggest to the reflexive implementation plan? Why?

ASSESSING OUTCOMES

PART 4

THINKING PROCESSES IN OUTCOME ASSESSMENT

CHAPTER 14

Introduction: Outcome Assessment as One Step in Evaluation Practice

Definitions

Essential Elements of Outcome Assessment

Main Points

Exercises

INTRODUCTION: OUTCOME ASSESSMENT AS ONE STEP IN EVALUATION PRACTICE

Outcome assessment is frequently considered the primary element in the evaluation process. Even though outcome assessment is essential, it cannot be comprehensive, soundly planned, and used without the thinking and action processes of problem statement, needs assessment, and formulation of goals and objectives. As we proceed through this chapter, note the strengths and limitations of outcome assessment. What can we come to know from this action process, and what can we not know? This chapter discusses the answers to these questions.

DEFINITIONS

An **outcome** is the result of being acted upon by or participating in an action process. We commonly think of outcomes as changes that occur following a planned intervention, although in some cases change may not be the intended result of an action. Think, for example, of prevention programs in which the status quo is the desired outcome. This point provides a segue to the important recognition of intended and unintended outcomes. Intended outcomes are those that are planned and elicited. Unintended outcomes are those that occur but were not named as desired. Unintended outcomes can range from extremely positive to harmful and are important to keep in mind throughout our discussion of outcome.

Outcome assessment is a set of thinking and action processes to ascertain and document what occurs as a result of being voluntarily or involuntarily exposed to a purposive process and to assess the worth of an intervention. Assessment of both planned and unintended occurrences is contained within outcome assessment. Let us look at *Joshua* to illustrate the notions of expected and unexpected outcomes.

To attain the long-term goal of elimination of substance abuse in Joshua's youth, two intermediate goals were established: to increase Joshua's awareness and acknowledgement of his problematic substance use and to be accepted to college.

Objectives for the second goal were established:

1. *Joshua will seek information about colleges, acceptance criteria, and college application procedures.*
2. *Joshua will identify three colleges to which he will apply and will indicate why he selected these institutions.*
3. *Joshua will complete and submit applications to three colleges.*

The expected outcomes were delimited to Joshua's application to three colleges. Why were acceptance and completion of college not included as expected outcomes? First, although these outcomes are desired and implicit, they would not necessarily result from actions that Joshua could take, and thus expecting what is outside one's control is not reasonable. Acceptance is a positive consequence that would occur from the completion of the objectives. Second, it was implied in the expected outcomes that Joshua would graduate from college, but what he would do with his degree was not defined. His advancement to law school and his commitment to work with the social issue of educational equity for poor students were therefore other unexpected positive consequences of the intervention. Interestingly, this legislative agenda emerged from Joshua's experience with negative attitudes about his ability to be successful in college in light of his poor test performance. An unexpected consequence of a negative experience turned into a lifelong career commitment for Joshua.

In social work, most outcome assessment focuses on the examination of the extent to which planned changes resulted from participation in an intervention. However, in evaluation practice, as indicated previously, we suggest a much broader definition than that provided in traditional approaches. Note that this definition, unlike the typical notion of cause-and-effect assessment between intervention and outcome, expands not only the scope of inquiry, but the methods that are acceptable in outcome assessment. These methods will be addressed later in the chapter. Direct measurement of cause-and-effect relationships is difficult in experimental-type evaluation designs due to constraints of investigation in the field and ethical dilemmas that accompany true experimentation. If we limited our outcome assessment only to the investigation of cause-and-effect relationships using traditional quantitative methods, our understanding of outcomes, as well as our methods for accountability, would be significantly limited.

Consider this example. What if Joshua had found literature that identified a curriculum that was documented as successful in producing significant increases in student scores on standardized tests? However, the curriculum was implemented with urban students only, and the school district wanted to test the curriculum before committing to it. We know that standardized test scores often have great influence over a student's school career, so how could Joshua test the outcome of the curriculum? If he used a true-experimental design, the control group would not have access to the curriculum. Would it be unethical to hypothesize that only one group of students would improve and the other would remain in the low range of scores?

ESSENTIAL ELEMENTS OF OUTCOME ASSESSMENT

Let us now look at the essential elements of outcome assessment in more detail.

Systematic Inquiry

Outcome assessment uses systematic inquiry to examine the relationship between an intervention and outcomes at multiple system levels, including the levels of individuals, groups, communities, and cultures. In outcome assessment, the design used should lay the groundwork for investigating the link between an intervention and its result, even if it is not feasible to conduct true experimentation.

We return to the issue of low test scores as an example. An experimental intervention was implemented in two schools, one in which teachers were given a financial incentive and one in which teachers were not. As we saw, test scores for students in both schools increased. How do we look at and make sense of these findings? We know that both schools participated in a new curriculum, after which the students improved on test scores. We also know that the "control" school improved significantly more than the experimental school. Although we cannot interpret these findings as causal, we can clearly see the association between curriculum and increases in test scores and note that something about resources was also associated with these increases. This information cannot tell us what caused the increase but serves as the basis for future scrutiny. At least we would know that the interventions were not followed by a decrease in scores, and thus we might be willing to implement the curriculum again, perhaps making some changes in the intervention as well as the outcome assessment. It might make sense to alter the curriculum and give a mock test that would not remain on a student's permanent record to observe how students fared following a change in intervention. Each piece of associational information gets us closer to an understanding of the correlates of outcome.

Obtaining a comprehensive picture of correlates allows the social worker to investigate these factors in the future through establishing a study to determine which individual or group of factors can predict outcome on test scores. Once predictors are known, we have important information to inform future intervention. Adding an observational element of inquiry could provide further evidence on how students respond to the intervention and to the testing condition. We might even ask the students to assess the degree to which they felt that the intervention helped them improve their test taking.

Articulation and Testing of an Intervention

In evaluation practice, measurement of results is in itself insufficient to depict outcome. A clear articulation of the intervention and its parts and an attempt to examine which part of an intervention relates to or caused a result are necessary. This point is critical when we consider intended and unintended outcomes. Without specification of the intervention parts and processes, it is not possible even to begin to ferret out the part or parts of an intervention to which an outcome is related.

In the previous example, if we had looked only at the financial incentive, we would have missed important information about the curriculum intervention. Thus, the curriculum had to be clearly described along with the experimental condition of incentive in order for us to identify a change that might be contributing to an increase in test scores.

Value-Based Inquiry

Outcome assessment specifies what should occur following an intervention, what should change or stay the same following an intervention, or what should be changed or not as a result of an intervention. Thus, outcome assessment both specifies and examines the extent to which what is valued and desired occurred following or as a result of a planned action. The desired outcome is the reduction or elimination of a problem, and problems are defined as statements of value.

Furthermore, how these desired outcomes are measured and how success criteria are specified are action processes that are dependent on values and opinions. As we discuss action processes in the next chapter, keep in mind that purpose is a driving influence in the choice of methods.

For example, to one provider in Joshua's case, success would have meant sobriety (the elimination of the undesirable condition of intoxication); to the other, success was defined as effort toward college entrance (the reduction in idle time leading to problem drinking).

Inquiry Informed by Description of the Interventive Approach, the Context of the Intervention, and the Change Agent

Clarification of the intervention and its variations is critical to understanding not only what happened but how and why the change occurred. Reflexive intervention therefore has an essential role in outcome assessment in that monitoring is a detailed and systematic analysis of what was done and how, when, and by whom it was done. When linked with outcomes, process assessment provides the detail about an intervention that allows the evaluator to look at how different parts and variations result in diverse outcomes.

As we saw in our example, if the curriculum had been omitted and resources beyond the base budget of each of the two schools were involved in the intervention to increase test scores, many errors in interpretation could have been made, and Joshua would not be any further along in his change effort.

Efficiency and Cost Analysis

Although cost analysis is an element of reflexive intervention, it is also a major part of outcome assessment. The focus of cost analysis in outcome assessment is the determination of worth. Worth refers to the degree to which the outcome warrants the expenditure of resources. Both value and efficiency are factored into the determination of worth.

Consider Jennifer. What if the cost of community education about universal access is not considered to be worthy, given the small number of individuals with mobility impairment in the community? Or, what if community education is considered to be valuable but does not produce the magnitude of desired results? In both cases, the worth of the intervention is limited. In the second case, efficiency is not obtained. To have positive worth, an intervention must maintain its value and achieve an accepted degree of success in an efficient manner as revealed in outcome assessment.

Investigation of Problem Resolution

In essence, all aspects of our evaluation practice model refer to the extent to which an identified problem has been resolved in part or in total as a result of or following an intervention. Assessment of outcome allows the social worker to make some judgments about problem resolution because each step of the evaluation practice process derives from the problem statement.

You are now familiar with the multiple problems identified in the cases of Joshua and Jennifer. For Joshua as a youth, the social worker would want to know the extent to which the intervention contributed to Joshua's self-esteem and worth and would direct outcome attention to reduction in alcohol abuse. In Jennifer's case, the first problem to solve would be comfort with intimacy. Second, the barriers to Jennifer's access to her workplace would be problems to be removed by the intervention. Third, the problem of systematic exclusion of individuals with disabilities from community environments would be a long-term problem to be addressed by intervention in Jennifer's case.

Contribution to Professional Knowledge Base

Although outcome assessment is traditionally and primarily initiated for the purpose of ascertaining the success of an intervention in achieving its goals, we agree with the position that this inquiry contributes to the overall professional knowledge base, in the ways listed in Box 14.1.

Examination of Multiple Direct and Indirect Targets

For evaluative as well as knowledge-building purposes, outcome assessment applies to numerous populations. Box 14.2, using both *Jennifer* and *Joshua* to illustrate, lists typical targets of outcome assessment. **Targets** are those individuals, groups, or units that are expected to demonstrate a desirable outcome due to participation in intervention. Direct targets are those who are addressed in the problem statement and identified in the needs assessment as needing change. Indirect targets are those who are not identified as needing change but who ultimately benefit from the change demonstrated by the direct targets.

MAIN POINTS

1. Outcome assessment was defined as the set of thinking and action processes that are enacted to document the reduction of a problem following or resulting from participation in an intervention.
2. Outcome assessment involves the application of research design to inquiry about intervention efficacy.

BOX 14.1 | OUTCOME ASSESSMENT AS KNOWLEDGE BUILDING

Allows for replication of successful interventions and planning of future services based on empirical evidence

Provides knowledge for comparison of interventions

Provides feedback for knowledge and advancement of individual practice

Allows for prediction of outcomes

Contributes to empirical practice knowledge

BOX 14.2 | TYPICAL TARGETS OF OUTCOME ASSESSMENT

Direct targets
   The client or service recipient—*Jennifer* and *Joshua* in counseling; teachers and students in the case of low test scores

Indirect targets
   The professional delivering the intervention—counselors working with *Jennifer* and *Joshua*; curriculum trainers working with teachers in Joshua's state; community educators working in Jennifer's community

   The intervention team—social worker and agency team working with Joshua as a youth; Joshua, the legislature, and the school district personnel in the problem of low test scores; community educators and the school district in the problem of limited access

   The payer—vocational rehabilitation in Joshua's youth; taxpayers in the problem of low test scores and limited community access

   The profession—social work; education

   The global professional community

   Policymakers and policy

3. Outcome assessment is informed by process assessment.
4. These are the essential elements of outcome assessment:
   a. Systematic inquiry
   b. Articulation and testing of an intervention
   c. Value-based inquiry
   d. Inquiry informed by description of the interventive approach, the context of the intervention, and the change agent
   e. Efficiency and cost analysis

f. Investigation of problem resolution
   g. Contribution to professional knowledge base
   h. Examination of multiple direct and indirect targets

EXERCISES

Analyze an outcome assessment from the literature for the following purposes:

1. Identify the problems to be reduced and/or resolved by the intervention.
2. State the explicit and implicit values.
3. Discuss the direct and indirect targets who are tested.
4. Identify the worth criteria if they are explicated.
5. Suggest how this inquiry can contribute to professional knowledge and apply to practice.

ACTION PROCESSES OF OUTCOME RESEARCH: LOOKING AT GROUP OUTCOME

CHAPTER 15

Four Steps of Outcome Assessment

True Experimental Design in Outcome Assessment

Using Nonexperimental to Quasi-Experimental Approaches in Outcome Assessment

Alternative Strategies to Attribute Outcome to Intervention

Main Points

Exercises

FOUR STEPS OF OUTCOME ASSESSMENT

In this chapter, we present and analyze methods of assessing group outcome. The purposive context of evaluation practice has been repeated throughout the text, but you must keep purpose in mind, especially as we discuss the processes that have been typically viewed as "objective."

Let us turn our focus to the discrete action elements of outcome assessment. Regardless of purpose or approach, all outcome assessment action processes involve the four major steps listed in Box 15.1.

In this chapter, we apply the four action processes to experimental-type approaches to outcome assessment. As discussed in Chapter 7 on clarifying need, experimental-type designs exist but are not always practical. Of course, using true experimental design to understand cause-and-effect relationships between an intervention and the desired outcome would be most desirable from a methodological standpoint. Let us look at how this design can be planned and implemented in the field.

TRUE EXPERIMENTAL DESIGN IN OUTCOME ASSESSMENT

Review the discussion in Chapter 7 on the logical foundation of true experimental design. To eliminate bias from your study and to obtain a clear picture of the degree to which an independent variable produced a change in the dependent variable, the three elements of randomization, control, and manipulation must be present. Evaluation practice presents ethical and practical challenges to structuring an inquiry with these three criteria. The condition of "withholding," necessary for control, is only one of the design elements that can pose an ethical dilemma when subjects are people who are in need of services. The example that we present shows you some of the techniques typically used to circumvent field constraints such as withholding.

Consider the example of a new education program designed to increase safe-sex behavior among teens. In evaluation practice, all steps from the articulation of the problem statement to reflexive intervention would ideally have preceded outcome assessment. To examine outcome, based on previous steps, purpose, resource needs, constraints, and so forth, you decide that true experimental design would be most useful. However, you have some ethical considerations to address, including your own belief that all students should have the opportunity to participate in the intervention, so you are careful in how you structure the experimental and control conditions.

To obtain a control group, you decide to randomly stagger participation rather than eliminate it altogether for the subjects who would serve as a control group. Thus, the control condition would be the waiting list; and the desired outcome, safe-sex behaviors, could be measured at pretest and posttest intervals for the experimental and waiting-list groups. By using a waiting list as a control, you are satisfied that the intervention would be available for all teens while you are also meeting the conditions of true experimentation.

> **BOX 15.1** | **FOUR ACTION PROCESSES IN OUTCOME ASSESSMENT**
>
> 1. Based on summative objectives, articulate lexical definitions (definitions expressed in words) of desired outcomes and criteria for success.
> 2. Delineate the exact evaluation questions.
> 3. Design the structure of assessment action processes with attention to field constraints.
> 4. Conduct the outcome assessment inquiry with attention to ethical, field, and resource constraints.

Unfortunately, the likelihood of implementing true experimentation with sufficient rigor is unlikely in most cases. Threats to validity and reliability, such as sampling bias, experimental mortality, and so forth, would be factors that compromise the efficacy of the findings. However, there are many ways to examine outcome even when attribution to the intervention is not directly observed.

USING NONEXPERIMENTAL TO QUASI-EXPERIMENTAL APPROACHES IN OUTCOME ASSESSMENT

In Table 15.1, we present nonexperimental to true experimental designs and the types of outcome questions that each can answer. As discussed previously, these designs are called nomothetic because they focus on group rather than individual phenomena. Thus, experimental-type designs are used to examine program outcome rather than individual outcome.

We use Campbell and Stanley (1963) notation in Table 15.1 to describe design structures. X always denotes the independent variable, which in outcome assessment is the intervention. O signifies the outcome or set of outcomes that you are testing. To depict the nature of randomization, we use uppercase R to denote both random selection of the sample and random assignment to experimental and control group. Lowercase r refers to random group assignment without random selection of the sample. If either uppercase or lowercase r is absent, then we know that randomization has not occurred at all.

Table 15.1 shows that experimental-type designs that do not meet the requirements for true experiments can answer important questions about an intervention. They cannot specify that the intervention created the outcome, but these approaches to inquiry can provide systematically derived evidence to measure desired phenomena or changes following an intervention. We will illustrate how each design in Table 15.1 can be structured and used to generate outcome knowledge.

| TABLE 15.1 | FREQUENTLY USED NOMOTHETIC DESIGNS AND QUESTIONS THAT THEY CAN ANSWER |

Design	Question*
XO (observation of the desired outcome following an intervention)	What happened following the intervention?
OXO (pretest, posttest, where the desired outcome is measured prior to and following an intervention)	What changed following the intervention?
O X O O O (pretest, posttest, with control group, no random assignment)	What comparative changes followed the intervention and control conditions?
rOXO rO O (true experimental design without random sample selection) A population is randomly assigned to experimental and control condition and pretested on the desired outcome. Following the delivery of the intervention to the experimental group only, both groups are posttested on desired outcome.	In the participating group, what changes were caused by the intervention?
ROXO RO O (true experimental design with random sample selection) A sample is randomly selected and assigned to experimental and control condition and pretested on the desired outcome. Following the delivery of the intervention to the experimental group only, both groups are posttested on desired outcome.	What changes were caused by the intervention in the population?
OOOXOOO A group is tested repeatedly on desired outcome, given the intervention, and then tested repeatedly after the intervention.	What changes were seen over time as a result of the intervention?

*Questions can be altered by statistical testing and manipulation.

We revisit Joshua in his quest to improve standardized test scores for elementary students in his state. The planned intervention was the implementation of teacher incentives to stimulate improvement in student scores. To begin the planned intervention, all students in grades 1–6 participated in a pilot program conducted in one school. To assess outcome, standard test scores were examined at the end of the pilot year. Given the field constraints, two outcome assessment designs were possible, one for students in first grade and one for all students in second through sixth grades.

For the first-grade class, an XO design had to be planned because no previous test scores were available for this group of students. For first-graders, the evaluation question was "What were student scores following the incentive program?" As you can see, the degree to which the teacher incentive caused the test scores cannot be answered by this design. All we can know from this approach is how well the first-grade students scored after the incentive program. Why use this type of assessment? What if the first-grade scores for the pilot program were much higher than scores for first-graders in previous years? Certainly, Joshua would have a sound basis on which to suggest that teacher incentives produced the improvement. Conversely, if scores were not higher than in previous years, the planned intervention might be reconsidered.

In the second- through sixth-grade classes, a more sophisticated design was possible as test scores from previous years were already available. An OXO design could therefore be implemented to test outcome using existing data for the pretest.

The outcome question answered by the OXO design was "To what extent did scores change following the intervention?" As you can see, the OXO design, although it still cannot attribute the cause of the outcome to the intervention, provides stronger support for the intervention if there is improvement in scores on posttest.

Let us look at more specifics so you can see how to plan and implement this type of inquiry. A pilot school in which the teachers were told that they would be paid a financial incentive for an increase in test scores was selected because of its traditionally low scores on the standardized tests given at the end of each school year in June. To conduct the outcome study, the social worker obtained the raw test scores for grades 2–6 for the year preceding the intervention (pretest) and for grades 1–6 the year of the intervention (posttest).

Two types of statistical tests were conducted, measures of central tendency to describe each group of scores (pretest and posttest) and an inferential statistic, the t-test for dependent samples, to examine the degree to which any significant change occurred in the test scores of students in grades 2–6. (See Appendix for more detail on these basic statistics.)

Table 15.2 presents the descriptive and inferential findings for grades 2–6.

The mean score for students in grades 2–6 on the pretest was 34, with a standard deviation of 12. Thus, approximately 66% of the scores in this school district fall between 22 and 46. Following the incentive intervention, the mean score rose to 42, with a standard deviation of 14. Although it appears that the scores increased, we cannot know if the increase was a chance occurrence or

TABLE 15.2 | DESCRIPTIVE AND INFERENTIAL FINDINGS FOR GRADES 2–6*

Pretest mean and standard deviation	Posttest mean and standard deviation	t-test and probability
M = 34, SD = 12	M = 42, SD = 14	t = 4.72, p = .002

*Test scores range from 0 to 100 with ascending scores indicating greater skill and knowledge.

not. The social worker therefore choose a t-test for dependent samples to analyze the data. A significant difference was found, and thus Joshua concluded that the students did actually improve after the intervention. The teachers were paid. (See Table 15.2.)

The second effort in improving test scores using an incentive system was conducted in two schools. The schools were chosen because they were similar to one another in composition and test score level. Each school implemented a "test-focused" curriculum. In the volunteer test school, the teachers were paid incentives for improvements in student test scores; in the other school, there was no incentive. Again, due to field constraints, two types of outcome assessment designs were conducted. The first-graders illustrate an $\frac{XO}{O}$ design, where X = incentive intervention and O = student test scores. This outcome assessment answered the question "How did student scores from the experimental school differ from student scores in the control school?"

The remainder of the grades could participate in an $\frac{O \times O}{O O}$ design as test scores were available prior to the intervention. For second grade and above, the outcome question was "How did scores change following the intervention compared to scores in which no incentive program was implemented?"

Unlike in the pilot program, once we add the control school, we are able to conduct an inquiry in which changes in scores following an intervention can be compared to changes in scores with no intervention.

Similar to the pilot program, scores at both schools were collected for two administrations of the test and subjected to analysis. This time, the social worker decided to conduct several analyses.

First, to describe the pretest scores for both schools for grades 2–6, means and standard deviations were computed. Table 15.3 presents these findings.

School 1 (experimental) had a mean pretest score of 42, with a standard deviation of 11. School 2 (control) had a mean pretest score of 39, with a standard deviation of 16. To examine whether the difference in pretest scores was significant or a chance occurrence, the social worker chose to conduct a t-test for independent samples. No significant difference was found, and thus the pretest scores were considered to be equivalent.

To compare the posttest outcome, the social worker decided to look at the mean change scores for grades 2–6. To do this, the pretest scores were sub-

TABLE 15.3 | PRETEST SCORES IN EXPERIMENTAL AND CONTROL SCHOOLS

	Pretest mean and SD
Experimental school (1)	M = 42, SD = 11
Control school (2)	M = 39, SD = 16
t-test	$t = 1.2, p = .12$

TABLE 15.4 | MEAN CHANGE SCORES, STANDARD DEVIATIONS, AND t-TEST FOR INDEPENDENT SAMPLES

Experimental school (1)	Control school (2)	t-test
M = 15, SD = 6	M = 21, SD = 7.2	$t = 7.3, p = .007$

tracted from the posttest scores. The mean and standard deviation for the changed scores were computed for each school and then compared with the t-test for independent samples. Table 15.4 presents these data.

A significant difference was noted, but not as expected. The school without the incentive improved significantly more than the school with the incentive. However, if we had interpreted these results as cause and effect, we may have concluded that the incentive did not produce an increase when compared to the control school. However, this design structure cannot answer questions about the cause of the outcome. No random assignment of the experimental condition was accomplished. There was no way to know if the schools were actually equivalent, and as we saw, the control school did not volunteer for the incentive because of the infusion of private money. If the schools were randomly assigned to experimental and control condition, you might be able to conclude that the change in scores was attributable to the intervention. However, in this case, it is clear that random assignment of two schools to either condition is not possible, as the schools themselves were in actuality not equivalent.

As you can see by the examples, many questions about interventions can be answered without true experimentation. The key to sound evaluation practice using these strategies is to make sure that when you interpret your findings, you do not exceed the capacity of the design. If you cannot support a causal relationship between intervention and outcome, do not make that claim.

Considering these examples and the likelihood that true experimentation will not be feasible, how can we structure nomothetic outcome assessment so that results can be attributed to the intervention?

ALTERNATIVE STRATEGIES TO
ATTRIBUTE OUTCOME TO INTERVENTION

Statistical manipulation and modeling are methods that can be used to examine cause-and-effect relationships in the absence of the ability to structure a true experiment mechanically, but they are often not feasible due to cost and practical constraints. It is not likely that the conduct of or the findings from these methods will be accessible to diverse audiences beyond those who are well versed in complex statistical methods. Moreover, because we see evaluation practice as integral to all arenas of social work, complex statistical modeling does not serve the majority of practitioners, as it is a skill that even few researchers possess. We do not want to suggest that statistical complexity should never be used. Rather, cautious and purposive use is indicated in situations where the targets, audiences, and purposes provide the rationale. For example, statistical modeling might be indicated in a medical setting where the actual manipulation of an intervention could pose some danger. The capacity to use a modeling technique to create conditions statistically would avoid risk while contributing to an understanding of the extent to which an outcome could be predicted by the presence, absence, or degree of an intervention offered.

There are some outcome assessment approaches that we have found extremely useful for examining cause and effect between the intervention and outcome if implementing true experimentation is not feasible. One strategy often overlooked is asking participants themselves to report their opinion of the degree to which an intervention caused an outcome. Although this approach does not allow empirical observation of change, it does address attribution through self-report. It is also reasonable to ask participants how and when they expect the change to be observed. This type of outcome assessment is particularly valuable in workshops where the desirable outcome is participant learning and use of learning in a specified context. Consider the following example.

In the community education on universal access in Jennifer's case, several methods were used to assess outcome. First, there was a brief quiz administered to participants after the session (XO, where X = educational session and O = quiz) to ascertain the extent to which participants understood the concepts discussed in the session. Second, the respondents were asked to rate the extent to which they increased their knowledge of universal access as a result of their participation (X = session and O = participant rating). Can you see that a simple XO design answers several questions, including "reported outcome" resulting from the intervention?

A second strategy, using observers to judge the extent to which a change occurred, can be a very useful approach to outcome assessment. Consider, for example, parent observation of a child. Parent report of change in the desired direction following the intervention is a strong case for attribution.

Third, triangulating methods, or using multiple approaches to investigate a single phenomenon, provides more than one data source upon which to suggest attribution of change to an intervention.

Let us consider the example of test score improvement addressed by Joshua. Suppose we were interested in testing the efficacy of the new curriculum designed to target learning to the skills and knowledge that are being tested on the standardized, year-end assessment. If the children were asked the same information that was on the standardized tests but in a different manner, mastery of the knowledge and skill that the standardized test purports to measure and to which the curriculum teaches would be assessed in two ways. The degree to which the scores are associated could yield important information on outcome. What if, for example, students did well on the alternative test but not on the standardized test? These findings would indicate that the curriculum could have contributed to the accomplishment of articulated knowledge and skill objectives but may not be addressing the other aspects of the standardized test, such as its structure. How would you look at this relationship?

The standardized test is scored on the scale 0–100. To obtain a score that could be compared to the standardized score, the social worker developed a checklist for observation. The checklist was carefully constructed to measure the same knowledge and skills that are tested by the standardized instrument. The scoring was also structured to yield a range of interval-level scores between 0 and 100, with ascending scores indicating greater knowledge and skill. Trained observers randomly selected the classes to observe in a single school. After observing classroom activity at regular intervals over the year, each student was scored on the observation. The observation scores were compared to the test scores through the computation of the Pearson's r correlation coefficient. This statistical test looks at the magnitude and direction of the relationship between two sets of scores (see Appendix). A score of $r = .23$ was obtained, indicating a small, positive relationship between the standard and observed measures. From this information, Joshua concluded that the testing conditions were not testing the same constructs. To find out what the tests were actually testing, more inquiry was indicated. It might be possible that the standardized test was measuring test taking, language, or some other factor; or it is possible that the observation measure might be problematic.

Finally, using multiple stakeholder or target groups to render opinions about the success of an intervention can be an important and compelling way to ascertain outcome.

Consider the adolescent transition project introduced earlier. In response to the problem of difficult transition to adulthood for adolescents with disabilities, the need was articulated to enhance the successful transition to adulthood, productivity, and financial independence for this diverse population through the development, implementation, evaluation, and expansion of a collaborative, accessible, comprehensive, culturally competent model program. A steering committee and a participatory action team (PAT) were created in the planning year to form an integrated model partnership. These entities oversaw and participated in intervention in a pilot region of the state that comprised the following activities: (a) using a force field analysis planning tool to develop an articulated set of adolescent-centered procedures through which adolescents were identified, their transitions were planned, and support and services necessary for successful transition were obtained; and (b) training those involved in adolescent transition about the special needs of this group and in the use of the newly codified adolescent-centered procedures.

To evaluate the pilot effort, a survey was developed and distributed to key respondents representing the stakeholder groups included in the project. The survey asked respondents to rate the importance of categorically arranged project activities on both meeting specific project goals and addressing performance indicators that were established for all programs in the nation funded under the same initiative. This strategy was used as an outcome assessment as the actual outcomes of the project were long-term, ideological, and not specifically aimed at meeting the performance indicators established by the federal government. The design allowed the project staff to ascertain the perspectives of multiple groups regarding the value of the activities in meeting statewide needs, addressing the problem of difficult transition, and linking the project activities to performance indicators.

As you can see, there are many methods that can be used to examine outcome, including true experimental design and other experimental-type approaches. The following chapters will discuss other methods that you can use to examine outcome, some of which can be mixed with experimental-type methods to strengthen and expand your knowledge of outcome.

MAIN POINTS

1. All outcome assessment consists of four essential steps.
2. True experimental design is difficult to implement but methodologically sound for attributing outcomes to interventions. Techniques such as staggering waiting lists can be ethical and reasonable ways of creating control conditions.
3. The use of true experimentation is infrequent due to field and ethical constraints.
4. Nonexperimental to quasi-experimental strategies for examining outcomes can answer important questions about description and change in desired outcomes but do not attribute change to the intervention.
5. Alternative inquiry approaches such as self-report and triangulation can be used to explore a causal relationship between an intervention and outcome when true experimentation is not possible.

EXERCISES

1. Pose an outcome assessment plan for the teen pregnancy prevention example discussed in this and the previous chapter.
2. Compare and contrast the use of true experimental strategies with quasi-experimental methods and alternatives for looking at a causal relationship between intervention and outcome.

3. Find an example of a true experimental outcome assessment in the literature. Critically analyze the ethical concerns presented. How would you address these concerns using an alternative nomothetic design?
4. List the ethical concerns that you believe can result from each of the outcome approaches we have discussed.
5. How would you address the ethical concerns that you listed in Exercise 4?

16

CHAPTER

OUTCOME ASSESSMENT USING IDIOGRAPHIC DESIGNS

Investigating Outcome Through Naturalistic, Mixed-Method, and Case Study Design

Definition of Idiographic Designs
Three Idiographic Design Types
Main Points
Exercises

DEFINITION OF IDIOGRAPHIC DESIGNS

In this chapter, we turn to the use of idiographic designs in outcome assessment. Unlike nomothetic approaches, which are intended to characterize what is most typical in groups, **idiographic** designs are those that investigate context-embedded phenomena. Usually these approaches are naturalistic in character and do not seek to generalize findings to populations beyond the single investigation. Many texts use the terms idiographic and qualitative interchangeably. We use idiographic in this chapter specifically to depict the contextual nature of the approach and its potential to focus on individual outcomes as well as outcomes in single instances of an intervention.

THREE IDIOGRAPHIC DESIGN TYPES

Many social workers and evaluators suggest that experimental-type strategies that rely on numeric data and sampling procedures are the only methods by which outcome can be examined. We believe that within the tradition of idiographic design, naturalistic methods, single case approaches, and mixed or multimethod designs are extremely valuable. Although many authors suggest that single case approaches are mixed-method designs, we treat them separately here since they are particular and characterized by their focus on a single unit of analysis. They describe the richness of the intervention process and provide data that can be used to examine causal relationships, particularly when external validity is not an aim, as is the case with most outcome assessment. We will explore each of the three design types in more detail.

Naturalistic Inquiry

Refer to the chapters on needs assessment and process assessment for detailed discussions of naturalistic design. As we have suggested, even though naturalistic design is not concerned with external validity, neither do the evaluation practitioners, for the most part, have the task of generalizability. Thus, the typical criticism of naturalistic design, that it is context-bound, is not relevant for evaluation practice unless a purpose of evaluation is to broaden the results of an inquiry to a population represented by the tested sample. The use of naturalistic inquiry can be powerful not only to examine what has happened following an intervention, but to ascertain why and to identify nuances in outcome that are related to specific characteristics of the intervention. Moreover, because naturalistic inquiry is pluralistic and inductive, complexity can be characterized and depicted in both intervention and outcome. However, in order to use naturalistic strategies to uncover cause-and-effect linkages between intervention and outcome, data analytic approaches that move beyond description are indicated (that is, taxonomic analysis, grounded theory, and so forth).

Naturalistic inquiry also provides the investigator with the flexibility to change approaches as the inquiry unfolds and can therefore be an excellent strategy to examine outcome when operational definitions of outcome criteria are vague.

Let us consider Jennifer in this example. Naturalistic inquiry strategies would be extremely valuable in assessing the extent to which community education in universal access contributes to community support for expanding public access to individuals with disabilities. Observation of community education would be important to ascertain the "culture" of the community and how that culture might shift and change in attitudes as a result of participating. But, would a simple attitude scale be more cogent in assessing attitude change? Although scales can measure articulated attitudes, they often cannot go beyond the rhetoric of social desirability (Fink, 1995d). Observation, however, which systematically examines patterned indicators of attitude in behavior and interaction (Denzin & Lincoln, 2000), can be triangulated with attitude measure or used by itself.

Despite the almost endless design possibilities offered by the naturalistic tradition, we suggest that evaluators consider the purposive use of strategies that can be explained to and understood by the evaluation audience. Complex and infrequently used approaches to naturalistic outcome assessment, such as semiotic analysis, heuristic methods, and so forth, should be reserved for audiences who are familiar with these naturalistic traditions.

We suggest that well-known strategies such as open-ended interview (face-to-face, Web-based, or paper-and-pencil, with one or more respondents), unstructured, nonparticipant observation, and/or qualitative analysis of documents be considered when asking for description of experiences before, during, and following intervention.

In Jennifer's case, assessing the extent to which attitudes toward universal access are favorably influenced by participation in the community education program might best be approached by face-to-face interview of selected participants or group interview in which participants discuss if and how to allocate resources to a universal design effort beginning in the school. Within the interview processes, the social worker would be looking for statements of attitude change and attribution of any change to the education intervention.

How might the social worker go about this type of inquiry? In this case, the social worker decides to conduct two types of interview: group interview and individual interview. For the group interview, key informants are identified by the educational program providers. One representative each from school administration, teachers, nondisabled parents of students with disabilities, and members of the community is recruited and asked to consent to audiotaped group interview. The social worker schedules the interview session, and after introducing its purpose of discussing opinions of universal access, guides the discussion with open-ended questions about the points made in the educational program, about the attitude toward universal design, and about any changes in opinion resulting from participation in the intervention. Audiotaped interviews are subjected to thematic analysis to reveal commonly held beliefs and changes in opinion, reported to have resulted from the intervention.

Representatives of the same interest groups are recruited for individual, face-to-face interviews, and audiotaped interviews are analyzed with thematic analysis. The social worker aggregates both data sets and conducts a third analysis. This type of inquiry can answer many questions, including differences in how individuals and groups report responding to an intervention on a culturally sensitive topic.

Artifact review, the examination of objects and their meanings, is also useful and can be fashioned to elicit rich description of how change occurred during and after an intervention.

Look at how these strategies are used by the evaluators in the curriculum intervention to improve test scores. In both schools, student assignments in reading, writing, and math can be collected and analyzed for their demonstration of knowledge and skills covered in the test. Comparisons of knowledge and skills between artifacts and tested data would yield important findings. If there is basic consistency between methods of assessing knowledge and skills, the evaluators could make the claim that the test actually measures what the curriculum is designed to teach. Thus, the scores on the test would be accepted as accurate indicators of student performance. On the other hand, inconsistency between test and assignment performance would indicate that different constructs were being assessed by each method. Further investigation would then be warranted to examine the accuracy of the test to assess what has been taught, assigned, and practiced in the curriculum. In the experimental condition, teacher efficacy in presenting the curriculum could be assessed as well through examining assignments, observing the teacher-student interaction, and even using another method of assessing student knowledge and skills.

A major consideration in the use of naturalistic outcome assessment is the perspective that one brings to the effort. Whether emic (insider) or etic (outsider), the investigator must be careful to be reflexive and look at his or her influence over the investigative process, findings, and use of outcome assessment knowledge. Let us look at what can happen when an investigator does not engage in reflexive analysis.

In a recent evaluation class, two students conducted an evaluation of an antiracism intervention by interviewing four individuals who attended the training. One of the students interpreted the results to mean that the training was not effective in increasing awareness of and activism to eliminate white racism. The other student saw the outcome of the training as an intersection between the beginning point of awareness, reason for entering the training, and process through which each individual journeyed. Why were the interpretations so disparate? Both students failed to reflect on their own experiential and theoretical perspectives and the way in which those lenses influenced their interpretations of an identical data set. Once the students looked at their personal lens, they came to consensus that the antiracism intervention could not be assessed by nomothetic strategies because participants brought such different perspectives, experiences, needs, and expected outcomes to the training. One individual, for example, wanted to validate her openness to all persons of color and in so doing, did not accept the premise of the training that everyone was racist. Another participant came to the training with the purpose of learning activist skills, since he had been a victim of oppression because of his sexual preference. In negotiating the interpretation of the data, the students were able to see the process of the training and identify numerous factors that theoretically predicted how participants might respond. They then agreed to test this theory with nomothetic methods.

Earlier in the chapter, we stated that cause and effect need to be established by analytic techniques beyond thematic analysis. Two of the more frequently used approaches are taxonomic analysis and grounded theory. **Taxonomic analysis** involves looking at the data set for relationships among themes. Because naturalistic analysis is inductive, cause and effect cannot be imposed. They must emerge from the data set. **Grounded theory** is a complex approach to theory development through which each datum is ultimately placed in a thematic category following an intensive inductive analysis called constant comparison. In constant comparison, the researcher examines a data set for initial categories and then determines the congruence of each datum with that category scheme. If a datum does not fit any category, the categories are revised until all data are explained. You can use a computer program such as NUD*IST 4 to conduct many types of inductive analyses (Qualitative Solutions and Research, 2000).

We now turn to a discussion of mixed-method designs. One approach that has shown increasing acceptance and utility in outcome assessment is single subject design. As mentioned early in this chapter, we treat these designs as a separate category, even though they use mixed methods, because of their special focus on a single unit of analysis. These designs are also referred to by many other terms, including single case, case study, and single system design. We use single system design as the category label.

Single System Designs

Single subject design has become increasingly used in social work practice to examine outcome of intervention in single units of analysis. These units may be individuals, a single group, a single organization, or some other single unit. Units of analysis may be whole single units or single units with multiple subparts. Let us first consider a definition of single subject design.

According to Bloom, Fischer, and Orme (1998, p. 5), **single case design** is "a set of empirical procedures designed to observe changes in an identified target (a specified problem or objective of the client) through the application of multiple methods of inquiry and multiple and repeated measures over time."

This definition has several important elements. First, data collection and analysis are not a one-shot approach as in the case of nonexperimental survey design. Second, single subject design is intended to measure change and therefore should be used when change is an outcome objective. Third, single subject design most frequently relies on multiple methods of data collection.

> **BOX 16.1** | **GUIDING QUESTIONS TO ASSURE QUALITY IN SINGLE SYSTEM DESIGN**
>
> 1. Are the study questions stated clearly and explicitly?
> 2. Is the type of single system design clearly described?
> 3. Is there a sound rationale for the selection of the case? design?
> 4. Are multiple measures used? Are measures consistent with the intended outcomes and justified by the theoretical approach to intervention?
> 5. Are the data analysis strategies justified?
> 6. Is the conclusion limited to the design capacity?

Consider the example of Joshua. Clearly, change was expected in his awareness and acceptance of his alcohol abuse. Moreover, once he was admitted to college, a good grade-point average, ongoing emotional growth, and an elimination of alcohol abuse were expected outcomes for each semester in order for Joshua to continue to receive tuition support. A single case design was implemented to measure each of these variables twice each year. Additionally, the social worker kept process recordings of regular counseling sessions and used them as naturalistic data for analysis of emotional growth. As you can see, this case study design relies on multiple points and methods of data collection and analysis.

As suggested by Tripodi (2000) and Alter and Even (1990), single case design is an excellent strategy for systematic evaluation practice in clinical work. We suggest that single case design not be limited to clinical work, however.

Look back at the outcome assessment for the universal access community education in Jennifer's case. This example was also a single case, in which the community was the case, and multiple measures over time were done to ascertain the degree to which the community education produced the desired outcome of a favorable attitude toward and support for allocation of resources for universal design in the schools.

As the tradition of single subject approaches gains acceptance among the evaluation practice community, it is critical to assure rigor in the conduct of this design tradition. The questions presented in Box 16.1 will guide you so that your single subject design will be based on rigorous, systematic action processes.

Now let us review the work of Yin (1994) to present common design structures of single case study. Table 16.1 presents Yin's taxonomy.

Joshua as a youth who was receiving intervention is an example of a holistic single case study. If all the individuals in Joshua's group therapy session were studied in the same way, the approach would exemplify a holistic multiple-case study.

Holistic case approaches, as implied in the name, see the unit of analysis as a "whole." Multiple-case studies are conducted as separate inquiries just as if

TABLE 16.1 | TAXONOMY OF CASE STUDY DESIGNS*

Type	Characteristics	Uses
Holistic single case study	Single unit of analysis that is seen as only one global phenomenon	• Illumination of critical case • Outcome for a single individual on a single indicator
Embedded single case study	Single case that is a conglomerate of multiple subparts or is a subpart itself placed within larger contexts	• Illumination of critical case • Outcome for a single individual on multiple indicators
Holistic multiple case study	Multiple units of analysis that are seen as only one global phenomenon	• Case comparison • Outcome for multiple units of analysis on a single indicator
Embedded multiple case study	Multiple cases that are a conglomerate of multiple subparts or are subparts themselves placed within larger contexts	• Case comparison • Outcome for multiple individuals on multiple indicators

*After Yin (1994)

one were replicating a group design. Sampling logic does not fit here because the case studies are not selected from a population nor do they represent one. Thus, nomothetic approaches to analysis are not indicated for case study design as they rely on sampling logic.

Now let's turn to Jennifer for an example of embedded case study. The community is considered to be a system with subsystems embedded within it. Employers, educators, individuals with disabilities, taxpayers, and so forth are all subgroups within the "case." Looking at the subgroup and total outcome of a single intervention would be considered as an embedded single case study. Systematic assessment of the outcomes of multiple interventions characterizes embedded multiple-case study. Again, here the iterations of outcome assessment should be considered as replications, not the incremental aggregation of a single data set.

Table 16.2 presents the structure of single subject designs and suggests what questions they can answer. A denotes the data collection, and B refers to the intervention.

This example of a single case study evaluation plan illustrates each design and what it can tell us. Let us revisit Jennifer and the access issue. Initially, a

TABLE 16.2 | FREQUENTLY USED SINGLE SUBJECT DESIGN STRUCTURES AND WHAT THEY CAN ANSWER

Design	Research question
ABA (pre-posttest design)	What changed following the intervention?
AABAA (can indicate cause and effect)	What patterns of change can be observed?
ABABA	What changes were produced by the intervention?
AABACAA	What comparative changes occurred as a result of the intervention?

single intervention was planned. Attitudes before the educational intervention were ascertained by attitude measurement and open-ended interview of purposively selected stakeholders in the community. Each was then invited to the community education program, and attitudes were reexamined using the same strategies. Movement toward a favorable attitude when measured and when observed within the interviews can tell us that attitudes changed in the desired direction following the intervention. However, with only two data points, we have no sense of the typical pattern of attitude change over time. To study change over time, two iterations of data collection were implemented both before and after the intervention, for a total of four iterations. Change in the pattern would be indicative of a causal relationship between intervention and outcome.

To study change over time, two iterations of data collection were implemented both before and after the intervention for a total of four iterations. Change in the pattern would indicate a causal relationship between intervention and outcome. In Data Charts A and B the line slopes indicate what changed, when, and whether the change was sustained. While both pretest and posttest lines in Data Chart A indicate an increase (between time 1 and time 2 and between time 3 and time 4), the pattern of increase is the same. No change in the slope of the line from pretest to posttest indicates that no change has resulted from the intervention, because what happened before the intervention also occurred following the intervention. In Chart B, intervention 1, there is a difference in the slope of the lines between the points in times 1 and 2 and between times 2 and 3. The increase in the slope of the line from time 2 to time 3 suggests a difference related to the intervention. A decrease in the change is indicated by the slope of the line from time 3 to 4. From time 4 to 5, however, the slope is less steep than the slope between times 2 and 3, but much steeper than the slope between times 1 and 2. This difference suggests that while the change decreased after time 3, it once again increased and was sustained from time 4 to 5. In Chart B, intervention 2, the slope between time 4 and time 5 looks very similar to the slope between times 1 and 2, suggesting a return to the

DATA CHART A | NO CHANGE

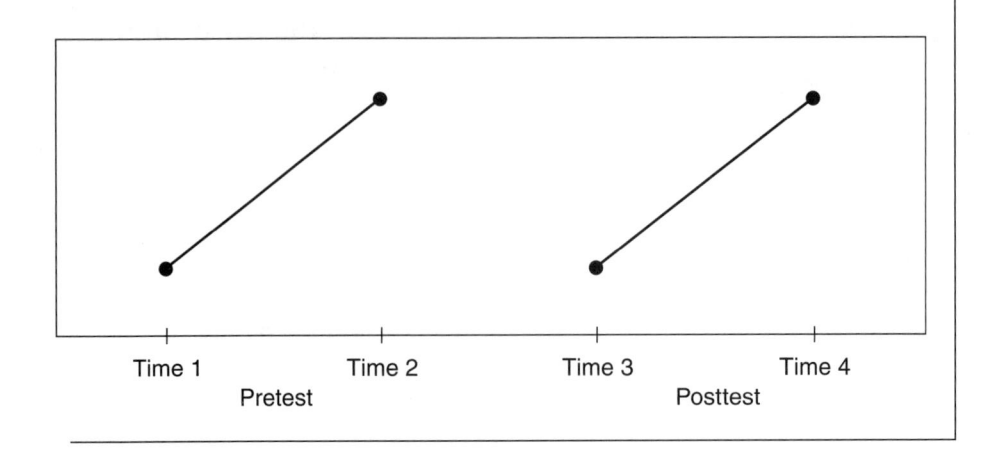

Time 1　　　Time 2　　　Time 3　　　Time 4
　　Pretest　　　　　　　　Posttest

DATA CHART B | COMPARISON OF INTERVENTIONS

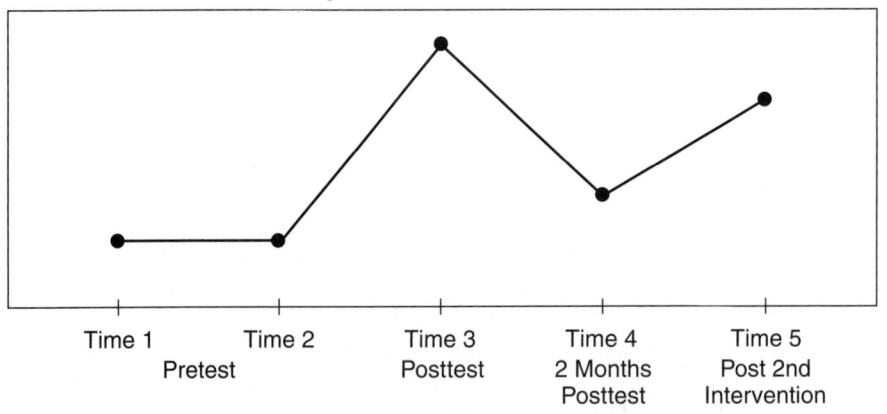

Intervention 1: Sustained Change

Time 1　　Time 2　　Time 3　　　Time 4　　　Time 5
　Pretest　　　　　Posttest　　2 Months　　Post 2nd
　　　　　　　　　　　　　　　Posttest　　Intervention

Intervention 2: No Sustained Change

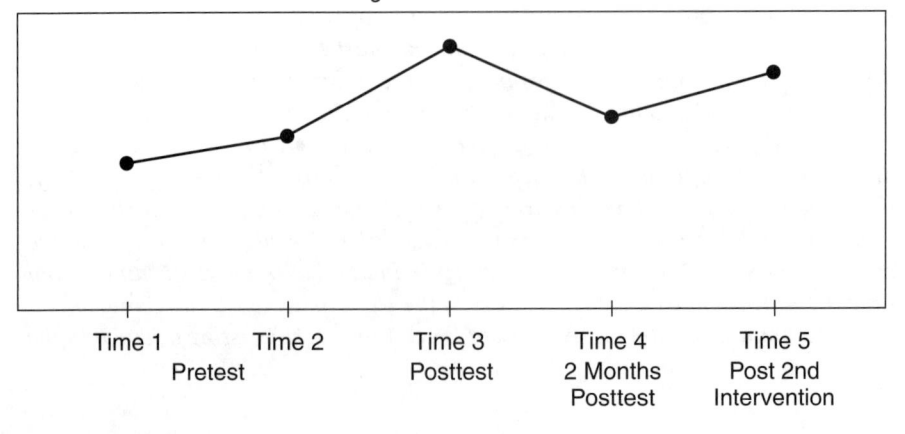

Time 1　　Time 2　　Time 3　　　Time 4　　　Time 5
　Pretest　　　　　Posttest　　2 Months　　Post 2nd
　　　　　　　　　　　　　　　Posttest　　Intervention

pretest pattern following the intervention. We can therefore conclude that no sustained change occurred.

A stronger design would involve measurement before and after the intervention and then after the intervention was removed and then reinstated. Changes in data points would tell us what the measure looked like with the intervention and then without it. Finally, adding a different intervention and measuring change in attitude would let us know whether the changes that we saw from the single intervention occurred after another intervention. If we saw similar change following two disparate interventions, we might surmise that the interventions were similar or that the change was due to attention rather than content.

Mixed-Method Designs

There are many configurations of mixed-method design. In our own evaluation practice, we attempt to mix naturalistic and experimental-type methods whenever purposive and possible. Mixing approaches is a powerful design in outcome assessment even when true experimentation can be used. Mixing methods allows for diversity of data and analytic methods and yields outcome information that captures both the linear sequence of intervention and outcome, as well as the complexity of the context that influences how the intervention is actualized. Moreover, use of diverse strategies renders it more likely that the epistemological preferences of multiple stakeholders will be met. This point will be discussed in more detail in the next chapter.

MAIN POINTS

1. Idiographic designs investigate context-embedded phenomena.
2. Most idiographic approaches are naturalistic, and thus external validity is not a goal.
3. Three design types—naturalistic, single system, and multimethod—are valuable in evaluation practice.
4. Idiographic designs can reveal complexity and valuable information that may not be captured in nomothetic approaches.
5. Single subject designs are gaining respect and popularity and can be used to examine changes in an individual unit of analysis.
6. Mixed-method designs bring the advantages of experimental-type and naturalistic inquiry to bear on evaluation practice.

EXERCISES

1. Obtain an outcome assessment from the literature that uses idiographic designs. Critically analyze the article for its efficacy in establishing cause-and-effect relationships between intervention and outcome.

2. Plan an idiographic approach to outcome evaluation for clinical, family, and large-system intervention. Begin with the problem statement, and proceed through each step of evaluation practice to justify your approach.
3. Find and analyze a mixed-method outcome assessment for its capacity to provide compelling evidence for a cause-and-effect relationship between the intervention and outcome.

CONCLUSION

PART 5

SHARING EVALUATION PRACTICE KNOWLEDGE

CHAPTER 17

Reporting and Using Knowledge

Evidence

Questions to Guide the Selection of a Reporting Format and Strategy

Structures

Use of Evaluation Practice Knowledge

Main Points

Exercises

REPORTING AND USING KNOWLEDGE

We have come to the part of evaluation practice that is the essence of its worth: reporting and using knowledge. There are many evaluation studies that have been completed, reported in written form, and then placed on a shelf, never to be seen again except perhaps in an academic journal article. We are not dismissing the critical importance of scholarly publication as one venue for dissemination. However, we assert that the process in evaluation practice has failed unless the knowledge derived from the systematic inquiry is used for the purposes for which the thinking and action processes were intended: informing the improvement and/or status of practice.

EVIDENCE

Before we discuss dissemination, we begin with an experience that sets the context for our discussion. Last summer, we attended a seminar on qualitative inquiry related to disability and work. The seminar was designed to bring together those who were well known in the field with those who were relatively new to the topic or the methodology. Each participant was asked to prepare a short description of a current or future project on which he or she was or wanted to work. The presentations and sessions in this week-long seminar were intended to inform the development of individuals' projects for implementation. Among the participants were attorneys, social workers, philosophers, educators, and health providers. Although we learned nothing new about methodology or content relating to disability and work, that summer session was one of the most valuable learning experiences that we have experienced. We did not learn what we expected, but we did learn an important principle that we now advance to you: *Because evidentiary standards differ so greatly across fields, communicating knowledge is a task that requires much more than clarity in the presentation of one's work.*

We have emphasized that the beauty of our evaluation meta-framework for practice is the set of organized, systematic, and substantiated thinking and action processes that it brings to social work practice. We assert that this set of processes would be an excellent organizing framework for any field. However, what we want to emphasize here is that the nature of the evidence that is sought and considered as credible within these thinking and action processes is quite diverse. Therefore, the action process of dissemination must be preceded by an understanding of what the audience will value as believable. This point, as the foundation of sound dissemination practice, will be discussed in detail.

Let us first look at social work practice and the different ways, even within our own field, that social workers accept a claim. We have written this text to urge social workers to think and act in concert with the principles of empirical inquiry. We have asserted that any claim made in social work should be linked to a value statement (problem) for which what is needed to resolve all or part of the problem is discovered through systematic inquiry. Each step that follows in the practice sequence, in our view, should systematically respond to the empirically supported need and show systematically obtained evidence that the action processes were sound, were well executed, and produced the desired outcome. Evidence to the contrary, therefore, highlights areas for social work practice improvement and/or change. In our model, it would be insufficient to develop an intervention without a logical, well-articulated, systematically supported reason to do so. However, this approach to social work practice is not espoused, at least on a surface examination, by all.

Let us think about other ways that social workers claim to know about practice. As discussed earlier, many clinical social workers espouse a theory or set of theories for practice, apply these theories to practice problems, and then look at the intervention processes from beginning to termination through theoretical lenses. Turning points and termination are often based on the degree to which the social worker and/or client believe(s) that the intervention has met its goal or cannot go further. Use of self and the relationship between client and social worker form the basis for practice. We frequently hear from practitioners that the focus on logical, systematic thinking interferes with the ability of the practitioner to "go with" the client. But does it really, or is the clinician using empirical evidence in practice but not articulating it? This question will be addressed later in this chapter.

Let us consider another example. A recent social work intervention was aimed at the development and passage of lemon-law legislation for assistive technology used by individuals with disabilities (wheelchairs, lifts, hearing aids, and so on). These devices were not protected by any legislation in the state of Virginia, and thus, if one's equipment malfunctioned, there was no recourse for repair or replacement. The empirical evidence collected about the frequency and consequences of malfunctioning was compelling. However, this set of evidence was not the evidentiary support directly reported to orchestrate the passage of the legislation. Rather, individual testimony and narratives about the devastation of broken equipment, alliances among agencies, and the recognition that other states had parallel laws served as the evidentiary foundation upon which arguments for the passage of the legislation were made.

In both of these examples, if we look at what was communicated by the practitioners as evidence, we may not immediately see systematically derived knowledge. However, peering below the articulated surface, we see systematic thinking and action processes that follow the principles of our model. Theory used by social workers, even if they do not articulate its research base, is grounded and tested with systematic inquiry. The magnitude of the failure of assistive technology, along with the significant financial costs, was clearly documented in the lemon-law example.

However, *at the point of communication about knowledge use in each example, the evidence used to justify an approach to action was not articulated in the form of formal research results. Rather, the empirical evidence was translated, transformed, or used as the basis to develop forms of communicated evidence that were credible and compelling for diverse audiences.*

This statement creates the context for our presentation of dissemination and use of knowledge. The thinking and action processes of evaluation practice are grounded in empirical evidence and systematic, logically developed inquiry.

Communicating the knowledge however is pluralistic in format and must consider why, who, what, where, when, and how.

QUESTIONS TO GUIDE THE SELECTION OF A REPORTING FORMAT AND STRATEGY

Why

This question identifies purpose and precedes any consideration of the structure, timing, format, and scope of dissemination. *In our example of community education on universal access in Jennifer's case, the social worker's purpose is to garner full support from the community for universal access and then use that support to leverage funds first to redesign school access and then to expand access to the public areas of the community.*

Who

Who communicates and to whom they communicate are critical considerations in the dissemination process. The fit between audience and communicator is an important determinant in the extent to which the knowledge will be heard, respected, and used. Consider this example.

As a result of the outcome assessment, the social worker found that the employers in Jennifer's community did not increase their favorable attitude toward universal access and design but the educators and school administrators did. The social worker decided to share this information with some participants in the community education intervention not only to inform the community of the outcome but to use the information in planning future intervention. Who should hear the results? Educators certainly would be in the audience because the intervention produced desired outcomes for them. But what about employers? The social worker decided to share evaluation results with them. Who else might hear evaluation results? What if the failure of the community education intervention to change the attitudes of employers dissuades community support for future intervention? What should be reported to whom? In this case, the social worker decided to enlist an employer to communicate the evaluation practice knowledge to the employer community. This choice was made so that it would not appear that the employers were being scolded for their attitudes and so that employers could be engaged in future intervention efforts. Note that those who have not participated were not considered in the initial audience. However, the social worker planned to share evaluation practice knowledge following the second intervention activity with individuals with disabilities who work and live in the community, with legislators, and with funders. This decision was made so that feedback to the participants occurred and could be addressed by them before other stakeholder groups brought pressure to bear on employers who were not yet favorable toward implementing universal design.

What, How, and Where

What and how are often intertwined because what is shared is dependent on how it is phrased and presented, and vice versa, phrasing is often dependent on what is shared. Where dissemination occurs is also considered in what and how.

Because the intervention elicited desired outcomes with only some of the participants, what should have been shared? Should the scores of each group and the actual empirical observations have been communicated with all audiences? If so, where should the findings be shared? Should they be reported in a group meeting and, if so, on whose turf? In this case, the social worker decided to write two reports, one in which the entire evaluation practice, from beginning through outcome assessment, was detailed in a formal reporting structure and one in which an executive summary was produced. In the formal report, the social worker focused on the problem, the need as it related to community access, and long-term cost of not expanding access, and then on the reflexive implementation. The outcome assessment was reported but was not a primary emphasis, and possible reasons for the outcome were advanced. These included the omission from the educational intervention of a discussion of long-term cost and consequences of not expanding access. In the conclusion of the report, the social worker linked employer attitude to this omission as a possible reason for the undesired outcome.

The executive summary reviewed the information contained in the report but limited the discussion of actual empirical evidence and highlighted the omission of important information from the educational intervention. The summary was given to an employer who was asked to distribute it in a local business meeting and to send it to all owners or chief executive officers of businesses within the community. As you can see, the content, the format, and the location of dissemination were well considered within the context of purpose.

When

The social worker in the above example decided to share the evaluation practice knowledge with those groups who participated in the educational intervention before expanding the knowledge. After the second educational intervention, the social worker was hoping that the introduction of new information would be a catalyst for the development of more favorable attitudes toward universal access on the part of employers.

As you can see from the example, sharing knowledge is an important action process in and of itself in contributing to problem resolution. Careful consideration of format, timing, audience, and communicator is important if the purpose of the intervention and its scrutiny are to be maximized. Most critical is to select the content and evidence that is compelling and credible and make a decision on how and when to disseminate it. As we found, what evidence is accepted by a group may differ from the evidence that you consider to be convincing. Thus, knowing what type of evidence to present in your reporting, and when and how to report it is one of the most important points to consider in any dissemination effort.

STRUCTURES

Now let us consider typical structures used to disseminate information. We support full accessibility of knowledge to all audiences. Attention to accessibility includes the presentation of information in diverse sensory modalities (for example, closed captioning or Braille) and in language that is understandable. Sharing evaluation practice knowledge in the form of a formal report with those who do not understand the language of statistics or naturalistic analysis does not result in transmission of knowledge.

Formal Evaluation Report

There are many formal structures to report systematic evaluation practice, and all have common elements. Each report includes a statement of the problem, need, goals and objectives, intervention and assessment methods, findings, and conclusions; however, we are not prescribing how these elements should be treated. A purpose statement may be clear and identified or may be implicit in how the report is framed and applied. It is unusual to see methods, data, and conclusions omitted from a formal written report, unless the structure is metaphoric—that is, representational rather than direct—or in a form that transmits knowledge in atypical ways. We discuss these later in the chapter. Box 17.1 presents the four basic principles that are used for formal presentation, regardless of format.

Given these four principles, we now look at typical styles for formal evaluation research reporting. Although reporting can occur anywhere in the process of evaluation practice, in this chapter we address reporting of all steps in the evaluation practice model from problem statement through outcome assessment. You can extrapolate the four principles to delimit your dissemination to specific parts of the model.

Because of the systematic and evidence-based foundations of evaluation practice, formal evaluation reports are usually written to follow the conventions of the inquiry traditions that the social worker employs. We address typical formats for experimental-type, naturalistic, and mixed-method reporting.

Preparing an Experimental-Type Evaluation Report Within the experimental-type tradition, language and structure for presentation are governed by standards of scientific reporting. The language used is logical, usually presented in the third person to allow the data to speak for themselves, detached from unsubstantiated personal opinion. All conclusions and interpretations must not exceed the data analysis; that is, interpretations must be clearly supported by and linked to the statistical evidence revealed in the findings section.

> **BOX 17.1 — FOUR PRINCIPLES FOR FORMAL REPORTING**
>
> **Clarity**
> One of the primary elements of all inquiry is clarity. If a report is vague, convoluted, or verbose, clarity is compromised and the knowledge cannot be understood.
>
> **Precision**
> Precision in this context means accuracy in reporting. No matter what venue or format, dissemination should clearly describe the thinking and action processes of the evaluation practice.
>
> **Parsimony**
> Although reports are often lengthy, one of the most important principles in writing is to be parsimonious. Writing too much, repeating your points, or just being too wordy are deterrents to readers. Keep your report as brief as possible, without compromising clarity and content.
>
> **Attention to Structure**
> Proper citations, heading formats, and overall format of the document are important aspects that can help the reader understand your report.

In the experimental-type report, there are usually six sections within the body of the report, an abstract, and a list of references used to support the inquiry.

The abstract precedes the narrative report and serves as a summary of each section of the evaluation. The reference list contains full citations of all literature identified in the report. Many citation formats exist. We suggest that you consider the use of a computerized program such as Procite or Endnote to keep track of your literature and to automatically format your references in your style of choice.

The introduction of an evaluation practice report contains a brief statement of the problem to which the intervention is addressed, a purpose statement, and an overview of the approach and questions answered in the report.

The section on problem and need varies depending on the point at which you are reporting. As we discussed in Chapter 5, the literature review provides the conceptual foundation and evidence for the problem statement. Review Chapter 5 for suggested formats for this section of your report. The limits and comprehensiveness of the literature section will depend on your audience. For example, in a journal article, the literature is usually bounded within five years unless historical references are made; whereas in an online report, the degree of detail varies. If the need was documented by existing literature, it is useful for that part of the literature to be discussed in detail. If a needs assessment inquiry was conducted, the methods and results of the study should be overviewed and located within current literature.

> **BOX 17.2** | **ELEMENTS IN THE EXPERIMENTAL-TYPE REPORT**
>
> Introduction
> Problem and need
> Intervention
> Assessment methods
> Results
> Discussion and conclusions

Following the section on problem and need, the intervention within the context of goals and objectives is presented. The degree of detail is dependent on venue and purpose of the report. In professional journals, it is customary to provide extensive detail in this section so that the reader knows what action processes were conducted. Monitoring methods may be discussed in this section, but they can also be detailed in the methods section.

The assessment methods section must contain the evaluation question or questions, the boundaries of the evaluation (that is, the respondents), a section on data collection and analysis, and the procedures used throughout reflexive implementation and outcome assessment. The degree of detail and specificity is once again determined by the purpose and audience.

In the findings or results section, the analyzed data are presented. Data may be presented in narrative, chart, graph, or table form.

The discussion and conclusions section aggregates and interprets reflexive implementation and outcome assessment data to address the extent to which goals and objectives were accomplished to meet needs and resolve the part of the problem that was addressed by the intervention. Within this section, conclusions about the efficacy of an intervention and changes that could improve outcome should be included.

Writing an experimental-type evaluation report involves a temporal and logical sequence detailing the steps in the evaluation practice model and drawing conclusions about the extent to which the process and outcome of an intervention demonstrated problem resolution. The degree of detail and precision in each section is dependent on the purpose and audience for the report.

Preparing a Naturalistic Report Because there are so many epistemologically and structurally different types of naturalistic designs, we cannot assert a single reporting structure. However, evaluation practice rarely covers the full spectrum of naturalistic designs. Thus, a formal report often conforms to commonalities contained in experimental-type evaluation reports. See Box 17.2 for the six elements that are usually contained in the report. The difference lies in the language, the nature of data, and data analysis.

Naturalistic reports rely heavily on narrative data. Thus, in reading the report, you may come across quotations in all sections from diverse informants, such as clients, providers, and administrators. We have seen visual representations in the form of taxonomies, as well as actual pictorial metaphors, such as trees, to depict an unfolding and growth process observed in an antiracism intervention. Regardless of the format, the four principles of clarity, precision, parsimony, and attention to structure should guide the reporting process.

Preparing a Mixed-Method Report   Review the two previous sections to guide the preparation of this type of report. Even if you are preparing a report of an intervention with a single client or client group, in which single subject methods were selected for outcome assessment, the same six sections need to be included. Data analysis is typically reported in graphic format, so that pre- and postintervention patterns can be visualized.

Other Reporting Formats

There are too many methods, structures, and venues for reporting evaluation practice knowledge to cover in this text. Purpose drives the choice of format. To help you structure reporting formats that do not follow the formal guidelines discussed, look at the questions in Box 17.3.

If you can answer all of these questions, you can begin to delimit report structures and venues. *For example, if in Jennifer's case you wanted to reach people with disabilities who were homebound, you might consider several venues, including newspaper, radio, television, and computer. If sensory access were a concern, you would attend to reporting that accommodated for visual and hearing impairments. If cognitive access was identified, you might prepare*

BOX 17.3 | **QUESTIONS TO GUIDE THE SELECTION OF A REPORTING FORMAT FOR NONTRADITIONAL REPORTS**

1. What is the purpose of the report?
2. Who is the audience? What role(s) do they play in the intervention? What do they want to know? What do you want them to know?
3. What evidence is compelling to your audiences?
4. What format and venues will be most likely to reach these audiences?
5. What type of reporting is most likely to attract and keep the attention of the audiences?
6. What do you expect to occur from sharing your report?
7. What do you want to avoid in sharing your report?
8. What access issues do you need to address in preparing your report?
9. How many formats will you need to prepare and for whom?

220 CONCLUSION

> **BOX 17.4** | **METHODS OF SHARING EVALUATION PRACTICE REPORTS**
>
> **Publishing Your Work in Print**
> > Professional journals
> > Newsletters
> > Monographs
> > Books and book chapters
> > Technical reports
> > Reporting for consumers
> > Executive summaries
> > Legislative brief
>
> **Oral Presentations**
> > Presentations at scholarly conferences
> > Continuing and in-service education
> > Presentations at professional meetings
> > Presentations at community meetings
> > Presentation at legislative sessions
>
> **Online Presentations**
>
> **Presentation Through Art and Literature**

your report in multiple formats, such as pictorial representations or with careful attention to the complexity of the syntax and reading level.

Box 17.4 lists some of the more frequent ways in which evaluation practice knowledge is shared. Each has its strengths and limitations, so if possible, sharing in multiple ways is most desirable if you want to reach diverse audiences.

As you can see, even a very limited list of methods to share evaluation practice knowledge is diverse. Purposive selection to accomplish dissemination goals is the key to selection of the most efficacious dissemination methods in evaluation practice.

USE OF EVALUATION PRACTICE KNOWLEDGE

There are multiple uses for evaluation practice knowledge. The intended use is important in shaping the format and nature of sharing of knowledge. Traditional uses fall into two categories: formative and summative. Formative uses apply evaluation knowledge to the improvement of interventions, while summative use of knowledge is aimed at determining the value of an intervention and the degree to which resources should be devoted to it.

In our model, the use of knowledge both completes and commences the sequence of steps in evaluation practice. Knowing the extent to which and how an intervention addressed a problem in essence redefines or reaffirms the problem. Let us consider an example.

We learned that test scores in Joshua's experimental district improved in both schools, but improvement was greater in the school in which the teachers did not receive the incentive for student score improvement. This information has redefined our problem statement and focus. From our evaluation practice knowledge, we learned that teacher incentive as structured was not a resolution to the problem as stated. We also learned that school resources had some association with student performance on standardized tests. A new problem statement might address the issue of resources in schools as a focus for student performance. With the problem reconceptualized, we begin the evaluation practice processes again.

MAIN POINTS

1. Different forms of evidence are credible for different professional and other stakeholder interest groups.
2. Answering *why, who, what, where, when,* and *how* questions helps you select a reporting format and strategy.
3. The four principles for formal reporting are clarity, precision, parsimony, and attention to structure.
4. Both formal and informal reporting should be considered.
5. The guiding questions are a valuable resource to help you select methods for purposively sharing evaluation practice knowledge.
6. Evaluation practice knowledge both completes and restarts the sequence of steps in the evaluation practice model.

EXERCISES

1. In the evaluation literature, identify and critically analyze an experimental-type report, a naturalistic report, and a mixed-method report. Compare and contrast the credibility of the evidence in supporting the claims of the authors.
2. Consider the multiple stakeholders in each report. How might you format and present the evaluation practice knowledge in each report to convince each stakeholder group to support the claims made by the author?
3. Find evaluation practice reports in unusual formats (art or literature, for example), and critically analyze them for their credibility.
4. Analyze the accessibility of each of the reports that you have found in Exercises 1 and 3 for diverse audiences.
5. Select a report, and use the knowledge presented in it to redefine or affirm the problem statement.

CHAPTER 18 CONCLUSIONS

Continuous Process of Evaluation Practice

Joshua

Individual Problem

Systemic Problem Identified by Joshua

Jennifer

Systemic Problem

Evaluation Practice: Upholding the Social Work Commitment

Go for It!

CONTINUOUS PROCESS OF EVALUATION PRACTICE

As stated in the last chapter, the final step in our evaluation practice model is the first step as well, and so we have come full circle. Each time a full round of thinking and action processes of the model is completed, the problem that was the focus of the intervention becomes redefined, reaffirmed, or perhaps at some point, eliminated. Of course, given the nature and expanse of social problems, they are never resolved in total. As the problem changes in nature, a new approach to intervention commences with clarification of the problem.

In this chapter, we put the model together by aggregating the content on *Joshua* and *Jennifer* and recapping it in one continuous narrative. We include both the macro- and microproblems that we followed throughout the text and integrate them to illustrate a round of the thinking and action processes that occur from problem clarification to use of evaluation practice knowledge. We then examine the model and its important uses in social work practice.

We begin with the microproblems faced by *Joshua*.

JOSHUA

Case Information

Joshua's youth was filled with what he terms "minor acts" of juvenile delinquency. These acts include shoplifting, drinking alcohol, breaking and entering, suspension from school, malicious mischief, vandalism, destruction of property, fighting with classmates, and school truancy. Also noteworthy was Joshua's poor performance in school, an important determinant of his future professional direction.

Joshua's use of alcohol increased significantly during high school with regular-to-daily use/abuse including periods of increased tolerance, blackouts, driving while drunk (though he was never arrested for such use), increased numbers of hangovers, public intoxication, and general perception by others that he was an active alcohol abuser. His use of alcohol interfered with his participation in and successful completion of high school, although at 17 years old, graduating from high school was not a priority for him; alcohol use was. Despite erratic attendance, poor assignment-completion rates, a general attitude of indifference, and periodic assignment to a counseling group by the school social worker, Joshua did graduate, but with poor grades and noncompetitive test scores on college entrance examinations.

The summer following his graduation from high school marked his first serious attempt at sobriety. Joshua signed himself into an inpatient detoxification unit, only to leave against medical advice a few days later. The next four years of his life were marked by several periods of voluntary inpatient and outpatient treatment, along with attendance at several meetings of Alcoholics Anonymous (AA). On his 22nd birthday, Joshua again signed himself into an inpatient, county-based alcohol treatment unit. This event marked his first sustained period of abstinence from substance use and continued participation in AA. This period of recovery continues into the present.

This time also marked the period of his attempt to secure vocational rehabilitation services in order to enroll in and complete his college education. His assigned vocational rehabilitation counselor was very reluctant to support Joshua in seeking an academic degree, documenting in his notes that Joshua was alcoholic, unreliable, and unprepared due to poor performance in school and on college entrance examinations. It was only after insisting that the full treatment team, including his social worker, meet that Joshua was able to obtain funding for his plan of recovery and sustained and substantive employment. Over the course of his efforts at recovery, his work to pursue the goals he wanted, and his undergraduate course work, Joshua developed an interest in political science and public policy. This interest led to his major in political science and minor in public policy. During his senior year, reflecting back on the critical role that grades and tests had on his life, Joshua decided that he wanted to pursue a law degree with a practice focus on public policy, with particular attention to public education law and policy.

INDIVIDUAL PROBLEM

Problem Clarification

Joshua abuses alcohol as a method to mediate depression and boredom.

Needs Assessment

Needs assessment was conducted using life history methodology. "Turnings" and patterns that influenced Joshua's substance abuse were identified. Substance abuse was exacerbated when Joshua spent time with other youth who drank on the weekends, and abated when Joshua was actively engaged in physical activity with some element of competition. Needs assessment revealed that Joshua required direction and challenge to resolve his problem.

Goals and Objectives

To attain the long-term goal of elimination of substance abuse, two intermediate goals were established: to increase Joshua's awareness and acknowledgement of his problematic substance use (see Table 18.1), and to be accepted to college.

Objectives for the second goal were established:

1. *Joshua will seek information about colleges, acceptance criteria, and college application procedures.*

TABLE 18.1 | INITIAL GOAL: AWARENESS AND ACKNOWLEDGEMENT OF SUBSTANCE USE PROBLEM

	Success criteria	Evidence	Time line
Will attend weekly group therapy with other youth with substance-abuse problems	Regular, weekly attendance at group	Attendance recordings	Ongoing
	Will participate in weekly indicator testing	Scores on indicator tests	Weekly
Will work with a peer mentor to identify future life goals and current barriers to achieving these goals	Regular meetings with peer mentor	Records of meetings documented by peer mentor	Ongoing

2. Joshua will identify three colleges to which he will apply and will indicate why he selected these institutions.
3. Joshua will complete and submit applications to three colleges.

Reflexive Implementation and Outcome Assessment

Semiannual systematic reports from Joshua, his grade-point average, and the results of measures of his alcohol awareness, use, and abuse were used by the social worker to evaluate Joshua's commitment to and progress with his sobriety. Given the social worker's previous experiences in working with individuals with similar problems with alcohol use, the social worker was able to analyze both the content of Joshua's reports and the test results to determine the probability that Joshua would maintain his sobriety.

Cost Analysis

Spending public money to support a college education for an individual who was considered an active alcohol abuser was not only a reasonable expense, but was the choice that would cost the least when considering the costs of lost work, public support, and healthcare expenses that result from chronic alcoholism.

SYSTEMIC PROBLEM IDENTIFIED BY JOSHUA

Problem Clarification

Poor standardized test scores limit children's future opportunities.

Needs Assessment

Joshua structured four separately conducted focus group sessions, three of which were homogeneous for each group and one of which included representatives from each of the three groups. He finds that parents express the need for more structured homework for their children, with specific attention to the academic skills of reading, writing, and math. Teachers suggest that parents need to become more involved in their children's education through assisting them with homework assignments and restricting television and other distractions from academic work. Administrators identify the need to increase the funding for teacher training to prepare students for testing. To further detail the needs, Joshua decided to conduct an open-ended survey with each group, posing the suggestions and asking each group to define specific strategies on how the needs could be filled. A range of responses, from disagreement with the identified needs to methods to implement after-school homework programs led by both teachers and parents, emerged from the survey.

Goals and Objectives

The goal for a five-year period is for students in a pilot school district to increase their scores. There are three objectives:

1. *Identify two elementary schools (grades 1–6) in similar parts of the district that will participate in the experimental program (to be done by the state department of education, based on aggregate demographic and school resource data). Randomly select one school for the experimental program and one as a control.*
2. *In August prior to the beginning of each school year, educate all head teachers (those who provide the supervision and oversight for academic work in each class) in both schools to implement a curriculum that focuses on the knowledge and skills contained within the test (teacher education to be delivered by state university faculty).*
3. *Test children in grades 1–6, once yearly in April, with the standardized state tests.*

Reflexive Implementation

Implement a financial incentive for teachers in the experimental school only. They will be paid a bonus of $3,000 at the end of each academic year for a significant increase in test scores (based on a formula that addresses differences in initial scores, demographics, number of students, and so forth). To monitor *the action processes, observation of teaching practices in each of the pilot schools was conducted and revealed that teachers in the experimental school saw a news program on a similar effort in which teachers received a $10,000 incentive. The observer/interviewer ascertained resentment and lackluster teaching stemming from the comparatively small sum of money being offered as an incentive. Observation of classroom teaching in the experimental school revealed that the teachers were choosing the time period just before lunch to implement the new curriculum. Students were anxious to get up from their seats and go to lunch. As a result of observation, a larger incentive was paid and a change in the curriculum was made, in which the teaching sessions were more interactive and delivered after students settled down in the morning.*

Cost Analysis

Base budget and yearly expenditures were monitored.

Outcome Assessment

Yearly test scores were obtained and compared in both schools to measure the outcome criterion of improved test scores. In both schools, student assignments in reading, writing, and math were collected and analyzed for their demonstration of knowledge and skills covered in the test. Comparisons of knowledge and skills between artifacts and tested data were conducted to examine the construct validity of the test in assessing specified knowledge and skills.

Results are not available and reporting strategy has not been developed.

JENNIFER

Case Information

Jennifer has a mobility impairment caused by post-polio syndrome. She spent much time at home as a child and youth and thus has limited social experience and confidence. Because much of her public school education took place prior to the 1978 formulation of regulations from the Rehabilitation Act of 1973, and her bachelor's and master's degrees were awarded prior to the enactment of the Americans with Disabilities Act of 1990, Jennifer's educational experiences have included little in the way of accommodation. Given the nature of early social experiences, and the general failure of community institutions to provide accommodations necessary for her to participate, Jennifer entered the worlds of higher education and career without some of the confidence necessary to push those systems to respond to her accommodation needs. Further, due to long periods of isolation from social contacts in her youth, Jennifer was not able to develop collaborative, peer partnerships with others with mobility-based conditions. As a consequence, Jennifer was inclined to view her access needs as her own inability to navigate steps and stairs, rather than as a broader environmental issue shared by many others, including, for example, parents using strollers to transport their children, or individuals needing to move packages or equipment with wheeled dollies or similar devices. Following receipt of her doctoral degree in 1995, Jennifer secured a position as a teacher in a public high school in her community. At that point, she sought help from a social worker to remediate issues of limited access that prevented her from doing her job.

SYSTEMIC PROBLEM
Problem Clarification

Physical and environmental inaccessibility interfere with or block participation in community activities (work, education, community living, securing healthcare services, and so forth) for people, like Jennifer, with physical disabilities.

Needs Assessment

Mixed methods were used for needs assessment. Initially, a focus group of disabled teachers and an ethnographic inquiry were conducted. Revealed in those elements of the needs assessment were the following:

1. *Access to educational environments expands beyond compliance with federal requirements for physical access.*
2. *Diverse time schedules require physical access to school buildings to fit individual needs.*
3. *Physical access is affected by the number of people in an environment and the weather (for example, wet floors on rainy days pose barriers).*
4. *Access is affected by attitudes of all individuals within environments, regardless of physical design.*

To ascertain attitudes toward universal access, the social worker administered a survey to key members of the community. From the survey, the social worker found that nonsupport for expanding access is related to beliefs that individuals with disabilities cannot work. The need to debunk myths about disability was therefore considered essential before the community would be supportive of and advocate for the allocation of resources to increasing access to the school environment.

Goals and Objectives

As part of a long-term goal to achieve universal access in educational environments, the following intermediate goal was asserted: Educate the community about universal designs and its benefits for all, including individuals with disabilities. There were seven intermediate objectives:

1. *Select a steering committee to represent community diversity.*
2. *Work with the steering committee to delimit the boundaries of the community (that is, who will be targeted for education?).*

3. *Develop curriculum for the diverse target groups.*
4. *Establish educational protocol and procedures.*
5. *Train all "trainers" to deliver the universal access curriculum to target groups.*
6. *Target-group participants will learn basic principles of universal access and suggest a plan to integrate universal design that can be integrated into the community.*
7. *Target-group participants will identify the specific benefits to the entire community of their suggested plan.*

Reflexive Implementation

The social worker began with a force field analysis process to identify steering committee members because the theoretical approach to "diversity" is too vague to select a diversity variable with no further inquiry. Driving forces impacting the attainment of this process objective included a large group of individuals interested in the problem of access and their desire to learn how to expand access. Restraining forces included not knowing which aspects of community diversity were important to consider. Based on empirical information in the literature on planning and operationalizing universal design, the social worker found evidence that diversity in age and disability were most critical to address in access issues.

The steering committee was therefore selected to represent these areas of diversity. The steering committee subsequently engaged in a force field analysis to complete objective 2. They identified restraining forces as time constraints of individuals who are employed full time or care for young children and the community's fear of the cost of environmental modifications to expand access. Driving forces included interest expressed by parents of children with disabilities in the issue of school access and increasing news coverage about disability issues including access. Based on the force field analysis, the steering committee decided to educate and work with adults with disabilities and parents of children with disabilities to learn and apply universal design principles to resolve access issues in the schools. A group of six key individuals worked online and within workshops throughout three months to learn universal design techniques. As part of the committee work, each member was asked to develop a universal design for his or her ideal school environment and present it to the work group. The most viable ideas were selected by the work group, synthesized into a plan, and sent to all adult taxpayers in the community. Along with the plan, the group developed public announcements for radio and television media on the project. An important part of the public announcement program was a short vignette about how limited access to schools affects not only those with mobility impairments, but all community members.

Process evaluation was conducted in these ways:

1. *Assessing the workgroup members on their knowledge of universal design through evaluating their plans*

2. Reporting the number of public announcements that were disseminated over radio and television
3. Randomly polling taxpayers to ascertain their exposure to the public announcements
4. Polling public attitudes toward improving school access

The social worker noted a large increase in awareness of access issues on the part of the community as a result of the public access campaign. The social worker used the evaluation information to establish a new goal of increasing community support for universal design in the public schools in the community. Monitoring occurred through narrative recording and observation of the steering committee process. To begin community awareness and support, educational interventions were developed and conducted for teachers and employers. Monitoring included narrative recordings of content and number of individuals from each interest group in attendance at the educational session.

Outcome Assessment

Several methods were used to assess outcome. First, there was a brief quiz administered to participants (XO, where X = educational session and O = quiz) to ascertain the extent to which participants understood the concepts discussed in the session. Second, the respondents were asked to rate the extent to which they increased their knowledge of universal access as a result of their participation (X = session and O = participant rating).

To evaluate subsequent session outcomes, single case methods were used in which the community was the case, and multiple measures over time were taken to ascertain the degree to which the community education produced the desired outcome of a favorable attitude toward and support for allocation of resources for universal design in the schools.

Sharing Information

As a result of the outcome assessment, the social worker found that the employers in Jennifer's community did not increase their favorable attitude toward universal access and design but the educators and school administrators did. The social worker decided to share evaluation results with all participants initially, but to enlist an employer to communicate the evaluation practice knowledge to the employer community. This choice was made so it would not appear that the employers were being scolded for their attitudes and for the purpose of engaging employers in future intervention efforts. Note that those who did not participate were not considered in the initial audience. However, the social worker planned to share evaluation practice knowledge with individuals with disabilities who work and live in the community, with legislators, and with funders following the second intervention activity. This decision was made so that feedback to the participants occurred and could be addressed by them before other stakeholder groups brought pressure to bear on employers who were not *yet favorable toward implementing universal design. All information was shared in accessible formats.*

New Problem Clarification

The evaluation practice process began again with a revised problem statement: "Negative community attitudes toward the costs of universal design impede expanding community access to all."

EVALUATION PRACTICE: UPHOLDING THE SOCIAL WORK COMMITMENT

In this text, we have advanced and illustrated evaluation practice. While the focus has been primarily on inquiry, we began by suggesting that evaluation practice is a meta-model for social work practice in all domains of professional concern. In this closing chapter, we attend to this claim. Contemporary social work practice is distinguished by its commitment to a person-in-environment perspective, to a multisystem approach to individual and social problems, and to advancement of social justice (Kirst-Ashman & Hull, 1999). As you read the summaries of both *Joshua* and *Jennifer* from beginning to end, consider how evaluation practice provides the framework through which these commitments are actualized.

Evaluation practice begins with the premise that social problems are value statements that are perceived differently by diverse interest groups. By definition, problems are therefore broadened beyond a single phenomenon. The problem-mapping approach that is foundational to evaluation practice expands a problem description from its broad sociocultural causes to consequences for individuals, regardless of what initial problem statement is articulated. Thus, even if a social worker does not enact an intervention at multiple points of a problem, conceptualizing the problem through the evaluation practice model provides an expanded view that can be addressed in subsequent work.

For the social worker, consideration of Jennifer's access issues expands beyond her individual experience, as the problem map is constructed upstream and verified with current knowledge. Conversely, the social worker, in seeking to address community access, understands the impact or consequence of environment barriers to individuals as the problem map proceeds downstream. The social worker who may decide to provide clinical intervention for Jennifer to address her lack of confidence and reluctance to advocate on her own behalf, would not restrict intervention merely to individual treatment.

Consistent with the commitments of social work, the social worker using evaluation practice as a guiding meta-framework, as illustrated in the previous example and in all examples throughout the text, would view professional intervention as multilevel and would practice accordingly. *Evaluation practice would provide the social justice context as well, just in the initial step of Jen-*

nifer's problem formulation, since the effect of discrimination and oppression resulting from access limitations would emerge in the problem analysis. As the social worker proceeds through the steps of evaluation practice, the attention to empirical support for need and all subsequent thinking and action processes to meet the identified need would be carefully conceptualized and scrutinized. *As illustrated by Joshua in his effort to increase students' standardized test scores, careful attention to process through reflexive intervention was the key in identifying the unanticipated external influences that changed the expected outcome and explained the unexpected outcomes. If limited attention were given to process, the intermediate failure of the experimental teacher-incentive program may have resulted in termination rather than modification of the intervention.*

The continuous nature of the model provides the framework for ongoing analysis and redefinition of complex social problems necessary to remain current and to provide relevant intervention. By using the evaluation practice model, attention to process and outcome of a single professional intervention, because of its insistence on systematic accountability, contributes not only to social action but to the continuous advancement of the knowledge base of social work practice. *Attempts to implement teacher incentives in similar educational districts would therefore be informed by the systematic scrutiny and findings of Joshua's project.*

GO FOR IT!

In this text, we have built upon social work theory, research, education, and practice to advance the evaluation practice model. We have presented case examples to you, each differing in nature, scope, and step in the evaluation practice model. We hope that *Jennifer, Joshua,* and others in the text have provided you with illustrations of the important thinking and action processes in evaluation practice. Now, go for it in your own practices!

APPENDIX

DATA ANALYSIS

Introduction

This appendix presents information to refresh your memory of data analytic concepts and techniques. Basic methods of experimental-type analysis (statistics) and naturalistic analysis (interpretive techniques) are included.

Statistical Analysis

Statistical analysis is a set of procedures, techniques, and rules that organizes and interprets data. The term *data* refers to numerical representation of concepts and/or observed phenomena obtained through systematic inquiry.

The selection of a statistical procedure is determined by five factors:

1. Specific research question(s) to be answered by analysis of the data set
2. Level of measurement
3. Quality of the information collected
4. Sampling procedures used
5. Sample size obtained

Statistical analysis can be categorized into three levels:

Descriptive—observations reduced and stated in numerical form

Inferential—drawing conclusions about population parameters based on findings from a sample selected from the population

234   APPENDIX

Associational—identifies relationships between multiple variables and determines the nature of those relationships

LEVEL 1: DESCRIPTIVE STATISTICS

Basic descriptive statistics describe the characteristics of a set of data. Box A.1 lists the techniques addressed in this appendix.

Frequency Distribution

- Definition—Frequency distribution refers to the range of values occurring for a given variable and the number of times each value occurs.
- How to compute—Frequency distributions are computed by listing all measured values and counting the number of times each occurs.
- How to report—Numeric charts, histograms, or bar graphs and polygons (dots connected by lines) are the usual reporting formats. Frequencies can be converted into percentages of the occurrence of each value relative to the total number of observations.

When to use—When you need to know the most frequently occurring class of scores and any pattern in the distribution of those scores. Use at the beginning of each data analysis session as a way to clean data.

Measures of Central Tendency

- Definition—Central tendency is the most typical or representative score in a distribution.
  Mode—Most frequently occurring value in a distribution of scores
  Median—Midpoint of a distribution; 50% of the scores fall above and 50% fall below value
  Mean—Average value
- How to compute
  Mode—Simple count
  Median—Rank order from lowest to highest score and identify the score below and above which 50% of all scores fall. In an odd number of values, the median is one of the values in the distribution. When an even number of values occur in a distribution, the median may or may not be one of the actual values because there is no middle number. Calculate as an average of the scores surrounding it.
  Mean—Sum all raw scores and divide by the number of scores

$$\sqrt{\frac{\Sigma(X - X_m)^2}{n - 1}}$$

| BOX A-1 | BASIC DESCRIPTIVE STATISTICS |

Frequencies
Central Tendencies (mean, mode, and median)
Variances
Contingency Tables
Correlational Analyses

- How to report
  Mode—Report as single most frequently occurring number(s)
  Median—Single score, or in the case of a frequency distribution based on grouped data, report as that interval in which the cumulative frequency equals 50% (or as a midpoint of that interval)
  Mean—Actual computed value
- When to use
  Mode—When you need to know the most frequently occurring score(s)
  Median—When you have an uneven distribution and you want a test that is insensitive to extreme scores
  Mean—When your data set is interval or ratio, when you want to know the most representative score, and as the basis for subsequent statistics. The major advantage of the mean over the mode and median is that all observations are used in the calculation.

Measures of Variability

- Definition—Variability is the degree of dispersion among a set of scores.
  Range—Difference between the highest and lowest observed value in a collection of data
  Standard Deviation—Average deviation of scores around the mean
- How to compute
  Range—Subtract lowest score from the highest
  Standard Deviation—

$$X_m = \frac{\Sigma X}{n}$$

X_m = mean $\quad$ X = raw scores
Σ = sum $\quad$ n = sample size

- How to report
  Range—As lowest to highest values
  Standard Deviation—Single computed value

- When to use
  Range—To present the simplest measure of variation
  Standard Deviation—To indicate how much scores deviate on the average from the mean

Contingency Tables

- Definition—Contingency tables are also referred to as cross tabulation, a two-dimensional frequency distribution that is used primarily with categorical data.
- How to compute—Identify vertical and horizontal variable values and compute frequencies for each separate group
- How to report—As two-dimensional table
- When to use—To examine frequencies in subgroups

Correlational Analysis

- Definition—Correlation analysis is a calculated index of the magnitude and direction of association between two variables. There are many correlational statistics. Selection is dependent primarily on level of measurement and sample size. Three types of directional relationships can exist among variables: positive correlation in which variable values move in the same direction, negative correlation in which variable values move in opposite directions, and no correlation, termed zero correlation.
- How to compute—Spearman's *rho*

$$rho = \frac{1 - 6\Sigma D^2}{N(N^2 - 1)}$$

where D = difference between a pair of ranks
N = number of pairs

Pearson's *r*

$$r_{xy} = \frac{N\Sigma xy - \Sigma x \Sigma y}{\sqrt{[N\Sigma x^2 - (\Sigma x^2)][N\Sigma y^2 - (\Sigma y^2)]}}$$

where x and y are variables under observation, and N = number of pairs
- How to report—To indicate magnitude or strength of a relationship, the value that is calculated in both Pearson's *r* and Spearman's *rho* ranges from −1 to +1, where −1 indicates a perfect negative correlation, and +1 signifies a perfect positive correlation. A value of 0 indicates no correlation.

- When to use—To examine how two sets of scores are related to one another. Pearson's r is calculated on interval-level data; Spearman's r_s is used with ordinal data.

LEVEL 2: DRAWING INFERENCES

These procedures examine the extent to which observations of the sample represent the population from which the sample was selected. Inferential statistics include statistical techniques for evaluating differences between sets of data. These techniques are used to evaluate the degree of precision and confidence of one's measurements.

Conduct the steps in Box A-2 for all inferential statistics:

BOX A-2 | STEPS FOR INFERENTIAL STATISTICS

Action 1: State the hypothesis.
Action 2: Select a significance level.
Action 3: Compute a calculated value.
Action 4: Obtain a critical value.
Action 5: Reject or fail to reject the null hypothesis.

Parametric statistics are mathematical formulas that test hypotheses based on three assumptions:

- The samples come from populations that are normally distributed.
- There is homogeneity of variance.
- The data are interval level.

Nonparametric statistical formulas are used when

- normality of variance in the population is not assumed
- homogeneity of variance is not assumed
- the data generated from measures are ordinal or nominal
- sample sizes may be small

Basic Parametric Statistical Procedures

Two basic techniques are used to compare two or more groups to see whether the differences between group means are large enough to assume that the corresponding population means are different: t-tests and analysis of variance.

The *t*-test
- Definition—A *t*-test is a statistical procedure used to compare two sample means. A *t*-test for independent samples is used when the two data sets to be compared are measured once in two separate groups. A *t*-test for dependent samples is used when the two sets of data are generated by two measures of the same group.
- How to compute—*t*-test for independent samples

$$t = \frac{(\bar{X}_1 - \bar{X}_2) - (\mu_1 - \mu_2)}{S_{\bar{x}_1 - \bar{x}_2}}$$

$\bar{X}_1$ = sample mean for group 1
$\bar{X}_2$ = sample mean for group 2
μ_1 = population mean for group 1
μ_2 = population mean for group 2

- How to report—Report *t* as a calculated value. Degrees of freedom and probability are reported with the calculated value of *t*. Degrees of freedom refer to the "number of values, which are free to vary" in a data set.
- When to use—When examining the difference between means of two groups of interval-level scores

One-Way Analysis of Variance (ANOVA)
- Definition—One-way ANOVA is a statistic used to compare two or more sample group means to determine if a significant difference can be inferred in the population.
- How to compute—ANOVA for two groups: F ratio is the square of the *t* value. They can be used interchangeably to compare the means of two groups.
- How to report—One-way ANOVA yields an *F* value that may be reported as $F(a, b) = x$, $p = 0.05$, where *x* equals computed *F* value, *a* equals group degrees of freedom, *b* equals sample degrees of freedom, and *p* equals level of significance.
- When to use—To compare differences among two or more groups of interval-level data. There are many variations of ANOVA, some of which test relationships when variables have multiple levels and some of which examine complex relationships among multiple levels of variables. When a one-way ANOVA is used to compare three or more groups, a significant *F* value means that the sample data indicate that the researcher should reject the null hypothesis. However, the *F* value in itself does not tell you which of the group means are significantly different. The selection of one of several procedures referred to as multiple comparison or *post hoc* comparison is necessary to determine which group is greater than the others. These procedures are computed if a significant *F* value is found.

Each of the tests mentioned thus far has a nonparametric analogue. See Bibliography for excellent texts that detail these procedures, for example, Babbie (2001), DePoy & Gitlin (1998), and Thyer (2001).

LEVEL 3: ASSOCIATIONS AND RELATIONSHIPS

Due to the complexity of these procedures, we mention only a few. The techniques in this group identify the nature of the relationships among variables. Included among these statistical tests are factor analyses, discriminant function analysis, multiple regression, and modeling. All seek to predict one or more outcomes from multiple variables.

Multiple regression is used to predict the effect that multiple independent (predictor) variables have on one dependent (outcome or criterion) variable. This approach is used only with interval-level data.

Discriminant function analysis is used with categorical or nominal data.

Other techniques, such as modeling, are frequently used to understand complex relationships.

NATURALISTIC DATA ANALYSIS

Naturalistic analysis is an inductive, dynamic set of processes. The techniques vary depending on one's approach to the inquiry.

Basic techniques involve four thinking and action processes: thinking inductively, developing categories, developing taxonomies, and discovering meaning and underlying themes. Unlike statistical analysis, the diversity of naturalistic techniques and their dependence on the data set are not consistent with the specification of detailed statistical analysis action processes at the beginning of the inquiry. We therefore provide a brief reminder of three frequently used analytic processes: thematic analysis, taxonomic analysis, and grounded theory.

Thematic analysis involves examining data for emergent patterns and themes. There is an iterative process in which the investigator critically and inductively reviews the data set. Emergent themes are identified and labeled and exemplars of each are used.

Taxonomic analysis builds on thematic analysis, in which relationships among themes are sought. Using a process similar to that of thematic analysis, the investigator looks for patterns of relationships and depicts them in multiple ways, including narrative and visual presentations.

Grounded theory, also called constant comparative method, compares and contrasts each datum to previous information and impressions. Examination of data reveals patterns that are coded. As new data are examined, they are coded and categorized. If data do not fit into previous categories, new or revised categories emerge.

GLOSSARY

Accessible design: a method to ensure that diverse respondents can participate

Audience: an individual or group of individuals who have a role in some or all thinking and action processes of an evaluation, including the initiation, receipt, and use of findings

Audit trail: explanation of how method was conceptualized and implemented, what evidence was used, and how it was used to support and verify an inductive claim

Bias: unplanned influence that confounds the outcome of a study

Categorical numbers (also called **nominal**): numbers assigned to phenomena for the purpose of labeling only

Closed-ended question: one that poses a limited range of responses from which the respondent chooses, all of which are posited by the researcher

Code: numbering assigned to observations of variables

Codebook: a list of directions denoting how labels and/or numbers to the survey responses were assigned

Concept: abstraction of observed or experienced phenomena

Control: a set of processes to eliminate sampling or experimental bias

Culture: the set of explicit and tacit rules, symbols, and rituals that guide patterns of human behavior within a group

Deductive reasoning: applying a general principle to explain a specific case or phenomenon

Dependent variable: the variable assumed to be the object of change

Design validity: assessment of the extent to which a study design answers the research question

Emic: the perspective of an investigator who occupies an integral role in the delivery of intervention being examined

Equivalence: the extent to which all of the indicators on an instrument aggregate to measure the construct to be tested

Error: inaccurate claim based on limitations in various parts of the research design

Ethics: guidelines for moral thinking and action processes

Etic: the perspective of a researcher who is external to the context of the object or subject of inquiry

Experimental-type design: research design based in positivist, logico-deductive philosophical framework and which relies on reduction and interpretation of numeric data

Ex post facto designs (literally translated as "after the fact"): methods to examine phenomena of interest that have already occurred and cannot be manipulated in any way

External validity: rigor criterion for the capacity of the sampling approach to answer the research question for the population from which the sample was selected

Force field analysis: a planning tool that provides a diagrammatic picture of all influences that maintain and/or impact a situation at a given moment

Formative evaluation: use of data about intervention input, conduct, and output to inform intervention improvement

Frequency: the number of times a value occurs in a data set

Goals: broad statements about the ideal or "hoped for"

Grounded theory: an inductive approach to theory generation relying on the constant comparative method of data analysis

Idiographic: an approach to design that reveals individual phenomena within a specified context

Independent variable: phenomenon that is presumed to cause an outcome

Indicator: an empirical representation of an underlying concept

Inductive reasoning: general rules evolve or develop from individual cases or observations of phenomena

Insider: see Emic

Instrument validity: the relationship between a concept and its measurement

Internal consistency: a measure of reliability that addresses the extent to which all the indicators on an instrument aggregate to measure the construct to be tested

Internal validity: rigor criterion for the capacity of the design structure to answer the research question within the units of analysis directly studied

Intervention processes: the set of actions that occurs to meet the goals and objectives of intervention

Likert-type response format: closed-ended response format in which the respondent is instructed to select one of five or seven categories, such as "strongly agree," "agree," "uncertain," "disagree," or "strongly disagree," to indicate his or her opinion or experience

Listserv: individuals who receive a body of information in electronic format

Literature review: the thinking and action step of critically examining literature and resources as a basis for formulating questions and approaches to answer them

Mean: the average value of a group of scores

Measurement: the translation of observations into numbers

Monitoring (also called **formative evaluation**): a set of thinking and action processes to ascertain, characterize, and document the relationship between articulated objectives and what occurs during an intervention, which factors impact the intervention, who is involved, and to what extent resources are used

Need statement: an empirical understanding of what is necessary to resolve all or part of a problem

Nominal numbers (also called **categorical**): numbers assigned to phenomena for the purpose of labeling only

Nomothetic: an approach to design that reveals commonalities within and/or among groups

Nonexperimental designs: experimental-type designs in which the criteria for true experimental design (random selection, control, and manipulation) cannot be met

Nonparametric statistics: statistical formulas used to analyze nominal and ordinal data in which the tenets of random selection, homogeneity of variance, and sufficient sample size are not present

Objectives: operationalized goal statements

Objectivity: belief that a single reality can be discovered by conforming to logico-deductive methods of observation

Open-ended question: one in which the respondent is asked to offer his or her comments on a topic without being directed to specific answers

Outcome: the result of being acted upon by or participating in an action process

Outcome assessment: a set of thinking and action processes to ascertain and document what occurs as a result of being voluntarily or involuntarily exposed to a purposive process; the application of rigorous research design to inquiry about intervention efficacy in producing desired results

Outsider: see **Etic**

Parametric statistics: data analytic procedures to ascertain population characteristics in which numeric data are homogeneous, interval, or ratio and have been generated through probability methods, normal distributions of variable values in units of analysis, and in which the minimum sample size criterion for use has been met

Passive observation designs: methods used to examine phenomena as they naturally occur and to discern the relationship between two or more variables

Population: the group of people (or other units of analysis) that are delimited by the investigator

Post hoc: after the occurrence of the phenomenon

Probability: theory that focuses on the likelihood of occurrence of an event

Probability sampling: sampling based on probability theory

Problem: a value statement about an undesirable that needs to be reduced or eliminated

Problem mapping: a method in which one expands a problem statement beyond its initial conceptualization by asking two questions repeatedly: What caused the problem? and What are the consequences of the problem?

Process assessment: monitoring the procedures of an intervention to determine efficacy and need for revision

Random: without bias

Random group assignment: probability method of placing subjects in groups as a means to eliminate bias and error

Random sample: sampling method in which all individuals in the studied population (or other units of analysis) have an equivalent chance of being selected for a study sample

Reflexivity: self-examination for the purpose of ascertaining how one's perspective influences the interpretation of data

Reliability: the rigor criterion that specifies the stability of an inquiry approach

Resource analysis: the full host of human and nonhuman resources that are used to conduct an intervention; instrument that measures the degree to which individuals possess a specific attribute or trait

Sample: a smaller number of units of analysis than those in the population, possessing the characteristics of the population and not possessing any of the exclusion criteria named by the inquirer, that are selected to directly participate in a study

Saturation: in naturalistic inquiry, the point at which new data do not provide any new insights

Science: a philosophical, theoretical, and epistemological lens through which one systematically examines phenomena, collects evidence, and uses evidence to develop, support, or refute a knowledge claim

Semistructured question: a data collection technique in which the respondent is delimited to a set of answers without being forced to choose an existing response

Single case design: use of multiple methods of data collection to examine change in a single unit of analysis

Stability: longitudinal accuracy of a measure

Subjectivity: the perspective of an individual, given his or her biases

Summative assessment: determination of the degree to which an intervention met its success criteria, its overall worth, and future existence

Survey designs: methods used primarily to measure characteristics of a population, including their knowledge, opinions, and attitudes

Surveys: questionnaires that are administered to ascertain the characteristics of a population or phenomenon

Target: individual, group, or unit that is expected to demonstrate a desirable outcome as a result of participation in intervention

Taxonomic analysis: inductive technique in which relationships among themes in a data set are identified

Theory: description, explanation, or prediction of phenomena through a set of interrelated concepts, constructs, and principles that can be verified or falsified by empirical approaches

Triangulation: the use of multiple approaches to investigate a single phenomenon

True experimental design: classic two-group (or variations thereof) design in which subjects are randomly selected and randomly assigned (R) to either an experimental or control group condition

Validity: rigor criterion that assesses the relationship between concept and evidence

Values: beliefs and opinions about what is desirable or undesirable, important or unimportant, and correct or incorrect

Variable: a concept or construct to which a numeric value is assigned. By definition, a variable must have more than one value, even if the investigator is interested in only one condition.

BIBLIOGRAPHY

Agar, M. (1996). *The professional stranger* (2nd ed.). New York: Academic Press.
Alkin, M. E. (1990). *Debates on evaluation.* Newbury Park, CA: Sage.
Alter, K., & Even, W. (1990). *Evaluating your practice: A guide to self assessment.* New York: Springer.
Anastas, J., & MacDonald, M. L. (2000). *Research design in social work and the human services* (2nd ed.). New York: Columbia University Press.
Atkinson, P., Coffey, A., & Delamont, S. (Eds.). (2001). *Handbook of ethnography.* Thousand Oaks, CA: Sage.
Babbie, E. (2001). *The practice of social research* (9th ed.). Belmont, CA: Wadsworth.
Bens, C. (1994). Effective citizen involvement: How to make it happen. *National Civic Review, 83,* 32–38.
Berlin, S. B., & Marsh, J. C. (1993). *Informing practice decision.* New York: Macmillan.
Bloom, M., Fischer, J., & Orme, J. (1998). *Evaluating practice: Guidelines for the accountable professional.* Boston: Allyn & Bacon.
Brager, G., & Holloway, S. (1992). Assessing prospects for organizational change: The uses of force field analysis. *Administration in Social Work, 16* (3–4), 15–29.
Buss, D. (1998). *Evolutionary psychology: The new science of the mind.* New York: Allyn & Bacon.
Campbell, D., & Stanley, J. (1963). *Experimental and quasi-experimental designs for research.* Chicago: Rand McNally.
Charlton, J. I. (1998). *Nothing about us without us: Disability oppression and empowerment.* Berkeley: University of California Press.
Chelimsky, E., & Sadish, W. (1997). *Evaluation for the 21st century: A handbook.* Thousand Oaks, CA: Sage.

Chen, H. T. S. (1992). *Theory driven evaluations*. Thousand Oaks, CA: Sage.
Cherin, D., & Meezan, W. (1998). Evaluation as a means of organizational learning. *Administration in Social Work*, 22 (2): 1–21.
Chronbach, L. J. (1982). *Designing evaluations of educational and social programs*. San Francisco: Jossey Bass.
Cohen, M. (1994). Overcoming obstacles to forming empowerment groups: A consumer advisory board for homeless clients. *Social Work*, 39, 742–748.
Coley, S. M., & Scheinberg, C. A. (2000). *Proposal writing*. Thousand Oaks, CA: Sage.
Commission on Accreditation. (2002). *Educational policy and accreditation standards*. Old Town, VA: Council on Social Work Education.
Connors, G. J., & Maisto, S. A. (1994). Alcohol beliefs scale. In J. Fischer & K. Corcoran (Eds.), *Resources for clinical practice: A sourcebook* (2nd ed., pp. 30–34). New York: Free Press.
Cournoyer, D. E., & Klein, W. C. (2000). *Research methods for social workers*. Boston: Allyn & Bacon.
Coutinho, M. J., & Repp, A. C. (1999). *Inclusion: The integration of students with disabilities*. Belmont, CA: Wadsworth.
Creswell, J. (1977). *Qualitative inquiry and research design: Choosing among five traditions*. Thousand Oaks, CA: Sage.
Denzin, N. K., & Lincoln, Y. S. (2000). *Handbook of qualitative research*. Thousand Oaks, CA: Sage.
De Panfilis, D. (1996). Implementing child mistreatment risk assessment systems: Lessons from theory. *Administration in Social Work*, 20 (2), 41–60.
DePoy, E., Gilmer, D., & Haslett, D. (2000). Adolescents with chronic illness and disability in transition: A community action needs assessment. *Disability Studies Quarterly*, 20, 17–25.
DePoy, E., & Gitlin, L. (1998). Introduction to research. St. Louis, MO: Mosby.
Fink, A. (1995a). *How to ask survey questions*. Thousand Oaks, CA: Sage.
Fink, A. (1995b). *How to design surveys*. Thousand Oaks, CA: Sage.
Fink, A. (1995c). *How to report on surveys*. Thousand Oaks, CA: Sage.
Fink, A. (1995d). *The survey handbook*. Thousand Oaks, CA: Sage.
Fischer, J. (1973). Is casework effective? A review. *Social Work*, 18 (1), 5–20.
Gambrill, E. (1997). *Social work practice: A critical thinker's guide*. New York, NY: Oxford University Press.
Gambrill, E. (2001). *Authority-based profession: Research on social work practice*, 11 (2), 166–175.
Gould, S. (1974). *Mismeasure of man*. New York: Norton.
Grinnell, R. M. (2001). *Social work research and evaluation* (6th ed.). Itasca, IL: Peacock.
Hartman, A. (1990). Many ways of knowing. *Social Work*, 35, 3–4.
Hartman, A., DePoy, E., Francis, C., & Gilmer, D. (2000). Adolescents with special health care needs in transition: Three life histories. *Social Work & Health Care*, 31 (4), 3–58.
Hess, P. M., & Mullen, E. J. (1997). *Practitioner-researcher partnerships: Building knowledge from, in, and for practice*. Washington, DC: NASW Press.
House, E. R., & Howe, K. R. (1999). *Values in evaluation and social research*. Thousand Oaks, CA: Sage.
Hustedde, R., & Score, M. (1995). *Force-field analysis: Incorporating critical thinking in goal setting* (No. 4, EDRS, ED384712, microfiche). Milwaukee, WI: Community Development Society.

Ippoliti, C., Peppy, B., & DePoy, E. (1994). Promoting self determination for persons with developmental disabilities. *Disability and Society, 9* (4), 453–460.

Kirst-Ashman, K. K., & Hull, G. H. (1999). *Understanding generalist practice* (2nd ed.). Chicago: Nelson Hall.

LaViolette, L. (2000). Evaluation practices of clinical social workers. Paper presented at the graduate student research symposium, 1998, University of Maine, Orono, Maine.

Lewin, K. (1951). *Field theory in social science.* New York: Harper & Row.

Mackelprang, R. W., & Salsgiver, R. O. (1997). *Disability: A diversity model approach in human service practice.* Pacific Grove, CA: Brooks Cole.

McCraken, G. (1988). *Long interview.* Thousand Oaks, CA: Sage.

Miles, M. B., & Huberman, A. M. (1994). *Qualitative data analysis: An expanded sourcebook.* Thousand Oaks, CA: Sage.

Murray C. A., & Hernstein, R. J. (1994). *The bell curve: Intelligence and class structure in American life.* New York: Free Press.

National Association of Social Workers. (2000). *Code of Ethics* [Online]. Available: NASWDC.org

Patton, M. Q. (1987). *Creative Evaluation.* Newbury Park, CA: Sage.

Patton, M. Q. (1997). *Utilization-focused evaluation.* Newbury Park, CA: Sage.

Qualitative Solutions and Research PTY. (2000). *QSR NUD*IST 4: Software for qualitative analysis.* Thousand Oaks, CA: Scholari.

Reamer, F. G. (1999). *Social work values and ethics.* New York: Columbia University Press.

Roche, S. E. (Ed.). (1999). *Contesting the boundaries in social work education: A liberatory approach to cooperative learning and teaching.* Alexandria, VA: CSWE.

Rokeach, M. (1973). *The nature of human values.* New York: Free Press.

Rossi, P., Freeman, H., & Lipsey, M. W. (1999). *Evaluation: A systematic approach.* Thousand Oaks, CA: Sage.

Royse, D., & Thyer, B. A. (1996). *Program evaluation: An introduction* (2nd ed.). Chicago: Nelson Hall.

Rubin, A., & Babbie, E. (2000). *Research methods for social work with Infotrac* (4th ed.). Belmont, CA: Wadsworth.

Sadish, W. R., Cook, T. D., & Levitan, L. C. (1991). *Foundations of program evaluation.* Newbury Park, CA: Sage.

Scriven, M. (1991). *The evaluation thesaurus.* Newbury Park, CA: Sage.

Steier, F. (1991.) *Research and reflexivity.* London: Sage.

Sullivan, T. (2001). *Methods of social research.* Fort Worth, FL: Harcourt College.

Thyer, B. (2001). *The handbook of social work research methods.* Thousand Oaks, CA: Sage.

Tripodi, T. (2000). *A primer on single-subject design for clinical social workers.* Washington, DC: NASW.

Unrau, Y. A., Gabor, P. A., & Grinnell, R. M. (2001). *Evaluation in the human services.* Itasca, IL: Peacock.

Wilson, J. (1973). *Thinking with concepts.* Cambridge, England: Cambridge University Press.

Yates, B. T. (1996). *Analyzing costs, procedures, processes, and outcomes in human services.* Thousand Oaks, CA: Sage.

Yegidis, B. L., Weinbach, R. W., & Morrison-Rodrigues, B. (1999). *Research methods for social workers* (3rd ed.). Boston: Allyn & Bacon.

Yin, R. (1994). *Case study research: Design and methods.* Thousand Oaks, CA: Sage.

Further Resources

Bourque, L. B., & Fielder, E. (1995). *How to conduct self-administered and mail surveys.* Thousand Oaks, CA: Sage.
Fetterman, D. L. (1989). *Ethnography step by step.* Newbury Park, CA: Sage.
Fischer, J., & Corcoran, K. (2000). *Resources for clinical practice: A sourcebook* (3rd ed.). New York: Free Press.
Frank, G. (1984). Life history model of adaptation to disability: The case of a congenital amputee. *Soc. Sci. Med. 19,* 639–645.
French, S. (1993). *Practical research: A guide for therapists.* Oxford, England: Butterworth Heinemann.
Glaser, B. G. (1978). *Theoretical sensitivity: Advances in the methodology of grounded theory.* Mill Valley, CA: Sociology Press.
Glaser B., & Strauss, A. (1967). *The discovery of grounded theory.* Chicago: Aldine.
Greenwood, D. J., & Levitan, M. (1998). *Introduction to action research.* Thousand Oaks, CA: Sage.
Greig, A., & Taylor, J. (1999). *Doing research with children.* Thousand Oaks, CA: Sage.
Guba, E. G. Criteria for assessing the trustworthiness of naturalistic inquiries. *Educ. Commun. Technol. J. 29,* 75–92.
Gubrium, J. (1988). *Analyzing field reality.* Newbury Park, CA: Sage.
Krefting, L. (1989). Reintegration into the community after head injury: The results of an ethnographic study. *Occup. Ther. J. Res. 9,* 67–83.
Liebow, E. (1967). *Tally's corner.* Boston: Little, Brown.
Lincoln, Y. S., & Guba, E. G. (1985). *Naturalistic inquiry.* Newbury Park, CA: Sage.
Lofland, J., & Lofland, L. (1984). *Analyzing social settings: A guide to qualitative observation and analysis* (2nd ed.). Belmont, CA: Wadsworth.
Mann, C., & Stewart, F. (2000). *Internet communication and qualitative research: A handbook for researching online.* Thousand Oaks, CA: Sage.
Miles, M. B., & Huberman, A. M. (1984). *Qualitative data analysis: A sourcebook of new methods.* Newbury Park, CA: Sage.
Royse, D., Thyer, B., Padgett, D. K., & Logan, T. K. (2000). *Program evaluation: An introduction.* Belmont, CA: Wadsworth.
Savishinsky, J. S. (1991). *The ends of time: Life and work in a nursing home.* New York: Bergen & Garvey.
Scriven, M. (1983). *Evaluation in education and human services.* Boston: Kluwer-Nijhoff.
Shaffir, W. B., & Stebbins, R. A. (Eds.) (1991). *Experiencing fieldwork: An inside view of qualitative research.* Newbury Park, CA: Sage.
Soriano, F. I. *Conducting needs assessments: A multidisciplinary approach.* Thousand Oaks, CA: Sage.
Spradley, J. P., & McCurdy, D. W. (1988). *The cultural experience: Ethnography in a complex society.* Prospect Heights, IL: Waveland Press.
Stecher, B. M., & Davis, W. A. *How to focus an evaluation.* Thousand Oaks, CA: Sage.
Strauss, A. L., & Corbin, J. M. (1990). *Basics of qualitative research: Grounded theory procedures and techniques.* Newbury Park, CA: Sage.
Stringer, E. (1996). *Action research: A handbook for practitioners.* Thousand Oaks, CA: Sage.
Wax, M. (1967). On misunderstanding verstechen: A reply to Abel. *Sociol. Soc. Res. 51,* 323–333.
Wuerst, J., & Stern, P. N. (1991). Empowerment in primary health care: The challenge for nurses. *Qualitative Health Res. 1,* 80–99.

INDEX

abstracts, 217
accessibility, 13–15, 20, 46, 48, 62, 76, 79, 82, 94, 124–125, 129, 144–146
accessible design, 109–110, 241
accountability, 7
action processes, 4, 128, 135–137, 143
administration of monitoring processes, 151
adolescent transition project, 128, 195
adolescents, 41, 81, 195
affirmative action, 15
Alcohol Beliefs Scale (ABS), 99, 101
Alcoholics Anonymous (AA), 8
alcoholism, 8–10, 38–39, 47, 48, 54–57, 61, 70, 98, 101
Americans with Disabilities Act of 1990 (ADA), 13, 20, 23, 51, 82
analysis: of nonresearch literature, 72; of research and evaluation sources, 71
analysis of variance (ANOVA), 105, 238
analytic axes: formative-summative, 37–40; insider-outsider, 32–35; scientist-practitioner, 35–37, 59
articulation, 182
artifact review, 201
assessment. *See* monitoring process
assistive technology, 213
associational statistics, 238
audience, 21, 23, 155–157, 217, 241
audit trail, 61, 241

barriers. *See* accessibility
behavioral intervention, 11
beliefs. *See* values
bias, 32, 88, 188, 241
browsers, 67

categorical numbers, 241
case studies (recaps): Jennifer Savoy, 227–230; Joshua Williams, 223–227
case study designs. *See* design, single subject
causal/predictive knowledge, 81
cause-and-effect linkages, 199
charting, 69–70
civil rights legislation, 53
citations, 217
clarification: of approach, 14, 183; of intervention points, 143; of problems and needs, 7–10, 18, 25, 46–57, 70, 75; of purpose, 64; of value base, 14
codebook, 105, 241
collaboration, 38
concepts, 98, 241
conflict of interest, 34
content, delimiting, 68–69, 98–99
contingency tables, 236
control groups, 89, 188, 241
consistency, internal, 242
correlational designs, 92–93, 236
cost analysis. *See* resource analysis
cost-effectiveness. *See* resource analysis

Council on Social Work Education, 143
culture 120, 241

data analysis, 233–239
databases, 65–68
Department of Justice, 82
Department of Vocational Rehabilitation Services (DVRS), 47, 48
descriptive knowledge, 79
descriptive statistics, 234–236
design: accessibility of, 209; comparative group, 164; experimental-type, 6, 86–87, 93–95, 163–167, 242, 243; ex post facto, 93, 242; idiographic, 199–208; mixed-method, 124–125, 172, 202, 207; naturalistic, 6, 199–202; nonexperimental, 91–93, 163, 243; passive observation, 164, 243; qualitative, 199–208; quasi-experimental, 163; selection for evaluation, 93–95, 123–125, 163; single subject, 202–207, 244; stakeholders, 207; survey, 92, 244; true experimental, 87–91
Diagnostic and Statistical Manual of Mental Disorders (DSM IV), 70
direct service (micropractice), 151
disabilities, 53, 77, 128–129, 154, 171, 213. *See also* accessibility; mobility impairment
discriminant function analysis, 238
discussion groups, 68
dissemination, 212
Dissertation Abstracts, 65
diverse groups, 172
document review, 171
Down's syndrome, 119
DSM IV (Diagnostic and Statistical Manual of Mental Disorders), 70

Educational Policy and Evaluation Standards (2001), 143
educational reform, 77
efficiency, 183
embedded case studies, 204
emic orientation, 114, 242
Endnote (computer program), 217
equivalence, 109, 242
error, 242
ethics, 40–41, 242
ethnography, 120–123
etic orientation, 114, 242
evaluation: areas of, 7–12, 18; distinct from research, 4; history of, 6–12; of information, 70; models, 4; political nature of, 13–14, 20–22
evaluation practice model: complexity of, 32; information in, 59–61; overview of, 4, 15, 20, 18–30; principles of, 19–24; processes of, 24; purpose in, 5–6, 22–23; reasoning in, 6; theoretical foundation of, 14–15; value-based 19–20
evaluators. *See* social workers
evidence, 212–214

251

evolutionary psychology, 6
ex post facto designs, 93
external influences, 12, 148, 160

field constraints, 188
focus groups, 115–118
Fogler Library, 65, 66
force field analysis, 52–57, 195, 242
formative evaluation, 37, 242. See also monitoring process
formative objectives, 129–134
frequency distributions, 102, 234, 242

goals, 128–130, 142, 242
graduation rates, 41
grounded theory, 202, 239, 242
group interviews, 115–118

holistic case approaches, 203

idiographic designs, 113, 198–208, 242
indicators, 98, 242
indirect service (mezzo- and macropractice), 151
inductive analysis, 123, 171, 202
inferential statistics, 236–238
information: authors of, 69; content of, 68–69; date of, 69; electronic, 65–68; evaluation of, 70, 77; organization of, 68–69; scope of, 77; sources of, 59, 60, 64–68; structure of, 69; venue, 69. See also measurement
information review: charting, 69–70; critical, 70–71; goals and objectives, 62–63; mechanics of, 63–72; needs assessment and, 78; purpose of, 59–61, 63–64; reporting on, 70; scope of, 64–65; thinking processes of, 59
inquiry: approaches to, 114–123; as distinct from practice, 24; empirical, 76; experimental-type, 79; naturalistic, 79, 113–126, 167–171; qualitative, 212; systematic, 212; value-based, 183. See also design
instrumentation structures, 101–110
instruments: nature of, 99; validity of, 242
intelligence, measurement of, 108
intermediate goals, 130
internet searches, 65–67
interval/ratio level of measurement, 100
intervention: behavioral, 11; external influences in, 12; integrity of, 22; processes, 151–153, 242. See also reflexive intervention
interviews, 114–118, 170–171, 200
intimacy, 30

key informant interviews, 115
knowledge: causal/predictive, 81; descriptive, 79; formative uses of, 220; nature of, 79; professional, 184–185; relational, 79–81; relevance of, 81; reporting and using, 212–221; scope of, 81; summative uses of, 220

language barriers, 10
legislation, 21–22, 53, 213
life history, 118–119

Likert-type response format, 100, 242
listservs, 68, 242
literature, 71, 72, 242
logic structures, 6

managing people, 32
manipulation, 89, 188
mapping, problem, 49–52
marker events, 118
measurement, 86; delimiting content in, 98–99; levels of, 99; overview of, 98–101; structure of, 99–101
measures of central tendency, 104, 234
mezzopractice, 151
micropractice (direct service), 151
mobility impairment, 13, 20, 50. See also accessibility; disabilities
monitoring intervention action processes, 147–148
monitoring objectives, 129–134
monitoring process, 10–11, 151–158, 163, 243, 244
multiple regression, 238

narrative data, 219
National Association of Social Work (NASW), 40
naturalistic data analysis, 234
need statements 46–47, 62; definition of, 75, 243; deriving goals from, 134–135; as distinct from problem statement, 75; identification of, 75–76
needs assessment: action strategies, 78–83, 86; experimental-type design, 86–91; goals and objectives, 82, 128–138, 147; guiding questions, 82–83; limitations, 83; naturalistic inquiry, 113–126; nonexperimental design, 91–93; obtaining information in, 97–111; selection of evaluation design, 86, 93–95, 123–125; thinking processes of, 93–95. See also need statements
nominal level of measurement, 99–100, 243
nomothetic designs. See design, experimental-type
nonparametric statistics, 237, 243
notation systems, 86
NUD*IST 4 (computer program), 202

objectives, 129–134, 142, 243
objectivity, 243
operationalization, 98
ordinal level of measurement, 100
outcome assessment: action processes in, 188–197; alternative strategies of, 194–196; essential elements in, 181–184; experimental-type approaches to, 188–197; nomothetic designs of, 189–193; overview of, 12, 180, 243; program outcome and, 189; thinking processes of, 179–186
outcome objectives, 129–134, 136–137

parametric statistics, 237, 243
participatory action team (PAT), 195
passive observation, 92–93, 171, 243

pluralism, 113
polio, 13, 29
political nature of evaluation, 13–14, 20–22
population, 92, 95, 243
post-traumatic stress disorder (PTSD), 33, 34, 38
practice wisdom, 68
probability sampling, 88, 243
problem mapping, 49–52, 243
problem resolution, 184
problem statement: clarification of, 46–48; common mistakes in, 48–49; definition of, 75, 243; as distinct from need statement, 75; in intervention planning, 147; supported by information review, 61–62
process assessment. *See* monitoring process
process assessment questions, 172–173
process objectives, 129–134, 135
process recordings, 171
Procite (computer program), 217
public concerns vs. individual concerns, 15, 29–30, 46, 50, 62, 76

qualitative designs, 199–208, 212
quantitative approaches. *See* design, experimental-type
questions, in surveys, 101

racism, 201
random group assignment, 87, 244
random samples, 87, 244
randomization, 88–89, 188
reasoning: deductive, 25–26, 27, 28, 241; direct practice, 28; inductive, 26–30, 242
Reeve, Christopher, 53
reflexive implementation, 131–132
reflexive intervention, 10–12, 18, 63, 131; action processes in, 163–175; force field analysis and, 143; implementation of goals and objectives in, 142–143; planning guidelines for, 147; processes of, 147–148; selection of an intervention approach and, 143–146; thinking processes of, 151–161
reflexivity, 12, 244 *See also* reflexive intervention
Rehabilitation Act of 1973, 13
relational knowledge, 79
reliability, 95, 108–109, 244
reporting strategies, 214–216
reporting structures, 216–220; experimental type, 216–218; formal evaluation reports, 216–219; methods of sharing, 220; mixed-method, 219; naturalistic, 218–219; non-traditional, 219
research design. *See* design
resource analysis, 11, 13, 20–21, 24, 46, 77, 83, 148, 158–160, 167, 183–184, 244
rigor, 20, 23, 95, 113, 154, 189

safe-sex behavior, 188
sample, definition of, 95, 244
saturation, 244

science, 35, 244
search engines, 67
single case designs. *See* design, single subject
single system designs. *See* design, single subject
skepticism, 7
social learning theory, 5
social justice theory, 15
social workers, roles and responsibilities, 32–42. *See also* analytic axes
special education 77
stability, 109, 244
staff development, 151
stakeholders, 20, 23, 40, 195
standard deviation, 104, 235
standardized testing, 21–22, 26, 27, 39, 80, 92, 107, 116, 142
statistics: analysis, 233–234; associational, 238; descriptive, 234–236; inferential, 236–238; manipulation, 194; modeling, 194; nonparametric, 237, 243; parametric, 237, 243; tests, 109
stress, 107
substance abuse, 5, 119, 133–134. *See also* alcoholism
summative assessment, 32, 37, 244
summative objectives, 129–134
surveys: analysis of responses in, 102–107; closed-ended questions in, 241; design and development of, 92, 106–110, 244; open-ended questions in, 120, 243; types of questions in, 101–102
systematic inquiry, 154, 181–182, 212
systemic interaction, 151

targets, 184–185, 195, 244
taxonomic analysis, 202, 239, 244
teacher performance, 80
teacher training, 142, 151
thematic analysis, 239
theoretical lenses, 14–15, 244
thinking processes of, 4, 27–28, 48–49, 59, 93–95, 144. *See also* reasoning
triangulating methods, 194, 244
true experimental design, 87–91, 244
turnings, 118

validity, 93–95, 107–108, 241, 242, 245
value base, 15
value statements, 212
values, 15, 19–20, 76, 79, 245
variability, 235
variables, 87, 99–101, 163, 189, 241, 245
venue, 69

Web sites, 67
withholding, 188
work skills, 11
worth, 183

YMCA, 75